The Puritan Cosmopolis

OXFORD STUDIES IN AMERICAN LITERARY HISTORY

Gordon Hutner, Series Editor

Family Money
Jeffory A. Clymer

America's England
Christopher Hanlon

Writing the Rebellion
Philip Gould

Antipodean America
Paul Giles

Living Oil
Stephanie LeMenager

Making Noise, Making News
Mary Chapman

Territories of Empire
Andy Doolen

Propaganda 1776
Russ Castronovo

Playing in the White
Stephanie Li

Literature in the Making
Nancy Glazener

Surveyors of Customs
Joel Pfister

The Moral Economies of American Authorship
Susan M. Ryan

After Critique
Mitchum Huehls

Unscripted America
Sarah Rivett

Forms of Dictatorship
Jennifer Harford Vargas

Anxieties of Experience
Jeffrey Lawrence

White Writers, Race Matters
Gregory S. Jay

The Civil War Dead and American Modernity
Ian Finseth

The Puritan Cosmopolis
Nan Goodman

The Puritan Cosmopolis

THE LAW OF NATIONS AND THE EARLY AMERICAN IMAGINATION

Nan Goodman

OXFORD UNIVERSITY PRESS

OXFORD
UNIVERSITY PRESS

Oxford University Press is a department of the University of Oxford.
It furthers the University's objective of excellence in research, scholarship,
and education by publishing worldwide. Oxford is a registered trade mark of
Oxford University Press in the UK and in certain other countries.

Published in the United States of America by Oxford University Press
198 Madison Avenue, New York, NY 10016, United States of America.

First issued as an Oxford University Press paperback, 2022

Library of Congress Cataloging-in-Publication Data
Names: Goodman, Nan, author.
Title: The Puritan cosmopolis : the law of nations and the early American
imagination / Nan Goodman.
Description: New York, NY : Oxford University Press, 2018. |
Series: Oxford studies in American literary history |
Includes bibliographical references and index.
Identifiers: LCCN 2017036775 | ISBN 9780190642822 (hardback) |
ISBN 9780197651209 (paperback)
Subjects: LCSH: American literature—Puritan authors—History and criticism. |
Law and literature—United States—History—17th century. |
Puritans—New England—Intellectual life—17th century. |
Puritan movements in literature. | New England—Civilization—17th century.
Classification: LCC PS153.P87 G66 2018 | DDC 810.9/3554—dc23
LC record available at https://lccn.loc.gov/2017036775

1 3 5 7 9 8 6 4 2

Paperback printed by Marquis, Canada

To The Honorable Norman Goodman,
My Dad

{ CONTENTS }

{ ACKNOWLEDGMENTS }

I conducted research for this book, fittingly enough given its cosmopolitan focus, in several different places, and I met individuals in all those places who are deserving of thanks.

I started the research for the book while I was a Visiting Professor of Law and Humanities at Georgetown Law Center, an opportunity made possible by Dean Robin West. At Georgetown I benefited from the services of amazing law librarians and of my research assistant, Sarka Havrankova. Eye-opening conversations about law, literature, and the humanities with Robin West and several other law school colleagues offered a fruitful environment for my initial thoughts about the book.

In Istanbul, where I first began to think about the links between the seventeenth-century New England Puritans and the Ottomans, I found many friends and colleagues. Cevza Sevgen paved the way for my discoveries by inviting me to teach and conduct research in the Western Languages and Literatures department at Boğaziçi University in 2011. Over the course of many visits, one of which was made possible by a Fulbright Fellowship, I benefited from conversations with Ayşen Candaş and the late Vangelis Kechriotis, who listened to my ideas about the cosmopolis with interest, kindness, and insight. I am also grateful for the things I learned from Ahmet Cem Durak, Edhem Eldem, Erol Köroğlu, and the late John Freely, and to Alpar Sevgen, who invited me to deliver two lectures on human rights at Boğaziçi, which helped me sharpen my understanding of cosmopolitanism and its relationship to human rights discourse over the centuries.

As a Scholar-in-Residence at the American Antiquarian Society, I was able to delve into many seventeenth-century texts, including the Mather Library collections, and to enjoy the welcoming intellectual community fostered by Paul Erickson, director of academic programs. Under the AAS reading room dome, I also exchanged ideas with, among others, Meredith Marie Neuman, Steve C. Bullock, John Demos, and Alex Socarides, all of whom taught me a lot about my own work by sharing elements of theirs. I also spent a wonderful month as a Huntington Fellow at the Huntington Library, where I was the beneficiary of the scholarly community directed by Steve Hindle.

I am grateful to the audiences at the many talks I gave while developing the ideas in this book. Four stand out: the Amherst Law and Social Thought seminar on the Utopian Imagination, the Race, Law, and American Literary Studies Conference at the University of Maryland, the English Literature and Linguistics Department talk series at the University of Glasgow, and the Jewish Studies Colloquium at the University of Colorado. At all four venues, I received incisive and generous advice, and I am indebted to Austin Sarat, Martha Umphrey, Edlie Wong, Robert Levine, Elizabeth Robertson, and David Shneer for invitations to present.

Cosmopolitanism, as affect and attitude, as this book and many before it suggest, is also a local phenomenon. The University of Colorado provided me with two invaluable opportunities—a Faculty Fellowship at the Center for Humanities and the Arts and a College Scholar Award—which allowed me to concentrate on my research and writing without interruption. Justin Saxby served as my tireless research assistant during some of this time and made some memorable suggestions.

Friends and colleagues on the home front withstood more regular requests for feedback. Janice Ho and Karen Jacobs read multiple drafts of several chapters and made comments that helped me reshape the book in significant ways. David Glimp, Katherine Eggert, William Kuskin, Richelle Munkhoff, Deborah Whitehead, and Sue Zemka also commented generously on various portions of the manuscript, which led to drastic improvements. Conversations with Sarah Barringer Gordon, Nomi Stolzenberg, Hilary Schor, and the late Robert Ferguson kept the book grounded in the law and humanities context, which has always been extraordinarily generative for me, and I thank them for listening attentively to various ideas over the years.

As the book was taking shape, Gordon Hutner was generous with his time and insight, making suggestions that helped me tighten the structure, reduce the verbiage, and home in on some of the major strands of argument without distraction. Gordon also did me the honor of accepting it for his Oxford Studies in American Literary History series. At Oxford, I am also grateful to editor Sarah Pirovitz, copy editor India Gray, and especially to Joellyn Ausanka, supervising senior production editor, who shepherded the book through the production process with care. I am also grateful to the anonymous readers for OUP, and a special note of gratitude to Lanny DeVuono, who agreed to let me feature one of her magnificent paintings on the jacket.

The many friends who populate my cosmopolis offered the love and support that kept me sane and happy over the years it took me to write this book. I am especially grateful to them for asking about the book without fearing the monologue that such a question often provoked and for knowing when not to ask about it. To Silva Chang, Jane Garrity, Janice Ho, Karen Jacobs, Karen Palmer, Edie Rosenberg, Nancy Sternbach, Betty Symington, and Sue Zemka, many heartfelt thanks. My world would be a far poorer place without you. Special thanks in this department to my compañera de viaje, Sandra Saltrese.

My most ardent and loving critics, Sam and Q, make everything I do more meaningful. Thank you for being in my life. And thanks finally to my dad, who taught me at an early age that the world is the large and exciting place I have come to call the cosmopolis and who did all he could to help me find my place in it. This book is dedicated to you, Dad, with love and gratitude.

The Puritan Cosmopolis

{ Prologue }

THE LITERARY COSMOPOLIS AND ITS LEGAL PAST

In the last analysis one is a member of a world community by the sheer fact of being human; this is one's "cosmopolitan" existence.

—HANNAH ARENDT

On May 13, 1698, people on the streets of the cities and towns of Puritan New England would have seen—and no doubt heard—hawkers selling copies of a broadside called "The Turkish Fast." Hot-off-the-press, one-page news sheets, colonial broadsides were printed on an occasional basis and regularly used to inform readers of urgent domestic or transatlantic news, such as the birth of a royal heir in England or a newly enacted colonial law.[1] "The Turkish Fast," by contrast, reported on an event that was foreign in the most fundamental sense of the word, having occurred in an empire that was geographically, culturally, politically, and theologically half a world away. Information about the military defeat by Christian forces that had prompted this imperial Ottoman fast would, no doubt, have been welcome news for colonial passersby, but the bulk of the broadside was devoted to a detailed description of the ritual procession that accompanied the fast, including who attended, what they wore, and the prayers they uttered. "Six thousand Turks shall lead the way cloath'd in Sackloth," the broadside noted, and "[a]fter them… [t]hree thousand Spahi's bareheaded, with long Beards, carrying the Prophet's Coffin." Why were such details included in this broadside, and why was it being sold on the street corners of New England? Other than to learn of the defeat itself, of which there was scant mention, why would anyone in late seventeenth-century New England have been willing to pay for a detailed description of the "weeping" and "bewailing" that characterized this outpouring of Ottoman grief?

One way to answer these questions would be to point to the extensive commercial and political contacts late seventeenth-century Puritans had with the rest of the world. Although once viewed as an isolated people with an exclusively religious agenda, the Puritans of New England, as recent scholarship has shown, were deeply engaged with world events, imperial politics, and global trade. In fact, while most broadsides from the 1680s reported on domestic or transatlantic events, such as the death of Charles II and the coronation of his successor, James II, broadsides of the 1690s often reported on events farther afield, such as the 1692 naval victory by the English over the French or the 1694 earthquake in Naples. In a Puritan domain characterized by this kind of curiosity and connectivity, a broadside reporting on a fast held in the Ottoman Empire might not have seemed unusual.

A connectivity based on the spread of knowledge about and investment in the commerce and politics of the world, however, does not fully account for the presence of "The Turkish Fast" or for other texts like it that were written, read, and circulated among a wide circle of Puritan elites and a smaller number of laypeople in the second half of the seventeenth century. It was neither commerce nor politics, for example, that "The Turkish Fast" addressed when it described how "every *Friday* of the New Moon, as also upon the 5th. 6th. and 7th. of the Month, that all Persons fast all the Day and that they go in that posture, first through the Streets, and then to the Churches, with their Eyes fix'd upon the Earth, lamenting and crying, *Ja Aagib, Allah, Allah*, that is to say,"*O Merciful God, O God*." Of course, in this and similar descriptions of Muslim rituals, some Puritans might well have found examples of what the broadside refers to as "Mahometan bigotry," which in this case consisted of the Ottomans' putting "too great confidence in [their] Strength and...Alliances against the Emperor of the Christians." Details of the Muslims' prayers and processions might also have fed the same hunger for information about the exotic other that had made proto-ethnographic narratives about the American Indians best sellers on both sides of the Atlantic in the earlier part of the century. But what of the details that registered the depth of grief the Turks suffered for their fallen comrades and the efforts they made to atone for their sins? Surely these descriptions, which would have resonated with some Puritans and put them in mind of their own transgressions and collective fasts, satisfied a different longing and had a different effect—one I argue here that contributed to an intellectual and affective orientation toward others on the part of many late seventeenth-century Puritans that went well beyond curiosity or political triumphalism.

In attending to this intellectual and affective orientation toward distant others in the work of some of the major Puritan writers in the second half of the seventeenth century, this book traces the emergence of a sense of kinship with and belonging to a larger, more inclusive world within Puritan literature. I call this sense the Puritan cosmopolis.[2] Connected to this cosmopolis in part through travel, trade, and politics, the Puritans in these pages were also thinking in terms that went beyond these parameters about what it meant to feel affiliated with people in remote places—of which the Ottoman Empire is the best, but not the only, example—and to experience what Bruce Robbins calls "attachment at a distance."[3] In those portions of "The Turkish Fast" that touched on the Turks' humility in defeat, charity for the poor, and respect for the dead, Puritan readers, this book argues, were not simply learning about others but also cultivating an awareness of themselves as "stand[ing]," as one theorist of cosmopolitanism has put it, "in an ethically significant relation" to people all around the world.[4]

The underlying source of these affective and ethical predilections was the law, specifically the law of nations, often considered the precursor to international law. Developed initially by Spanish Scholastic philosophers, who were working within a Catholic context, the law of nations, around which the legal significance of this study revolves, was reworked by Protestant legal and political theorists, such as Alberico Gentili, Hugo Grotius, and John Selden in the late sixteenth and seventeenth centuries just as the Puritans were putting down stakes in New England. Committed to understanding the law as a mechanism that would regulate conduct among political entities and facilitate cooperation among nations in the face of nearly a century of religious wars, the law of nations theorists revived the ancient idea of a cosmopolis by positing a sphere above the state to which all people belonged. Through the terms for sovereignty, obligation, and society, which were made available by this turn toward the cosmopolitan in the law, the Puritans experimented with concepts of extended obligation and ideas about a society consisting of all humans, not simply those living along certain trade routes or within certain foreign communities. By mapping these thought experiments, *The Puritan Cosmopolis* uncovers Puritans reconceptualizing war, contemplating new ways of cultivating peace and, perhaps most importantly, rewriting the rules for being Puritan by internalizing legal theories about living in a larger, more inclusive world.

The Scholarly Context

A general focus on the global and the cosmopolitan situates this book firmly within the scholarly tradition of the last two decades or more in which historians and literary critics have reconceptualized the Puritans as deeply engaged with the outside world. Beginning with Stephen Foster's The *Long Argument: English Puritanism and the Shaping of New England Culture, 1570–1700* (1991) and Francis Bremer's *Puritanism: Transatlantic Perspectives on a Seventeenth Century Anglo-American Faith* (1993) and moving through Michael Winship's *Seers of God: Puritan Providentialism in the Restoration and Early Enlightenment* (1996) and Philip Round's *By Nature and Custom Cursed: Transatlantic Civil Discourse and New England Cultural Production, 1620–1660* (1999), scholars have revealed the extent to which the Puritans were for reasons having nothing to do with the law of nations connected to a transatlantic culture in which a breadth of thought and a reciprocity of communication were already deeply engrained habits of mind. So profoundly has this scholarship changed our view of the Puritans that even the so-called Antinomian Controversy—an event that originally fueled characterizations of the Puritans as an isolated people concerned only with the rivalry of intramural theologies—has been recontextualized as a movement with roots in and consequences for the transatlantic world.[5]

Linking the transatlantic to the world at large, another group of Americanist scholars has allowed us to see the transatlantic turn as only one of many axes in the expanded communication network the New World Puritans shared with the rest of the world. Answering a call for global histories of America, many scholars, from William Spengemann and Wai Chee Dimock on the literary side to David Armitage and Thomas Bender on the historical and political side, have focused on reinserting America into the global arena.[6] In fact, scholars of a global Puritanism link the inhabitants of early New England with the geoculture of centrist liberalism that created what Immanuel Wallerstein has called a "world-system."[7] As a result of their participation in this "world-system," the Puritans understood what they called the "Worlds Market" to be, as Mark Valeri writes, "infused with transcendent meaning."[8] They also developed a taste for information about and products from remote locations that by the late seventeenth century made New England a magnet for a diverse population and Boston a "cosmopolitan" city.[9]

To the rich insights gained from scholarship on the commercial and political axes of globalization referenced here we must add a third category of scholars working on Puritan and Native-American relations. These scholars have laid the groundwork for the more internalized cosmopolitanism with which this book is concerned. The work of scholars in this area, including Laura Stevens, Jenny Hale Pulsipher, Andrew Newman, Hilary Wyss, Kristina Bross, Sarah Rivett, Matt Cohen, and Birgit Rasmussen, among others, has opened our eyes to the ways in which the Puritans, though not necessarily looking outward to a world beyond their immediate borders, were in their relations with their indigenous neighbors expanding their understanding of cultural and ethnic differences and repositioning themselves in a network that went beyond the Protestant world. To the extent that the scholarship on these Native-Anglo relations represents a Puritan capacity, however imperfect, to accommodate, integrate, and adapt to the ethnic, religious, and cultural outsider, it is crucial to my claims about how the Puritans came to cultivate a sense of cosmopolitan belonging.[10]

While much of this work on commerce, politics, culture, and an increasingly global Protestantism has helped us see the Puritans as embedded in transatlantic and global structures, however, *The Puritan Cosmopolis* shifts the focus to show how through the operation of the law these structures also came to be embedded in the Puritans themselves. My more particular focus on the law and its ability to induce people—in this case the Puritans—to adopt ethical and affective orientations previously unknown to them constitutes *The Puritan Cosmopolis*'s most important critical intervention.

Globalization versus the Legal Cosmopolis

We can begin to understand the difference law makes between the kind of globalization at stake in the works cited earlier and that in *The Puritan Cosmopolis* by reference to an ontology of global history articulated by Samuel Moyn and Andrew Sartori. For Moyn and

Sartori, there are three kinds of global histories. The first deploys the global as an a priori or "meta-analytical" category imposed by historians on the material at hand. Examples of this include world histories that span centuries and address events in comparative terms. The second understands the global as a concern within a given period of history that, like climate change or concurrent revolutions, affects much or all the world at once. Moyn and Sartori consider this version of the global a "substantive scale of historical process."[11] The third pertains to the subjective experience of historical agents.[12] In this sense—the sense I adopt here—the legally cosmopolitan and global is internal, an attitude shared by the individuals in question and experienced as a sense of belonging to the world on the part of the "historical agents" or participants themselves.

To associate the law with an internalization of ethical orientation and affect that helped engender cosmopolitanism, I engage the law on the level of what Panu Minkkinen calls its "deep structure," or the principles that give it coherence without necessarily implying design.[13] Focusing on this internalizable feature of the law, however, does not suggest that other versions of globalization were not internalized as well. Many of the global processes central to Moyn and Sartori's first two categories, including infrastructural events of long duration or of universal scope, might well have induced subjective experiences of cosmopolitanism in many people. Such subjectivity, however, would have been different from that engendered by the law. In contrast to these relatively impersonal processes, I argue, the law would have served the Puritans in the way it serves us all, as a normative discourse that not only offers models for making sense of the world, but also asks those for whom it is relevant to internalize that sense and to make it their own. The internalization of the law of nations occurred on an individual and society-wide basis as well where, as will be apparent in chapter 4, the outward facing norms of cosmopolitanism become in the late seventeenth-century Puritan commonwealth a norm for the evidentiary elements of domestic, internal law as well. Internalizing the law of nations then raised crucial questions for the Puritans about the lines between external and internal law, which in turn helped usher in the era in which we find ourselves today—where it is difficult to tell where domestic policies leave off and international policies begin.

To help us further understand how the law of nations came to make a Puritan cosmopolitan subjectivity possible, I turn to Seneca, the Roman Stoic, whose political and philosophical theories played a central role in the development of cosmopolitanism and the law of nations. Inheriting notions of cosmopolitanism from his ancient Greek forebears, including Diogenes, who is credited with coming up with the idea of the *kosmopolites* in the first place, Seneca defines cosmopolitanism in quintessentially legal terms. He writes:

> Let us embrace with our minds two commonwealths: one great and truly common—in which gods and men are contained, in which we look not to this or that corner, but measure the bounds of our state with the sun; the other to which the particular circumstances of birth have assigned us—the commonwealth of the Athenians or the Carthaginians or some other city which pertains not to all men but to a particular group of them.[14]

Here we see the cosmopolis emerge in the terms most germane to this study: embraced by "our minds," it lives in our imagination; described as a "commonwealth," it occupies a jurisdictional imaginary; "truly common," it is shared by men and gods; "bounded" only by the sun, it is planetary. Finally and perhaps most importantly, as one of two worlds, the cosmopolis demands of us a sense of membership and belonging commensurate with the polis or civil state alongside which it exists.

Two features stand out in my précis of this passage from Seneca—belonging and imagination. Both are central to understanding how the texts and concepts of the law of nations functioned for the Puritans. When it comes to the law, belonging and imagination are inextricably linked since the law, foreign or domestic, is centrally concerned with imaginary constructions of belonging. As James Boyd White argued in his 1973 book, *The Legal Imagination* (in what may have been the first use of that term), to the extent that the law consists of language, it exists in the imagination. Language, after all, is processed in our minds, and lawyers more than most rely on their audiences' imaginations not only to listen but also to conjure scenes—of accidents and crimes, for example—that have otherwise vanished from sight. The imaginary belonging to which Seneca refers, however, expresses a truth about the law's operation and purpose that goes beyond this shared linguistic legacy, for what the law does above all else is to reinforce our sense of belonging to a place, or what the law calls a jurisdiction. Even when the law does not appear to be concerned with belonging—when it is meting out punishments, assigning compensation for injuries, or even ordering people out of its jurisdictions—it is always reminding its constituents that belonging is the most important and valuable identity it can confer. In this sense the law does not simply apply to people within its jurisdictions; it creates the jurisdictions to which people belong.[15] To embrace the law as "two commonwealths," therefore, is to embrace a subjective, internalized identity of multiple belonging at one's core. It follows that while parts of the Puritans' internalized identity as citizens of the cosmopolis would naturally manifest with respect to their dealings with the rest of the world, as described primarily in chapters 2 and 3, we will also see evidence of how their cosmopolitan sensibilities affected their domestic polis as well in chapters 4 and 5.

Worlds and the Imagination

Worlds—plural—had lived in the Puritan imagination for some time. Most pertinent for the Puritans, perhaps, was the world of Christendom, which existed alongside the Puritans' godly commonwealth in the New World. In *Sympathetic Puritans*, Abram Van Engen reminds us of the co-relational nature of Puritanism's "Calvinist theology of fellow feeling," which actively worked to bring people into the Christian fold.[16] Embodying the dictates of fellow feeling, Van Engen argues, allowed the Puritans to build a transatlantic community at a time when their flight from England was often seen as a source of division on both sides of the Atlantic. For Van Engen, however, this sense is emotional and devotional, not legal. Van Engen writes: "Most New England Puritans dealt with sympathy on a personal level: it spoke directly to anxieties raised by election." Admittedly, later in the century Van Engen's version of fellow feeling allowed the Puritans to develop affective affiliations with each other across certain territorial borders, but this too was a fellow feeling defined by religious uniformity. My interest, by contrast, is in a feeling that has less to do with people in one's immediate vicinity or extended religious sphere than with the more attenuated feeling we might have for someone whose existence we had not previously contemplated. The fellow feeling I am concerned with arose in those instances when, for example, the Puritans began to think about the Ottomans as part of the same planetary jurisdiction without approving of their religious practices or wanting to convert them. Indeed cosmopolitanism refers to a belonging without any assumptions about fellow feeling beyond those engendered by what Hannah Arendt calls in the epigraph to this chapter "the sheer fact of being human."

The law of nations made the "sheer fact of being human" the key component of early modern cosmopolitanism. Still bound to certain notions, such as sovereignty, and never truly universal in its scope (among other things, it was grounded in a Western intellectual tradition that left out wide swaths of the world as we know it today), the law of nations nevertheless rested on a more expansive sense of the world than ever before. The two major manifestations of this expansiveness would have had particular significance for the Puritans, who were as legally minded as they were godly. From the time of John Winthrop's "Model of Christian Charity" (1630), written on board the ship that carried the first white settlers of the Massachusetts Bay Colony across the Atlantic, the law proved an intimate partner to the Puritans' religious desires and goals. The first manifestation of this legal expansiveness had to do with Jewish law, adopted nearly a century earlier by the Puritans, yet given a completely new reading by Alberico Gentili, Hugo Grotius, and John Selden, the three most influential law of nations theorists in England. The second had to do with the history and culture of diplomatic negotiation within the Ottoman Empire, whose salience as a source for the law of nations and whose inclusion within the newly enlarged understanding of the world, enabled a new vision of a part of the world the Puritans had traditionally seen as pernicious and expendable.

It would be difficult to exaggerate the significance of these legal moves for the world at large or for the Puritans in particular. When Selden, for example, pointed not to the Jewish Decalogue, which was delivered at Sinai to the Jews, but to the Noahide laws—the seven laws given to the non-Jewish Noah and his sons after the flood—as the basis for the law of nations, he opened up new vistas in Jewish thought and Jewish law that would have been meaningful to the Puritans in their role as the "surrogate Israel." Similarly, when Gentili dismissed the medieval notion of the just war and introduced a new sense of justice based on empirically verifiable formalities and negotiation, the world known to the Puritans and other early moderns as irreconcilably divided by war was permanently altered. Finally when Grotius encouraged Christian sovereigns to make and honor peace treaties with the "infidel," he broke with a powerful religious and legal tradition that would have had its own significance for the Puritans, who had long considered the idea of a war with the "Turks" as a prerequisite for ushering in the millennium.

A Civil Law Tradition

To consider the law of nations as central to Puritan thinking and writing in the second half of the seventeenth century has important implications for understanding the Puritans' relationship to the law in general. Specifically, the focus on the law of nations entails a shift away from the common law, which has dominated scholarship on Puritan legal history, and toward the civil law, which informed and inflected Puritan thought in previously unseen ways.[17] Much recent work has opened up the early American period to a plurality of legal practices—formal and informal, Indian and English, local and imperial—but it rarely touches on the civil law.[18] There is good reason for this since most of the law the Puritans brought with them from England and turned to their advantage in the New World was based on the common law.[19] Following in the footsteps of their common law counterparts and forebears, the Puritans instituted a common law regime that closely followed English precepts and, thanks to the flexibility embedded in the system of precedent on which the common law was based, could be altered as conditions required. The charter originally issued to the first white settlers in New England, for example, gave them the authority to make laws as they saw fit so long as they were not "repugnant to the laws of England." Originally known as an exclusively English creation, the capacious common law soon became known as a mixed Anglo-American creation as the Puritans reworked it for their purposes.

The law of nations, by contrast, was not a creature of the common law. Related to Roman law—from which the law of nations took its cosmopolitan impulse, as the passage cited from Seneca suggests—the law of nations belonged to what the English called civil law, which was largely legislative and prevailed on the continent of

Europe. In the Anglo-American tradition, this law has been unjustly overlooked. As Brian Levack has shown, the civil law tradition, contrary to popular opinion, was not only well integrated into the common law of England, especially in the areas of merchant and admiralty law, but was also a significant factor in the development of English common law throughout the seventeenth century.[20] Other scholars have called for the reintroduction of international law—the modern heir to the law of nations—in eighteenth-century American historiography.[21] To date, however, little to no work has been done on the civil law's influence on the prerevolutionary American colonies, where it served, as this book demonstrates, as a conduit for the law of nations and the Puritan cosmopolis.

The one important exception to this rule has come from Native-Americanist scholars concerned with law and politics, including Jeffrey Glover, Colin Calloway, James Merrill, Stuart Banner, and Andrew Newman. The work of these scholars addresses to varying degrees the laws that governed the making of treaties with the Indians. In particular from their work we gain invaluable insights into how treaties between Anglo-American and Native-American settlers were given voice and interpreted by the Native Americans, who have so often been left out of the picture. In *Paper Sovereign: Anglo-Native Treaties and the Law of Nations, 1604–1664*, Jeffrey Glover explicitly calls our attention to the law of nations as a source for some of those treaties, and in this way Glover's book provides the closest parallel to my own. Glover's book, however, differs substantially from mine in three ways. First, it deals with an earlier period in which the law of nations was still largely dominated by Spanish Catholicism, while my account is grounded in a law of nations developed by Protestant thinkers, who like the Puritans relied on Hebrew sources. Second, it concerns treaties between the Anglo-American settlers and Native-American,inhabitants, which were often creations of a specifically Anglo-Native devising, while I examine treaties that adhered to a standard form of legality and generated relatively self-similar treaties across sovereign entities. Third, Glover's argument about treaties revolves around their reinforcement of territorial claims, while I study the ways the law of nations helped bring people into a communal, cosmopolitan sphere where territorial claims were often secondary concerns.[22] Governed in general by the law of nations, as Glover suggests, Puritan-Native diplomacy and treaty making nevertheless belong to a different, earlier phase of the law of nations in which the features central to my analysis—standardization, neutrality, and the primacy of procedural and written consent—were not yet in play. Recognized as a nation for the purposes of invoking treaty law, the Indians in Glover's account were arguably not yet understood as a nation in the context of other nations, a fact that came back to haunt Indian law in the notorious Indian removal cases of the nineteenth century.

Contributing to what remains a common law bias in the study of Puritan literary and legal history is an overly constrained view of the legal archive of colonial America itself. We know, for example, from a comment preserved in the records of the General Court of the Massachusetts Bay Colony that the Puritans "procured" and read the works of Sir Edward "Cooke [*sic*] upon Littleton," a masterpiece of the common law. We lack such an anecdotal nugget concerning their knowledge of the civil law.[23] Solid evidence of the widespread dissemination of the law of nations, however, and a general familiarity among the Puritan elites with the work of Gentili, Grotius, and Selden is available. We start with textual evidence from some of the earliest narratives by Roger Williams and John Eliot about the Indians, which suggests that these writers and their many readers were aware of the contributions of the Spanish Scholastics whose work in the middle of the sixteenth century laid the foundation for the Protestant law of nations a half-century later. In particular, the Scholastic discourse about whether the natives inhabiting New England qualified as humans with rights to life and liberty permeates these works, while many of the court records acknowledging Indian land ownership and political autonomy are based on a theory of a shared human nature.[24] In fact, for Williams the Indians emerge at times as better Christians than the Puritans, making their natural entitlements as "humans" all too clear.[25]

Did the Puritans Know about the Law of Nations?

Because of the diversity of sources from which they were drawn, law of nations texts were also easily assimilated by groups of different critical and cultural persuasions. As the legal scholar David Kennedy points out, one of the distinctive characteristics of law of nations texts is that they were rarely if ever seen as being in competition with one another by their contemporaneous readers.[26] If the work of the

Spanish philosophers, who wrote about the natural rights of indigenous people within a Catholic context, was familiar to some Puritan writers, there can be little doubt that those same writers and their peers would have known the works of the three major Protestant writers, who reworked the Catholic contributions for their own religious purposes. That Increase Mather and his son, Cotton Mather, arguably the most prolific and influential ministers in Puritan New England (and discussed at length throughout the book), owned a copy of a Grotian text on clerical administration and at least one other volume that included a text devoted in part to a refutation of the ideas of "H. Grotius" confirms that at least some Puritan ministers knew Grotius's works well.[27] Explicit references to Grotius in Cotton Mather's biography of his father, Increase, as "that Great Man, Grotius" known for his "great erudition and great experience" further suggest that the Mathers not only read Grotius but also admired him and would have introduced their many friends and colleagues to his work.

From the many Puritan sermons that are shot through with the fruits of Selden's labor as the chief expositor of Christian Hebraism comes evidence that the Puritan reading elite knew of Selden's contributions to Protestant thought and scholarship as well. Sermons of the 1680s and 1690s, in particular, demonstrate a familiarity with Selden's resurrection of the Noahide laws as a source for the law of nations. That the Puritans, as Mark Peterson reminds us, did not distinguish between "Christian history and secular politics," as we do today, only increases the likelihood that the political texts of Grotius, Gentili, and Selden were widely read alongside their theological offerings.[28] The whole point of Selden's *De jure naturali et gentium, juxta disciplinam Ebraeorum* (*The Law of Nature and Nations According to the Hebrews*), after all, was to mine the Hebrew Bible as a source for the contemporary Protestant republic, indicating that, in Selden's case at the very least, theology and politics were one and the same.

The most incontrovertible evidence that many Puritans, elite and otherwise, were familiar with the law of nations comes, however, not from what we know of their library holdings or even from internal references to the works of the law's most important Protestant proponents, but rather from the treaties that were made between England and other nations and among other nations outside the English imperial sphere. These treaties, which set out the terms for peace, were the signature textual production of the law of nations and became, curiously enough, the basis for a popular literature.[29] Multiple copies of the 1648 Peace of Westphalia, for example, could be found in the stalls of many London booksellers that year, while news of diplomatic efforts in subsequent years flooded printing presses and newspapers all over Europe, putting treaty negotiations on everyone's minds, including in the far-flung American colonies. In 1659, for example, public demand for the Peace of the Pyrenees was such that copies were printed for collective and individual purchase. Soon after, printers started publishing treaties in compilations, such as Leibniz's *Codex juris gentium diplomaticus* in 1693.

Literary Texts and Cosmopolitan Authors

The circulation of these treaties and the stories they told about the making and breaking of multiple connections between and among nations help clarify the literary stakes of this study. Looking past the strict sense of cause and effect that characterized the Puritan jeremiad, the narrative form that famously threatened punishment for bad behavior, we can see in a literature shaped by and in dialogue with the many treaties inspired by the law of nations a different type of Puritan narrative that gives voice to stories of renewals and multiple jurisdictional belongings that went far beyond the domestic sphere.

In an earlier book, *Banished: Common Law and the Rhetoric of Social Exclusion in Early New England*, I wrote about the Puritans' understanding of domestic and transatlantic jurisdiction. In that book I was interested in how the Puritans, notorious for spelling out in explicit and affirmative terms what one had to do to be a Puritan, also invested a lot of energy in developing their communities by spelling out who was not allowed to be a Puritan, no matter how hard they tried. The procedures associated with identificatory affirmation—or determining who was in—and identificatory negation—or determining who was out—were admittedly intertwined, but the Puritans, I argued, turned to banishment and exclusion as the more accessible and efficient method of creating community just as people were starting to sort out the bewildering concepts of citizenship and belonging. In England, especially, classifications that tried to tease out various degrees of belonging were profuse. You could, for example, be a denizen, a subject (natural born or naturalized), or an alien (enemy or friend), and in this environment, I argued, the dos and don'ts of Puritanism proved dangerously ambiguous.[30]

In *The Puritan Cosmopolis*, which forms something of an intellectual sequel to *Banished*, I continue my investigation of belonging, but I turn here to the essence of the law as it pertained not to the domestic or transatlantic world but to a world where borders no longer existed as such. In researching the rhetoric of belonging and membership for *Banished* I found unexpected evidence of a more inclusive sense of Puritan belonging alongside the exclusionary one. Initially I found this puzzling. What I have since come to realize, however, is that this dual cosmopolitan orientation—of simultaneous inclusion and exclusion as well as simultaneous belonging on different levels—makes a good deal of sense. Thus one of the more general theses of this book is that in taking on a cosmopolitan identity, the Puritans took on the possibility of belonging to more than one legal sphere and managing more than one identity at the same time.

The presence of this combination of two or more senses of affiliation within one individual began in earnest in the period under examination here, from the eve of colonial charter revocation in 1680 (although hints of this expanded sense of affiliation surface as early as 1660 and are covered here as well) to about 1702 (the year King William III died). It was in these years, in the sermons, treatises, and pamphlets of the most influential ministers of the time, including Increase Mather, Cotton Mather, and Samuel Willard, that the Puritan elites wrestled most visibly with the twin poles of polis and cosmopolis that made up Seneca's two commonwealths. Having been robbed of their autonomy by the charter revocation, the Puritans naturally clung to their local affiliations, trying to shore up the commonwealth they worked for more than half a century to establish. At the same time, however, they also developed affiliations with the wider legal sphere made possible by the law of nations. Chapter 5, which examines the rise of Puritan Pietism, admittedly extends beyond this time frame, but it too tells a story that had its roots in the earlier period and was explicitly focused on the maintenance of a person's inner and outer orientations.

To say that the law of nations was the primary conduit for the development and expression of these wider affiliations is not to say that it was the only one. It is possible, for example, to read the sacramental openness of the Halfway Covenant that loosened restrictions for membership in the Puritan religious community in the 1660s as an early example of Puritan openness toward the world as well. On this account, even Solomon Stoddard, one of the greatest proponents of the Halfway Covenant but far from a cosmopolitan in any conventional sense, demonstrated a limited sort of cosmopolitanism by encouraging the widest possible membership in the church and participation in communion. After reminding his parishioners that he had written his "small" treatise, "The Safety of Appearing at the Day of Judgement" (1687), primarily for them and thus with an obviously insular purpose, Stoddard gives voice in a parenthetical remark to his outward looking concerns as well. "([N]ot that my care is confined to your Selves," he adds, "[but] I owe a regard to the prosperity of other places)." Prompted perhaps to think about those outside the limits of his congregation or the Colony of Massachusetts by the prospect of a universal "Judgement Day," Stoddard hints at a cosmopolitan affect here that comports with that espoused by the law of nations. Such an affect rooted, in this case, in a theological compromise would at the very least have smoothed the way for the spread among a relatively wide audience of the more legally informed cosmopolitanism promulgated by Willard and the Mathers.

If certain expressions of religious reform, such as the Halfway Covenant, helped at times to spread cosmopolitan thought patterns among a larger ministerial and lay audience in this period, they did not necessarily have consensus or consistent support, however. Some of the greatest exponents of cosmopolitan thinking, such as Increase Mather, could be inward looking at times, outward looking at others, and many second- and third-generation ministers remained indifferent to anything outside the Puritan settlements altogether.[31] The minister William Hubbard, for example, and the magistrate Simon Bradstreet, contemporaries of Willard and the Mathers, spent little time, judging from their own writings and the many writings about them, thinking about extra-colonial affairs. Hubbard, who wrote about the wars with the Indians and the history of New England, even went so far to express his disapproval of expansive trade policies, calling the commodities transported to the colony "superfluous vanities." Although he served as the governor of the Massachusetts Bay Colony for two interim periods—the first after the charter was revoked, and the second after Edmund Andros was deposed by a popular Puritan uprising—Simon Bradstreet was equally resistant to outward-looking thought and generally set his sights no further than royal appeasement.[32] Finally, it is possible to read the witchcraft crisis of 1692, an event that occurred well into the period in which, as I argue here, cosmopolitanism took root, as the supreme expression of a Puritan insularity characterized by the legally unpopular if not already anomalous admission of spectral evidence. Because cosmopolitanism was capacious enough to exist alongside these local, exclusionary orientations, however, it remained a powerful component of the Puritan mindset in these years.

Chapters to Come

Intersecting as they did with many common Puritan subjects and genres, such as the sermon, political pamphlet, and broadside, it makes sense that Puritan stories of cosmopolitanism issued not from a single discursive portal but from multiple discursive sites, including, most prominently, the covenant, the millennium, evidence, and Pietism, the four sites examined here. It makes sense too, given that the vast majority of Puritan textual production was dedicated to the expression of their faith, that three of these four discursive sites are nominally religious. The Puritans often explored legal, political, and social notions in the context of their faith, and religion and the law were also inextricably bound up with each other as sites of world creation. For readers unfamiliar with Puritan theology, background information on each of the theological contexts—the millennium, the covenant, and Pietism—is provided in the relevant chapters. For readers steeped in Puritan history and theology, the hope is that revisiting these touchstones in the context of cosmopolitanism will cast them in a new light.

Because the law of nations serves as both the material and epistemological ground for the Puritan cosmopolis and because its history is not well-known even among many legal historians, chapter 1 addresses the law of nations in detail. The argument made in this chapter as well as in the book as a whole is literary and historical: the law of nations ushered in a vision of cosmopolitanism that was taken up in a variety of discursive areas by the legally savvy Puritans in New England. The tools I use to explore this cosmopolitanism, however, often come from the work of twentieth- and twenty-first century theorists, who have returned to the problem of cosmopolitanism with renewed interest as a possible source for solving many of the problems of modern globalism. Although much of this work is geared toward contemporaneous forms of cosmopolitanism, we find definitions and ideas that help us make sense of early modern Puritan cosmopolitanism as well. Just as contemporaneous theorists refer back to the ancient and medieval notions of cosmopolitanism, I refer forward to them for the concepts central to the cosmopolitanism elaborated by the law of nations theorists and adopted by the Puritans, which have changed little over time. Drawing on the work of Bruce Robbins, Kwame Anthony Appiah, Martha Nussbaum, and others, chapter 1 looks at the law of nations in the seventeenth century as the imaginative source for the construction of a cosmopolis tailored to the early modern age. In a period obsessed with questions of belonging, sovereignty, and state formation, the cosmopolis imagined by the law of nations comes into being as a parallel world with its own answers to the pressing questions of the day: How to stop war and bring about peace? How to link people in distant places to each other? How to respect difference while also fostering unity?

Chapter 2, which together with chapter 3 forms the heart of the book's contribution to Puritan legal history, begins with the covenant, the image of corporate identity around which the Puritans' understanding of religion and the law revolved. The Puritans' notion of the covenant, chapter 2 demonstrates, found new life in a treaty-based sense of renewal. Searching for a more treaty-oriented sense of the covenant, I argue, the Puritans revived the covenant of renewal, which had its roots in the Hebrew Bible and was central to the law of nations. In sermons from the time of their first settlements through the 1660s, the Puritans had looked to the covenant as a way to understand obligation and reinforce their social order, finding in it just the right prescription for their status as God's newly chosen people. In the second half of the seventeenth century, from about 1660 to 1710, however, Puritan ministers, such as Samuel Willard, turned to the covenant not as a way to reinforce the Puritans' domestic order, as they had in previous years, but as a way to remind their audiences how deeply their covenantal form of community was indebted to and dependent on communities across the globe. Returning the covenant, as many of the law of nations theorists did, to its original moment when God offered it to the ancient Jews, the Puritans read it anew as a conduit for understanding attachment at a distance. As they came to understand in this period, to have been designated as

God's chosen people involved a choice made in the context of others, which formed a strong basis for cosmopolitan thought. That the covenant was renewable, a feature of covenantal relations the Puritans stressed in their late century sermons, added to the idea of distant attachment the possibility of what Bruce Robbins has called "the reality of (re) attachment [and] multiple attachment," which furthered cosmopolitan ends.

World creation continued for the Puritans in the context of the millennium, the discursive subject of chapter 3. The critical component of cosmopolitanism in that chapter occurs in an altered understanding of peace, which had both legal and religious significance for the Puritans and drove the law of nations work of Grotius and Gentili, in particular. In the three book-length sermons by Cotton Mather examined in this chapter, we witness a transformation in the image of millennial peace that moves from religion to the law and back again and that resonates far beyond these particular texts to inform the thoughts and relationships from which a fully comprehended cosmopolitanism took shape. The crux of the cosmopolitan reading advanced in this chapter comes in an examination of those passages that deal with the "Turks," the catchall designation used for people then living in the Ottoman Empire. What is most noteworthy about Mather's account is that the Turks emerge as a hated entity and as a culturally and legal acceptable "other," who in the context of war appeared uniquely capable of bringing about peace. This latter representation of the Turks takes precedence in this sermon over that of the Turks as the Eastern Antichrist—the image from Revelation that was commonplace in most millennialist sermons.[33] The manifestation of chapter 3's cosmopolitanism inheres as well in the repositioning of peace from an image rooted in religious history and bound up with a form of narrative predictability (common, for instance, to the readings of Revelation that spell out the end of time) to an image contingent on an unknowable number of things rooted in the law, including the actual progress of hostilities and the skill of negotiators. The integration of negotiation—one of the most important treaty conventions—informs the representation of peace within the sermon as manufactured rather than discovered with a meaning already intact.

Chapter 4 takes up the implications of having distant attachments and obligations in the legal realm by examining the discourse about truth in the pamphlet wars that developed around the revocation of the Puritans' charter. The discourse in that chapter also plays a large role in explaining how the Puritans understood the law in the late seventeenth century. To belong to a world that included distant others meant that knowledge and truth were matters for the whole world to determine. Under the influence of the law of nations and cosmopolitanism, the legal standards determining what it meant to know the truth of something, especially something that affected the planet as a whole, changed from thinking about evidence as issuing from a small group of people in a local area—the standard to which domestic law had long been committed—to insisting on garnering evidence from people around the world. This concept of what I am calling cosmopolitan evidence was of particular moment to the Puritans in their responses to the revocation of their charter and the imposition of direct supervision by Edmund Andros beginning in the 1680s. Appointed by King James II to take over as governor of the Massachusetts Bay Colony in the newly formed Dominion of New England in 1686, Andros had ignited the Puritans' anger by commandeering space in the Puritan churches for Anglican services, voiding land titles that the Puritans had upheld, abrogating laws passed by the Puritan Assembly, and starting a war with the Indians that the Puritans believed could have been avoided. Since Andros's installation, the Puritans had made numerous appeals to the king to stop him from mistreating them, but on April 18, 1689, finding no other recourse, several hundred took to the streets of Boston and brought about a "revolution," which ended with the jailing of Andros and the reinstallation of their governor, Simon Bradstreet.

The application of cosmopolitan evidence to these events demonstrates the extent to which cosmopolitan thinking proved relevant not simply to external events but also to internal, Anglo-American relations. Relying on new cosmopolitan standards for telling the truth, the Puritans, including, Increase Mather, an author known only as A.B., and several other anonymous authors of the documents written before, during, and after this "revolution," accused the royal commissioners of lying about the ostensible atrocities they claimed to have witnessed in the colonies and about themselves. Edmund Andros, the Puritans argued, was nothing more than an impostor whose lies could be effectively countered only by testimony from witnesses around the world. The cosmopolis finds expression in these texts in the association of truth with a demand not just for any evidence but for corroboration from a worldwide population now defined in cosmopolitan terms by its shared knowledge and concern for truth.

The final and fifth chapter makes a case for cosmopolitanism in the development of Pietism, a movement of the late seventeenth and early eighteenth centuries that put the Puritans in touch with what has come to be known, auspiciously for our purposes, as the Protestant International. Unlike more conventional readings of the "internationalism" of Pietism, which focus on the networks the Puritans established with coreligionists across the world, this chapter links Pietism to the creation of a cosmopolitan language. A highly literate and language-based people, who developed what was known as the "plain style," an essentially stripped down form of expression that while not always plain in the literal sense was nevertheless based on direct and unadorned explication of the Bible, the Puritans had long been interested not only in what people said but how they were saying it. In the context of late seventeenth-century Pietism, a movement aimed at revitalizing Protestant practice by creating a community of Protestants around the globe, Cotton Mather, as chapter 5 shows, turned to a similarly simple form of expression that was indebted to the law of nations and was visible in the many treaties penned in its wake. In *Bonifacius* and *Notitia Indiarum*, as well as in various letters and journal entries from the time, Mather reflects on what it would take to create a language that would not only be understood by many, distinguishing his efforts from contemporaries working on translation or universal language schemes, but also foster "Harmony [in] Persons that are in many Sentiments as well as Regions, distant from one another."[34] To this cosmopolitan end, Mather follows the model provided by the law of nations, which, along with its better-known precepts for global cooperation, established a new understanding of how language could work in and for the world. Treaties, I argue here, ushered in a new kind of literary reductionism in which words functioned as placeholders for interpretive agreement. In much of their pietistic literature the Puritans followed suit, minimizing the number and meaning of words and turning words from semantic sites of persuasion into material conduits that could cover unimaginably large cultural and linguistic gaps. An examination of this technique closes out the book's new view of Puritan literature in the context of the law of nations.

Presentist Possibilities

The law of nations constructed many possibilities for imagining a new, epoch-making world that allowed the Puritans to forge a sense of distant belonging. Returning to Seneca's remarks, however, we are reminded that this new world, the cosmopolis, was one of two: "one great and truly common"—that is, large and world encompassing—"the other to which the particular circumstances of birth have assigned us"—commonly understood as the colony or nation. The Puritans were of course familiar with the idea of multiple worlds long before the law of nations emerged. They were as a result of their shifting corporate status—from company to colony to province and from chartered to rogue—accustomed to juggling political and legal affiliations. In coming to grips with the terms put forward by the law of nations, however, those who were so inclined might have felt authorized for the first time to hold these seemingly antithetical identities simultaneously. In a legal sphere that was far more fluid than we have been led to believe, both legal tendencies—toward distant attachment and belonging on the one hand and toward exclusivity and self-involvement on the other—seemed to coexist.

As a condition of social possibility and an implicit form of governance that put the world as a whole on a par with the political and legal affiliations elicited by the many smaller communities familiar to early modern populations across Europe and beyond, the law of nations would have offered the Puritans an opportunity to manage their increasingly fraught relations with England from a perspective that went beyond the common law. In recognizing a new constellation of relations—between New England and England, but also between New England and the rest of the world—in emphasizing the mutual dependencies of those relationships, and in welcoming for the first time the legal and political actions of a covenanted "people" with or without an absolute sovereign, the Puritans adopted an identity that was, like the law of nations itself, cosmopolitan.

The Puritan Cosmopolis demonstrates the impact of a cosmopolitan reading of the Puritans for our critical recognition of the early American past as literary and legal historians have typically depicted it. To read the Puritan past as embodying a cosmopolitan potential based in the law, however, is to read against the grain of much previous scholarship. To construct such a counter-narrative, moreover, is particularly controversial in the period under scrutiny here, for it is widely accepted that in this period, marked by waning religious fervor and political power, and general dissatisfaction with royal rule, the Puritans showed their true colors and staged on a small scale what would ultimately become a coherent platform for independence and nationhood some eighty years after their commonwealth had come to an end.

At the beginning of the eighteenth century, the sermons and political pamphlets that issued from the Massachusetts Bay Colony, which had by then been incorporated into the Province of Massachusetts Bay, continued to give voice to cosmopolitan principles. As the century wore on, however, there was a noticeable shift away from the Puritans' expression of interest in the world at large (except perhaps with respect to external enemies) and toward their own civil government. For minsters such as Benjamin Colman and John Wise, who were writing in the first two decades of the century, the key issue was internal governance, religious and secular. As heirs to the late seventeenth-century struggle represented here, these ministers demonstrated their cosmopolitan outlook less by developing a sense of belonging to a larger world and more by adhering to the Enlightenment principles of tolerance and equality within their smaller one. It might be an exaggeration to say that in this trajectory Puritan cosmopolitanism disappeared, but it definitely took a back seat to domestic developments.

By the late eighteenth century, the law of nations had given way to what we now call international law, which was more positivistic and, I think it fair to say, less imaginative than its predecessor. The epilogue to this book addresses this transition—from law of nations to international law—in terms of its impact on cosmopolitanism and the lessons the Puritan engagement with the law of nations may hold for us going forward. If the Puritans, however provisionally and inchoately, lent their energies to both forms of community building—to the nation and to the cosmopolis—then perhaps we can more readily understand how we might do so today. As others have noted, "the cosmopolitanization of memory does not mean the end of national perspectives, so much as their transformation into more complex entities with different relations to the universal."[35] Following this dictum and keeping the Puritans in mind, it may be possible for us to move beyond the clash between nation and cosmopolis that still dominates the scholarship on the subject. Even as we work toward denationalization, as Saskia Sassen suggests, we can also look to a past where complementary versions of both types of social order and both types of belonging were cultivated simultaneously.[36] It is not for me to say whether the American nation that developed in the eighteenth century and became dominant in the nineteenth century contributed to the loss of this decidedly cosmopolitan chapter in our legal and literary past or whether this loss merely became a victim of the triumphalist story we decided to tell about it. I simply leave it to the following pages to raise the question in a fruitful way.

{1}

The Law of Nations and the Sources of the Cosmopolis

Once someone has said, I am an Indian first, a citizen of the world second, once he or she has made that morally questionable move of self-definition by a morally irrelevant characteristic, then what, indeed, will stop that person from saying . . . I am a Hindu first and an Indian second, or I am an upper caste landlord first, and Hindu second?

—MARTHA NUSSBAUM

The cosmopolitan thought of the Puritans in late seventeenth-century New England had its source in the cosmopolitanism of a law of nations that was as much about the world as a whole as it was about the nation-state it later came to epitomize. With the nation-state not yet a consolidated entity, the seventeenth-century law of nations was far more open-ended than the international law to which it gave rise more than a century later. In the absence of a fixed idea of sovereignty, the law of nations was able to articulate multiple historical possibilities for social, political, and legal communities, one of which—the cosmopolitan—is fundamental to the reading I offer here. In my account, the cosmopolis emerges as a central part of the intellectual project of the law of nations put forth by the Protestant thinkers Alberico Gentili, Hugo Grotius, and John Selden, with the main features of the law recast as the building blocks of the cosmopolis.

Thinking of the law of nations as the source for an early modern cosmopolitanism, of which the Puritans were prime exemplars, however, is neither common nor traditional. The majority view holds that the law of nations was antithetical to cosmopolitanism. Far from being about a shared universe, the law of nations in the majority view was a starting point for the birth of the nation, with its impassable borders and compartmentalized conception of identities. Admittedly, all three of the law of nations' theorists examined here were partially complicit in this construction. According to Hedley Bull, Grotius laid the foundation for thinking about the globe as "a society of states."[1] To the extent that a global system such as the law of nations issued from the establishment of the modern state, it was the result of sovereign states confronting each other rather than subordinating themselves to a more universal authority such as an emperor or the pope. Although it was an unquestionable improvement on the centralization of authority in the medieval period, the upshot of this sovereign contestation was an interstate system that enabled states to interact to resolve interstate differences. This system fell short, however, when it came to matters of global concern. Each state on this account was, in the words of one legal historian, a "monad living by itself and ready to link up with another State only to the extent that this serves its own interests."[2]

This monadic, interstate view of the law of nations stems largely from the law's association with the most celebrated mechanism for its enforcement, the Treaty of Westphalia, which was a series of treaties signed by the Holy Roman Empire, the Dutch Republic, Sweden, and France in 1648. As Olaf Asbach and Peter Schröder observe, "the peace of Westphalia is a symbol for a specific set of new social and political actors . . . and the symbolic year '1648' in particular stands for the establishment of the 'modern state.'"[3] Under the terms of the Treaty of Westphalia, the Hapsburgs' goal of creating a universal monarchy over all Europe was disrupted, and in its place came a complex of sovereign states defined as having absolute control over the citizens within their borders. The key to the association of the law of nations with Westphalia and of Westphalia with the birth of the nation is a product in part of the replacement of the confessional state—determined by its religious identity--with the territorially defined one. As K. J. Holsti notes, Westphalia provided a "legal basis for the developing territorial particularism of Europe, and by terminating the vestiges of relations between superiors and inferiors, with authority emanating downward from the Emperor and the Pope."[4]

Some historians have delved beneath the surface of this account and helped us see beyond it. As William Grewe points out, while the trend over the course of the century was away from confessional states and toward territorially demarcated states with systems of general sovereignty, this was hardly an accurate description of the contemporaneous state system. The seventeenth century was marked by rival models of states, including the parliamentary and aristocratic models that developed in England, as well as the absolutist models that seemed to predominate across continental Europe and in frontier areas that were coping with unclear loyalties. This multiplicity of models remained in place after Westphalia and well into the latter part of the century. Despite the Treaty of Westphalia's efforts to reinforce territorial boundaries, the treaty itself, brokered among several nations and the Holy Roman Empire, was a testament to the plurality of parties that would need to be invoked and consulted to make the law work. While Westphalia may have contributed to cementing what later became a dominant nationalism in the nineteenth century, alternative histories reveal that the reality on the ground in the seventeenth century was scarcely altered as people continued to move across territorial borders without awareness of them.

This recognition of the facts on the ground, however, has done little to distinguish between the early modern iterations of the law of nations and international law, which is a discrete area of law that like other jurisdictional divides within the law, including canon law and admiralty law, came into being in its modern incarnation in the 1790s when European states instituted a security system of vast proportions. In most legal histories of international law, the law of nations is still represented as a precursor to this more reified notion of the law, a legal counterpart to Immanuel Wallerstein's world system, geared toward competition and the development of nationalisms for the purposes of distinction and rivalry.[5] Sovereign states in Wallerstein's model and in most legal histories of the law of nations vied with each other to create an interstate system in which states had to recognize each other, but they did so only for the purposes of gaining advantages over one another.

Given this dominant view, the challenge of this chapter lies in conveying a sense of the law of nations as a legal entity that served in its own day—a period that coincided with the Puritans' rule in New England—as a source for a legal and political sphere far more inclusive and cosmopolitan than the "international law" system it eventually became. To be clear: identifying a burgeoning cosmopolis within the ideas of Gentili, Grotius, and Selden is not to suggest that these theorists were engaged in the kind of lawmaking that, as David Held writes, "create[s] powers, rights and constraints that go beyond the claims of nation-states and which have far-reaching consequences, in principle, for the nature and form of political power."[6] For Held this kind of cosmopolitanism was not possible until the rise of a coherent multilateral social and political order after the Second World War. But if the seventeenth-century law of nations did not give rise to or coincide with such an order, it did redefine the bonds between and among states to create a sphere in which multiple players, including players of indeterminate sovereignty, such as the Massachusetts Bay Colony, could theoretically participate. Regularly misconstrued as a system devoted exclusively to strengthening the sovereign entities involved, the legal and political sphere imagined by seventeenth-century law of nations theorists conferred on its participants a new status within a body of law founded on a concept of belonging to a supranational world, which remains one of the hallmarks of cosmopolitanism today.

General Principles

There were three related ways in which the seventeenth-century law of nations contributed to the theory and practice of cosmopolitanism. The first was by redefining universalism to include people outside Christendom. The second was by replacing culture-bound notions of justice with the formal language of the law. The third was by considering individuals not necessarily as the repository of human rights, as we understand them today, but as sources of law-making equal in importance to the sovereign or the state.[7] Not coincidentally, all three of these features—universalism, linguistic formalism, and the primacy of the individual—were focal points for the Puritans in the development of their church-state in New England, putting them in conversation with the law of nations and cosmopolitanism from the start. Developments around all three of these axes within Puritan theology coincided with these legal developments in the second half of the seventeenth century, pushing the Puritan commonwealth toward greater cosmopolitanism in many areas. In the wake of the Halfway Covenant in 1662, for example, Puritan congregations moved closer to the kind of universalism theorists of the law of nations had in mind. Needless to say, Puritan churches never contemplated admitting non-Christian members, yet there was a growing tolerance over time for people who called themselves Puritans but whose ideas about conversion and worship did not conform to the stricter standards that had prevailed in the first half of the century. Loosening membership requirements contributed to a religious and legal shift that allowed the community to expand its boundaries and to accommodate individual difference, both of which were law of nations' dictates. The focus on individualism within the law of nations also corresponded to a long-standing Puritan emphasis on individual hermeneutics and conversion, a by-product of the Protestant Reformation. In addition, as Francis Bremer points out, an emphasis on the Puritan clergy has in part obscured the role of the Puritan laity, many of whom played a part in creating a religious practice that depended on individual volunteers.[8] That the communication and correspondence of Puritan ministers with this larger community, including Puritans in distant countries, required the development of a stripped down language also helped the Colony move closer to cosmopolitan goals. To promote communication with people in distant countries whose practices, though nominally Protestant, often differed from that of the Bay Colonists, Cotton Mather, for example, advanced linguistic reforms that aimed to transcend language practices more obviously tied to particular cultural formulations.

Did the law of nations promote an ideal cosmopolitanism with no restrictions on membership and the equal participation of all? Far from it. But the efforts made by the seventeenth-century law of nations theorists toward these ends and the effects they had on the their Puritans counterparts in New England were far greater than those of their predecessors in sixteenth-century Spain or their immediate heirs in the eighteenth and nineteenth centuries. A normative theory that posits the existence of a world to which all human beings belong, cosmopolitanism was rooted in the theories of the ancient Greek and Roman Stoics, but by the seventeenth century, its sources themselves had become cosmopolitan, which made the seventeenth-century iteration of the law especially well-suited to promoting cosmopolitan goals. From Spain came the work of the fifteenth- and sixteenth-century Spanish Scholastics, Francisco de Vitoria and Francisco Suarez, which became a mainstay of political theory in the Protestant world by the early seventeenth century. From the Near East came the Hebrew Bible, which formed the basis not only for the Puritans' sense of themselves as the chosen people but also and paradoxically for the much more inclusive sense of covenant central to the law of nations. From the Ottomans came the elaboration of covenant as the basis for treaty negotiations (also present in the Hebrew Bible). Finally, from the Netherlands and England came the law merchant and the elaboration of these various other influences into the body of law known to the Puritans as the law of nations.

The law of nations most familiar to the Puritans was based on the legal theories of Hugo Grotius, Alberico Gentili, and John Selden—all Protestant, the latter two inhabitants of England. Gentili, who was Italian by birth, taught civil law at Oxford University from 1580 to 1608 and theorized new relationships among sovereign entities in his *De jure belli libri tres*, or *The Law of War* (1598). In this landmark publication, Gentili promoted just war and addressed the precarious relationships among countries that were in a state of neutrality. Grotius, a Dutch legal theorist and diplomat, reinforced Gentili's ideas about war but added a system for instituting peace within a global sphere in his *De jure belli ac pacis*, or *The Rights of War and Peace* (1625). Finally, Selden, who served as a government consultant and scholar, brought the theories of Gentili and Grotius to bear on the development of civil society more generally in his *De jure naturali et gentium, juxta disciplinam Ebraeorum*, or *The Law of Nature and Nations According to the Hebrews* (1640). While not typically associated with the law of nations or the writings of Gentili and Grotius, for whom the title of founding fathers is typically reserved, Selden's work was enormously influential in England and formed a touchstone for the cosmopolitan thought of the Puritans in particular.

Dedicated to crafting laws that would regulate conduct among political entities, all three theorists looked to the ancient idea of a cosmopolis, a larger, more inclusive sphere to which all people naturally belonged—regardless of their legal affiliations to municipality, state, or nation. The law of nations theorists also crucially extended that sphere, making the world more cosmopolitan than it had ever been before. As Gentili's ideas about a shared humanity informed Grotius's vision of a secular universalism and Selden's notion of a biblical law that encompassed Jews and gentiles alike, the cosmopolis around which the law of nations revolved began to take on a more inclusive and legally plausible shape.

Grounded firmly, as it always had been, in natural law—a legal and philosophical theory that looked to nature as the source of all laws and to human reason as the mechanism by which such laws could be ascertained—the seventeenth-century law of nations nevertheless moved beyond some of the problems that had plagued the exercise of natural law in the medieval period. Specifically, the law of nations added a fundamental formality to legal regulations about war and peace that had under the natural law regimes of the past been tied to concepts within the overly capacious understanding of "nature" and "reason," defined in morally ambiguous ways. Many wars in the Middle Ages, for example, never came to a proper end because both sides assumed the moral high ground based on different interpretations of natural law. Under the law of nations, by contrast, a line was drawn between law and morality, giving law, newly rendered as an adherence to written rules, the final word. Under the law of nations and the treaty provisions that gave it voice, the only thing that mattered was whether and to what extent each side had followed the rules about (1) who could go to war, (2) how belligerents were to be treated during war, and (3) how to restore peace after hostilities ended. Assessing the justness of each side's claim (which had long been central to the just war tradition) according to clearly written rules about war's conduct turned what had previously been vague moral parameters into relatively clear procedural ones, allowing parties from a much wider range of belief systems, including those outside Christendom, to share in a juridical process.

To this same end—enlarging the number of meaningful parties in the global sphere—the rules of war and peace laid out by the law of nations also worked to disaggregate the aims of the state and the aims of its individual inhabitants, affording people the chance to sustain their own cross-cultural affiliations even when the sovereign entity to which they owed allegiance was at war. Gentili articulated this disaggregation in part by reminding readers that the sovereign's authority was contingent on the consent of his or her subjects. A monarch, Gentili wrote, may not "alienate his subjects nor give them to another king; for a people is free even though it be under a king."[9] Grotius articulated a similar notion of disaggregation by distinguishing between private law—concerned with individuals—and public law—concerned with matters of state. "The most general and most necessary Divisions of War is this, that one War is private," he writes, "another publick."[10] In contrast to medieval warfare where one or another prince might declare war on behalf of the political entity as a whole without clear authorization to do so (blurring the line between private and public war), Grotius's rules of war were applicable only to an explicitly public war undertaken by a recognized sovereign. Permitting individuals to maintain the private, nonstate affiliations that would ultimately contribute to and strengthen the cosmopolitan sphere left them free to honor their obligations to Seneca's two commonwealths—the state and the cosmopolis—as well as, potentially, a host of other commonwealths even in wartime.

All of these innovations were possible in part because of conditions on the ground, which make the claims offered here historically and conceptually specific. By the early seventeenth century, when Gentili, Grotius, and Selden were formulating their theories, many ancient texts were newly available and a greater ecumenism within religiously inflected legal thought prevailed. Compared with their predecessors in the Middle Ages, seventeenth-century law of nations theorists were able to choose from among a number of less restrictive and less homogenous historical sources when thinking through the concept of a world-encompassing law. By the same token, when the law of nations theorists were thinking through a law for the world, the world itself was in a state of disarray and the issue of sovereignty unsettled.[11] Compared with their heirs, then, seventeenth-century thinkers were able to contemplate the idea of a sovereign legal sphere that was not necessarily bound by the nation, the concept that dominated later eighteenth- and nineteenth-century legal thought.

To already outward looking third-generation Puritan ministers, magistrates, and merchants, the ideas embodied by the law of nations would have made a good deal of sense. Having reconciled themselves to the theological compromise represented by the Halfway Covenant, which allowed the children of baptized church members into the church with far fewer requirements, a majority of third-generation community leaders and laypeople (who had also given their consent to the Halfway Covenant in large numbers), had already opened themselves up to the possibility of a wider community. After the Glorious Revolution, moreover, which replaced the crypto-Catholic James II with the Protestant William and Mary, the Puritans could reasonably expect to strengthen their alliances with people in distant places. With a Protestant power back on the throne, it was now possible, as Mark Peterson writes, "for Bostonians to believe their own ambitions might no longer be limited to their remote corner of the Atlantic world."[12] The link between the Puritans and the law of nations, however, had still deeper roots in their shared interest in universalism, individualism, and linguistic formalism, the three components of cosmopolitanism mentioned above. The rest of this chapter outlines the ways in which the law of nations embodied those particular components and the ways in which they intersected with and influenced already existing Puritan concerns.

Universalism

The law of nations inaugurated a new conception of universalism on four planes, all of which intersected with already existing Puritan beliefs and practices. The first was a shift from a Christian universalism to a universalism that could accommodate the Turks. The second was the emergence of a double affiliation, local and global. The third was a planetary sense of the law in which some events affected the world regardless of where they happened. The fourth was the turn to Jewish sources (specifically the Noahide laws), which were promulgated to all humankind without restriction. The Puritans reworked all four manifestations of universalism as they revised their ideas about the millennium, the covenant, evidence, and Pietism. To varying degrees, each feature of universalism helped the Puritans imagine a place above and beyond their local commonwealth to which they could appeal legally and on which they could rely for an alternate sense of themselves as members of a cosmopolitan community.

Universalism has always been one of cosmopolitanism's greatest and yet most controversial features. The ancient Greek understanding of cosmopolitanism included a fellowship among all people on the basis of a shared humanity. If being human was a universal condition, it followed that all humans belonged to a shared universe. With this sense of universalism in mind, Roman lawmakers such as Cicero posited a law of universal application, rooting it in human nature and in the essence of human fellowship. Within the bounds of nature, Cicero explained, lay all the rules of good government, domestic and global. "True law is right reason in agreement with Nature," he wrote. "It summons to duty by its commands and averts from wrong-doing by its prohibitions."[13] Derived from nature, such a law was universal, immutable, and irrefutable. It was, as Cicero went on to say, "impossible to abolish it."[14]

Cicero may have been right about the impossibility of abolishing natural law, but as medieval developments revealed, natural law proved highly susceptible to alteration and manipulation. For Thomas

Aquinas, the greatest medieval exponent of natural law, the central component of the law was not the quality of being human, but the human's ability to participate in and channel the expression of God. In the hands of Aquinas and other Christian philosophers, natural law took a back seat to God's law, and the emphasis on the human element went underground. In its place the universalism immanent in humans was ascribed to a heavenly realm, a city of God, as Augustine called it, where humans who were by nature corrupt and thus incapable of providing the basis for any kind of law could nevertheless aspire toward Christian perfection. Christian universalism, as it was called, became a compelling form of universalism throughout the Middle Ages and lingered well into the sixteenth century as the West incorporated the Americas into the global vision of an *Orbis Christianus*. So powerful was the reach of the Christian church in this period that many dismissed the exclusivity of Christian universalism as a temporary impediment to world domination.

The School of Salamanca to which the sixteenth-century Spanish philosophers Francisco de Vitoria and Francisco Suarez belonged laid the groundwork for a modern law of nations that was steeped in Christian universalism. Suarez spoke of a "universal society" built on "mutual aid and association," and both men posited a global community to which all smaller polities belonged.[15] For both Vitoria and Suarez, however, law was ultimately a theological concept, a Christian interpretation of natural law predicated on a Christian sense of human rights and dignity. Human rights, the Spanish scholastics insisted, belonged to all people, and even wars waged against allegedly "uncivilized" peoples—a theory that had relevance for the indigenous populations of the New World conquered by Spain—were deemed just only if they conformed to Christian dictates.

As part of the theory of universalism, the drawbacks of Vitoria's and Suarez's law of nations, the City of God, and its secular counterpart, the *res publica Christiana*, are self-evident. An ideal determined by Christian morality, Christian universalism may have transcended territorial borders, but it remained confined by the borders of faith. How could a sphere confined to individuals of the Christian faith make a legitimate claim to being universal? Despite its proponents, who argued that it was only a matter of time until Christianity became universal in name and in practice, realities on the ground suggested otherwise. Muslims and Jews, for example, proved largely impervious to the allure of Christianity, and those who did convert often did so under duress, giving rise to a universalism that had more to do with the imposition of one people's values on another's than with any shared, innate quality common to humankind.

Unsurprisingly, one of the strongest contemporary critiques of cosmopolitanism rests on the claim that in imagining one world to which we all belong, universalism has become synonymous with cultural or religious imposition, leading to the production of a homogenous whole that elides important differences among people. The notion of cultural or religious imposition masquerading as universalism may have plagued Christian universalism more visibly than any other form of universalism in history, and in subscribing to it, the New England Puritans were not exempt from these limitations. Yet signs that a capacious, legally informed notion of universalism began to push against the Puritans' more parochial, theologically informed vision can be seen in the adjustments they made to the worn concepts of the millennium, the covenant, and piety discussed in subsequent chapters.

Other forms of universalism from ancient Rome to today continue to suggest that a cosmopolitanism based on universalism is nothing more than a veil for homogenizing operations, which have less to do with Christianity or domestic law than with the imposition of Western values on the rest of the world. Acknowledging the shortcomings of all versions of universalism, Bruce Robbins has nevertheless come to its defense as the starting point for legal and political reformation. "[T]here never can be a universalism that is not 'under the aegis of some definite power or agent,'" Robbins writes. "To disqualify it on these grounds, in the hopes of eventually finding a 'clean' universalism independent of all partial powers and agents, is to condemn oneself to an infinite wait and, in effect, to withdraw from the project of political change. In short, all universalisms are dirty."[16] The goal, following Robbins, would be to accept the inevitability of universalism while remaining vigilant about its homogenizing tendencies and reducing them whenever possible. As part of its cosmopolitan vision, the law of nations did just that.

The first, and from the Puritans' perspective arguably the most appealing, way in which the law of nations reduced the homogenizing effects of universalism was by removing the need for an absolutist power from the global scene. This represented a real change from the absolutism that had resided in the power of the pope during Christendom. In place of a supreme imperial power, the law of nations required legal entities to subscribe to an overriding theory of a global sphere, replacing one authority in possession of immutable power with many voices and an understanding of the contingencies that defined the world. This alone would have predisposed the aggressively anti-papist Puritans to the law of nations. The Puritans' penchant for "gathered" churches that would govern themselves in a decentralized system of church hierarchy made them early adapters of a nonhomogenized universalism. In the gathered church, as the Puritans defined it, congregants managed their own affairs, chose their own ministers, and developed their own rules about ritual. To be sure, the gathered or congregational churches favored by the Puritans created almost as many problems as they solved since each church was capable in theory of insisting on the superiority of its own practice, potentially undercutting the establishment of any larger, universal community. Just such claims from several congregations, including most conspicuously the congregation in Salem, led to problems with church authority in the early years of the Bay Colony. By the second half of the seventeenth century, however, the idea of the gathered church had largely coalesced into a way of accommodating difference—as in the Halfway Covenant—while fostering unity overall, bringing the Puritan church-state that much closer to the cosmopolitan ideal of the law of nations.

The second feature of the law of nations that moved universalism away from homogenization and toward greater heterogeneity was the injunction to negotiate with entities that were outside the old confessional borders. As Richard Tuck explains, this was one of Grotius's major innovations. While Gentili sided with Peter Martyr, a Reformation theologian and compatriot of Gentili's, who believed that it was "never right to make an alliance with infidels," Grotius expressly endorsed such alliances. "Do we perhaps believe that we have nothing in common with persons who have not accepted the Christian faith?" Grotius asked. Grounding his answer in his insistence that the universe of law was truly cosmopolitan and "includes every human being," Grotius also saw a practical benefit to negotiating with infidels. "Not only is it universally admitted that the protection of infidels from injury (even from injury by Christians) is never unjust," he explained, "but it is furthermore maintained . . . that alliances and treaties with infidels may in many cases be justly contracted for the purpose of defending one's own rights, too."[17] This statement reveals a practical motive for treating with the infidel on whom one might later have to depend that nevertheless advances the universalist agenda of the law of nations. "[T]here is no State so strong or well provided," Grotius reminds his readers, "but what may sometimes stand in need of Foreign Assistance, either in the Business of Commerce, or to repel the joint Forces of several Foreign Nations Confederate against it."[18]

Guided by a sense of practicality, Grotius's injunction to treat with infidels had real-world implications for the Puritans and for Europe as a whole. The Ottoman Empire had been accreting Western territories from the time of the fall of Constantinople in 1453. By 1521, the Ottomans had seized Belgrade and would soon take key cities that had formerly belonged to the Hapsburg Empire in what is now known as Hungary.[19] For years afterward the Ottomans continued moving further west until 1688, when they found themselves on the outskirts of Vienna, the heart of Western civilization. In their territorial encroachments, the Ottomans posed what was arguably the most significant challenge to a law that had up until that time been seen as universal but had in reality been reserved for entities within the bounds of Christendom alone.

Dismissed for centuries by Western historians as being of little importance in the development of Western law or literature, the Ottomans actually played an enormously influential role in the early modern history of the West, as more recent historians and literary scholars have pointed out. Trade had been a major conduit of interaction with the Ottomans from the fifteenth century on, and the Ottoman system of capitulations—agreements drawn up with the sultan allowing foreigners who paid a tax to the government to live in peace in Ottoman lands—had encouraged even deeper cultural and political ties. As the sixteenth century wore on, however, the presence of the Ottomans as a potentially hostile force with a highly trained army became unavoidable. It was at this point that the law of nations reconfigured them as potential partners in peace. This reconfiguration came in the form of a new model of diplomacy characterized by diplomats who did not wait until hostilities broke out to treat with the legal entity in question but resided abroad for long periods of time and became political and cultural fixtures in foreign societies.

The role of the new diplomat, the "resident ambassador," altered the climate of global relations considerably and sent it in a more cosmopolitan direction. In part this was due to the primacy of legal over commercial relations that now accompanied the diplomat's role. With diplomats living in foreign countries for years, if not for the greater part of a lifetime, the stream of information transmitted to the home country was not only more frequent and more detailed but also more focused on keeping the peace than on increasing trade revenues. This new, legally oriented diplomatic information was based on a deep and constantly changing understanding of foreign cultures and their inhabitants.[20] When fully developed, this diplomatic system concerned itself with matters that went beyond commerce, rumors of assassinations, or governmental coups—the stuff of medieval embassies—to include information about the culture's attitudes toward marriage, tax paying, and religious practices, which appeared in the form of dispatches and became the basis of a popular literature.[21]

Voraciously consumed by people on both sides of the Atlantic, this literature, such as Richard Knolles's *Turkish History* from 1687, to which the British consul, Paul Rycaut's, account was appended, or "The Sum of the Nine Articles," a treaty signed between the Ottoman Emperor and a Hungarian leader in 1683 (copies of which were held by the Mathers), led many Puritans to see the customs of the Ottomans in a new light.[22] As chapter 3 reveals, where many leading Puritans ministers had once tied their vision of the millennium to the inevitability of a war with the Turks, they were, under the auspices of the new diplomacy, more inclined to find continuities between them and their own social and legal orders. In particular, in several of Cotton Mather's millennialist sermons, we see evidence of Grotius's advice to see the Turks as partners, who might just as easily have played a part in protecting the Protestants as in harming them. In "The Turkish Fast," the broadside discussed in the prologue, we see additional evidence of how such a practical approach to the prospect of peace had the potential to translate, for some Puritans, into a cultural orientation in which the Turks emerged as partners in devotion, atonement, and human sympathy. Dovetailing with the Puritans' acceptance of an ever-widening sphere of Christian universalism, but reaching a much wider audience, this new, diplomatically inspired stream of information increased the level of legal cooperation among countries and reinforced the idea that the world was a social and legal sphere unto itself. Such an expansive sense of community also gave rise to the spread of a late seventeenth- to early eighteenth-century Puritan Pietism that embraced Christians all over, including in Muslim lands. This pietistic community is the subject of chapter 5.

The spread of information garnered from diplomatic reports and treaties also gave rise to a sense shared by numerous legal bodies that some events had the ability to affect the world as a whole, regardless of where they originated. The law of nations developed to regulate such matters, influencing neighboring countries as well as all sovereign entities whether they had contiguous borders or not. This connectivity led to an early form of what I earlier called a planetary universalism. A planetary sense of community would have been all too familiar to the Puritans by the 1680s, if not earlier, when they were placed under the supervision of a royal governor and became increasingly aware that decisions made in England, not to mention in a place as far away as the Ottoman Empire, could have an immediate effect on them. In the interconnected world of the early modern period, in which social, legal, and political dependencies went from the territorially proximate to the remote, more things qualified as matters of worldly concern. For the Puritans this expanded sense of worldly concern found expression in their thoughts about evidence, especially in the context of claims to sovereignty, a matter that was by definition of worldly concern. If more things mattered to the world as a whole, the Puritans reasoned, only evidence from the world and its various inhabitants could accurately tell the truth about them. In their negotiations with the Crown after their charter had been revoked, the Puritans availed themselves of this planetary universality by calling on people from all over the world to weigh in on their claims to autonomy. Chapter 4 takes up this reckoning in more detail.

Of a piece with the changing tide of truth-telling among the Puritans, treaties in the early modern period often worked together with the law of nations to reinforce the need for an infinitely complex understanding of contingencies to maintain peace and order. "An acceptance of contingency in general," as one political theorist writes, "would become the study of international law."[23] Piracy is often taken as an example of an early modern phenomenon that revealed contingencies among states and affected the world as a whole. Yet piracy was not an isolated phenomenon. There was an accompanying recognition that the sinking of an important cargo ship in one place or the spread of plague in another might determine commercial and political fortunes across the globe. Even war, which had long been the subject of and impetus for treatises on the law of nations, by the seventeenth century could no longer be seen as a matter of interest to warring parties alone. Unlike the Scholastics, who did not believe that conflicts between two or more sovereign nations could threaten the world order, Gentili and Grotius considered war in one place a concern for legal and political bodies the world over.[24] As Arthur Nussbaum explains, "the most urgent and troublesome problem of international law of the seventeenth century bore upon neutrality. The legal position of states not participants in a present war was most obscure and precarious."[25] For Nussbaum, treaties outlining the rights and duties that various countries had toward others were essential in this regard. Neutrals were important for an additional reason as well—because they represented more visibly than countries actively engaged in war how the principles of the law of nations could be maintained through separate affiliations to a cosmopolitan sphere. Thinking about the possibility of remaining neutral would have certainly been on the Puritans' minds in the later seventeenth century as the wars between England and France came to their shores, causing battles between New England and New France from 1688 to 1697 that might, at least as far as they were concerned, not otherwise have erupted.

If negotiating with the Ottomans and instituting a diplomatic corps responsive to cultural differences of political and legal entities around the world helped reduce the homogenizing tendency of the universalism on which cosmopolitanism was based, it did not, however, address another charge relevant to the early modern world and of concern to contemporary critics of cosmopolitanism as well; namely, universalism unrealistically imagines an affiliation above and beyond the local. According to these critics, Richard Rorty preeminent among them, local affiliations are the only plausible source of morality and law. We cannot feel for people we have never seen, Rorty implies, or conduct ourselves in accordance with customs we have never experienced. Taking up a position in conflict with Martha Nussbaum's repeated assertions that the defining characteristic of cosmopolitanism is a primary affiliation with the world at large, Rorty contends that our primary affiliations will inevitably be local since the local alone fuels the feeling of attachment around which social community revolves.[26] Conceding that there is a germ of truth in Rorty's formulation, Nussbaum writes: "Becoming a citizen of the world is often a lonely business. It is, as Diogenes said, a kind of exile—from the comfort of local truths, from the warm, nestling feeling of patriotism, from the absorbing pride in oneself and one's own." Yet to Rorty's entrenched position against cosmopolitan affiliations, Nussbaum wonders why we should "think of people from China as our fellows the minute they dwell in the United States, but not when they dwell in a certain other place, namely China?"[27]

Kwame Anthony Appiah, another contemporary cosmopolitan theorist, has taken up a middle ground between Nussbaum's primary affiliation with the world and Rorty's primary, if not exclusive, affiliation with the local. Acknowledging the importance of difference in the form of local affiliations with the neighborhood, community, city, or state alongside affiliations with the world, Appiah's solution is to promote what he calls a liberal cosmopolitanism that acknowledges differences together with national loyalties. Liberal cosmopolitans, Appiah writes, "value the variety of human forms of social and cultural life, [and] do not want everybody to become part of a homogenous global culture." Local differences, he goes on to say, "must meet certain general ethical constraints," but as long as this happens, "we are happy to let them be."[28]

Rorty's presumption that a national affiliation is the only kind of social affiliation that makes sense is countered by Appiah's notion of a dual system of affiliations that are not mutually exclusive. Writing more than four hundred years earlier, Gentili's and Grotius's versions of cosmopolitanism anticipate Appiah's to a striking degree. That these early modern theorists had a strong sense of two worlds—the local and the cosmopolitan—rooted in their many references to Seneca's theory of "two commonwealths," cannot be disputed. But their theories of the local and of the cosmopolitan also went beyond the categorical. For Grotius, for example, one of the purposes of the law of nations was to serve as a counterpoint to the local affiliations that distinguished large sovereign entities from each other. According to Grotius, people in different countries acted in predictably homogenous and locally defined ways; people in Spain acted like Spaniards, in England like the English, and so on. Paradoxically, it was this notion of intramural homogeneity—with which many have taken issue today—that gave rise to Grotius's sense that a more universal bond across legal entities should be cultivated.

For Grotius a sense of this legal bond across various political entities would express itself in the form of covenants from which, he notes, both religious and civil laws, including treaties, arose. "Again, since the fulfilling of Covenants belongs to the Law of Nature," Grotius wrote, "(for it was necessary there should be some Means of obliging Men among themselves, and we cannot conceive any other more conformable to Nature) from this very Foundation Civil Laws were derived."[29] This emphasis on covenants—civil and religious—went on to inform the Puritans' understanding of covenant in the context of treaty literature as well. As important to the Puritans as it had been to the ancient Jews, the idea of a covenant between the individual and God, as well as among individuals, underwrote Puritan religious and civil society. Much work has been done on the close relationship between the Puritan covenant and the social contract, which was associated with the commonwealth they established and later with the nation to come, but less has been said about the covenant's connection to a treaty as a legal and literary text.[30] Covenants differ from contracts and treaties in similar ways. God is a party to a covenant, while contracts and treaties are drawn up exclusively among humans. Yet, just as covenant conventions pervade early modern and Enlightenment theories of contract, so too do early modern treaty conventions and assumptions underwrite theories of the covenant in later seventeenth-century New England.[31]

The most important influence of early modern treaties on the Puritan covenant can be traced to the concept of renewal, which distinguishes the Puritan covenant of the second half of the seventeenth century from its earlier counterpart (and is the subject of chapter 2) as much as it distinguishes the later seventeenth-century treaty from its medieval antecedent. As Randall Lesaffer observes, the language of many later seventeenth-century treaties reveals an interest that was absent in earlier treaties in maintaining the larger legal order. Grotius compared this overarching legal order to the smaller civil power that lay with the sovereign of the state. "But the *more extensive* Right, is the *Right of Nations*," he wrote, "which derives its Authority from the Will of all, or at least of many nations."[32] For Lesaffer this "more extensive right" only becomes apparent after Westphalia, but in putting an end to the religious wars that had troubled the sixteenth century, earlier seventeenth-century treaties also demonstrate this concern. In the absence of the unifying figure of the pope, the law of nations served as his replacement.

Evidence of an allegiance to the international legal order established by the law of nations is visible in several features of late seventeenth-century treaties, including their frequent references to "amity"—the principle of friendliness that would ensure the larger peace—the limitations placed on the destruction any given party could wreak on another in the name of war, and the decrease in the personal references to particular sovereigns and their heirs that had populated medieval treaties in favor of references to the state or legal entity as keepers of the peace.[33] Finally, the allegiance to a cosmopolitan order was visible in the references to a restoration of a peace that had preexisted the hostilities, as if the act of adhering to a larger legal order made each treaty into a symbol of continuity, which marked not a new beginning, but a resumption of the old. Article II of the Treaty of the Pyrenees (1659), for example, speaks of the "good, firm and lasting Peace, Confederation, and perpetual Alliance and Amity" between the parties as "that good Re-union," which would put the parties back to a status quo ante that made the treaty a kind of renewal ritual itself.[34] This principle of continuity is at the heart of the Puritans' concept of covenant renewal in chapter 2.

Considered an aspiration of all humans everywhere, peace—the goal of treaty law and of the law of nations as a whole—also informs the evolution of the Puritan covenant from a symbol of their exclusivity to a symbol later in the seventeenth century of their participation in the human community as a whole. What made the law of nations universal, Gentili and Grotius agreed, was that it was rooted in the quality of *being* human as opposed to how humans behaved, which was, depending on where people lived, thought to be hopelessly incoherent. "All this universe which you see," Gentili wrote, "in which things divine and human are included, is one, and we are members of a great body. And in truth the world is one body. Moreover nature has made us all kindred, since we have the same origin and the same abode. She has implanted in us love for one another and made us inclined to union."[35] In Gentili's theory of the cosmopolis, we see a precursor to Robbins's sense that "there are emotional solidarities beyond the nation that are continuous with the emotions elicited in the process of nation building."[36] Grotius gave voice to a similar idea with an even greater focus on the social. "Among the things which are unique to man," Grotius wrote, "is the desire for society, that is for community with those who belong to his species."[37]

This species-wide sensibility receives a final validation in the uses the law of nations made of Jewish sources and their original articulation of universal law. Previously excluded along with Muslim texts from the intellectual precincts of the West, Jewish sources were rediscovered as part of a larger movement among Christian Hebraists in England and

Holland.[38] In the context of the law of nations these sources served to open up the law to global differences and interdependencies. It is thus not a coincidence that in the very statement in which Grotius endorses making alliances with the infidels, he invokes the ancient Jewish precedent for doing so. Making alliances with infidels, Grotius explains, is supported not only by reference to "the pious doctrine of Augustine," whose theories presumably trumped those of Peter Martyr in Gentili's thought, but also "(so we are told) by Abraham, Isaac, David, Solomon, and the Macabbees."[39]

Of all three law of nations' theorists under examination here, John Selden made the most of Jewish sources. His major contribution to the expanded notion of universality within the context of the law of nations came from the Hebrew sources that discussed the Noahide covenant, the laws given to Noah and his sons after the flood for the benefit of all humans everywhere regardless of race, creed, or nation. The seven Noahide laws include six prohibitions—against idolatry, blasphemy, bloodshed, sexual violations, theft, and eating flesh cut from a living animal—and one positive injunction, the establishment of a legal system.[40] The Noahide laws became the centerpiece of Selden's law of nations treatise, *De jure naturali et gentium juxta disciplinam Ebraeorum*. So important were these laws to Selden's scheme that each of the seven books of his *De jure* is devoted to one of the seven Noahide laws. Called the most learned of the Christian Hebraists of his day—Jason Rosenblatt goes so far to call him a rabbi in his own right—Selden was an active member of Parliament, a scholar, and the author of a number of influential works on divorce, tithes, and the right of ownership over the sea. Almost all of these works were based on Selden's profound knowledge of Hebrew sources, including the Talmud and Maimonides's *Mishneh Torah* to which Selden turned for the elaboration of the Noahide laws.

The Noahide laws were central to Selden's theory of the law of nations because they were in his opinion the only law that had been given to the people of the world as a whole and that established in sufficiently minimalist terms the conditions that would allow them to live in peace. They were, as it says in Genesis, part of the covenant God made with Noah "and all flesh that is on earth" (Gen. 9:17). Grotius, who had also written about the Noahide laws, believed they had been given as universal laws three times: once to Adam, once to Noah, and then again in the law of the gospel. For Selden, by contrast, the laws given to Noah took precedence over the others because they were, unlike the laws given to Adam, written down, and unlike the gospel of Christ, not associated with any one religious creed or people.

For Selden, the Noahide laws preceded the delivery of the Decalogue to Moses, which made the pre-Sinaitic Jews adherents of the universal Noahide laws as well. This timeline becomes an important basis for Selden's belief in the universality of the Noahide laws. Again and again in the service of his universalist argument, Selden insists that non-Jews were allowed to follow what later became known as exclusively Jewish laws because they were part of the Noahide system. To take one example of such a law, Selden noted, "*Gentilibius licet Holcausta offere Domino quocunque locurum*," which translates roughly as "the Gentiles are allowed to offer sacrifices to God in whatever place."[41] Like the Decalogue, the Noahide laws issued from specifically Jewish sources, but as Selden stressed, they were promulgated to all humankind without limit.

Already immersed in Jewish law through a deeply perceived kinship with the Jews, the Puritans of seventeenth-century New England would have been aware of and influenced by Selden's work on the Noahide laws. We can, for example, read in their reconsideration of the covenant an admission of the dual legal formation that lay at the heart of the Noahide laws, for the covenant they came to embrace was forged in the context of the larger uncovenanted world. That there was a covenant for the Jews and by extension for their Puritan heirs and another for the rest of the world was central to the Puritans' late seventeenth-century understanding of what it meant to be in covenant with God. To be among the chosen in this sense never ceased to mean that they–the Jews or the Puritans—were favored, but it now also required recognizing that to be among those who were not chosen was not necessarily to be among the damned. As the Noahide laws made clear, there was a universal law for everyone, chosen or not. Appreciating them because they were given to humankind as a whole, Selden also seemed drawn to the Noahide laws for their substantive universality. For one thing, there were fewer of them than other laws, which made it far more likely that they would be adopted universally. For another, they addressed situations that were fundamental to all social orders. The first six Noahide injunctions, for example, all of which have their counterpart in the Decalogue, revolve around people's relationships not to God but to each other. In this, they embodied the kind of shared moral rules that could provide a basis for relationships among humans all over the world.

We can consider the promotion of laws that were minimalist in form and content to be Selden's second contribution to the universalist project of which the law of nations was a part. Selden's universal laws, however, retained an ambiguity that was built into the Jewish tradition. The Noahide laws, after all, were a source of controversy in the rabbinic commentaries where Selden had first discovered them. It was not Selden, then, but Grotius who followed through on the impulse they both shared to draft a law that was so stripped down that it would make the prospect of worldwide adoption virtually inevitable. The first move Grotius made toward this end was to distinguish between what was truly legal and what had long passed as law but had in the end had more to do with morality. "And even in the Law of Nations, I have made a Distinction between that which is truly and in every Respect lawful, and that which only produces a certain external Effect after the Manner of that primitive Law."[42] Going even further, Grotius reduced what was "truly and in every Respect lawful" to a few simple rules that would not only extend the law's universal reach but also complete the shift from the moral to the juridical realm. Without written rules and a positive law that avoided the moral ambiguity of divine law or its natural law descendent, the law of nations would remain forever at the level of a *theory* of agreement. For Grotius, adding a crucial formality to the common set of rules would ensure the practice of agreement as well.

Formality

If natural law is the articulation of human reason grounded in nature, positive law is its antithesis. Unlike natural law, positive law is a cultural production, written down, typically rooted in practicality as opposed to morality, and subject to change. For this reason positive law is rarely associated with the law of nations. From the time of the Scholastics until the late eighteenth century and the work of Immanuel Kant, the law of nations was, like the civil law propounded in the social contract theories of Hobbes and Locke, associated with natural law. Like the assumptions about the early modern legal understanding of universalism, however, this reading of the seventeenth-century law of nations overlooks one of its crucial features: its reconciliation of natural law with written rules. Never reaching the level of the late eighteenth- or nineteenth-century iterations of international law, which many people identify with the rise of legal positivism, the law of nations in the hands of Gentili, Grotius, and Selden nevertheless incorporated aspects of positive law that made the world more cosmopolitan in the process.

In making an argument that the seventeenth-century law of nations helped instigate a greater sense of cosmopolitanism through its turn to positive law, I present a paradox: In what way does positive law, typically taken to be culture specific and inflexible, serve this end? How can a move away from the morality in which cosmopolitanism is rooted foster cosmopolitanism? The answer, which emerges directly from the writing of Grotius and Gentili, is twofold: positive law increases cosmopolitanism by reimagining morality as obedience to the law, while at the same time avoiding the ambiguity of or a possible conflict between moral injunctions; and in the absence of an agreed upon arbiter of morality, such as the pope or the Holy Roman Emperor, positive law provides a source of legal authority that though voluntary and consensus based offers an alternative to the traditional model of sovereign authority. As Kant and Bentham came to realize when the eighteenth century proved every bit as war torn as the centuries before it, precepts grounded solely in natural or divine law were not helping to unite the world. What was necessary instead (although far from sufficient) were measures written out in clear-cut, formal prose.

The turn toward positive law was on some level a recognition of the need for a cosmopolitan language, a language that would be understood by everyone around the world. The decreasing popularity of Latin, even among the learned, as well as a growing awareness of non-European-language speakers prompted many philosophers, including Descartes, Comenius, and Newton, to think about creating a universal language, with all new characters, which could be easily learned by people from different linguistic backgrounds. The goal of the law of nations theorists, however, who turned their attention to the language component of the law, including Gentili, Grotius, and Samuel Pufendorf (whose work on language was of particular importance and is discussed at greater length in chapter 5), was not to invent a new tongue but to streamline existing channels of communication by paring texts and using customary language practices as semantic signposts. "If no conjecture guides us otherwise," Grotius wrote, "the Words are to be understood according to their Propriety, not the grammatical one . . . but what is vulgar and most in Use."[43] This Grotian dictate about language usage was especially important in the interpretation of treaties where achieving a consensus about meaning was imperative.

A similar recognition about paring language and relying on popular usage drove much of the Puritan turn toward pietism in the late seventeenth century. In order to forge a Pietism movement that encompassed people in all parts of the world, Protestant leaders in Europe and North America tried to tailor their Christian precepts to a broad spectrum of Protestant denominations. Understandably, this entailed a good deal of theological compromise.[44] By the late seventeenth century and well into the first two decades of the eighteenth century, Cotton Mather, the greatest Puritan exponent of an international Pietism had joined in this effort, but his most salient contributions to Pietism focused less on theological compromise and more on streamlining the language in which Christian precepts were expressed to make them more comprehensible to begin with. To this end, Mather invoked the principles of linguistic formality, which would have been familiar to him from the Grotian imperatives of *The Rights of War and Peace* and from the language used in the many treaties we know he read. Mather would have been aware of the importance of linguistic simplicity not only from the treaties that were being made regularly between foreign powers but also from the many treaties that had been signed between the white Anglo-American settlers and the American Indians in New England, Virginia, and elsewhere during the first half of the seventeenth century. Mirroring the turn toward positive law in the law of nations, Mather transformed the pietistic message from one of intricate and often incomprehensible religious doctrine to one of simple and easily understood belief, moving like the law of nations away from the ambiguous notion of justice in the concept of the just war toward a minimalist language that fostered common meaning. Reducing dozens of precepts to a minimal two or three, Mather integrated the principle of formality into the Puritans' most essential beliefs about God and Christian fellowship. The results of Mather's experiments with this literary reductionism are most visible in his *Bonifacius*, *India notitia*, and *Nuncia bona*, explored in chapter 5.

To understand exactly what the law of nations theorists had to say about the language of the law with which they were concerned, we must start with Alberico Gentili, who published his three books on the law of war in 1588 and was the first to attempt to do away with the moral ambiguity that had plagued global relations in the past. Gone from Gentili's treatise were the moral ambiguities and subjective determinations of the Middle Ages whose theory of just war, for instance, provided a rationale for war as long as it served good over evil, yet left open the question of how to define good and evil. In place of these ambiguities, Gentili suggested laws based on clearly stated definitions on which all nations might agree. Justice in Gentili's work was no longer tethered to religious claims or even to the progress of a given war but to the processes through which war was conducted. Just war theory remained a major feature of the law of nations as it migrated from Spain and the Catholic world to England, the Netherlands, and Protestantism, but in Gentili's revised understanding, the justness of war was to be evaluated on the basis not of a vague moral code but of a clearly articulated law.[45] Instead of giving power to decide wars to the pope, Gentili gave it to the jurists. To Gentili, the law of nations remained grounded in the natural law but articulated through and represented by the compilation of written laws most nations shared. "Our jurists, then," he wrote, "have been able to compile this law [of nations] from absolutely all nations; for if the Romans, Greek, Jews and barbarians, in short, all known peoples, have made use of a certain code of laws, it must be assumed that all men have made use of that same code."[46] In this way Gentili effectively fused the idea of positive law with natural law and gave natural law an immutable status.

If Gentili moved the law of nations away from morality by hypothesizing a peace that would not rely on "a confession of wrongs" by the parties, Grotius went even further. "A definite formality in the conduct of war was introduced by the law of nations, and . . . particular effects follow wars waged in accordance with such formality," he wrote. "Hence arises the distinction . . . between a war which, according to the law of nations, is formally declared and is called legal, that is a complete war; and a war not formally declared, which nevertheless does not on that account cease to be a legal war."[47] If the question of what made a war just in the Middle Ages was too often left to the moral arbiters on both sides of the question, just war in Grotius's hands became a matter of empirical and verifiable investigation. Perhaps the boldest move Grotius made in the first edition of his *The Rights of War and Peace* was in the opening gambit in which God, the ultimate source of morality in the past, was nowhere to be seen. "Few people have tackled the law that mediates between different countries or their rulers," he explains, "whether that law stems from nature itself or from custom and tacit agreement."[48] While Grotius reinserted God into his second edition of *The Rights of War and Peace*, adding the possibility that the law might, after nature and before custom and tacit agreement, be "instituted by Divine Commands," he never abandoned the premise that the law of nations could operate with or, more significantly, without divine sanction.

It was Grotius, moreover, who systematized Gentili's ideas and gave the cover of rights to his assertions about formality. To this end Grotius specified what elements of the law had to be present to make a war just and formalized those elements so that each side would be aware of them. So intent was Grotius on presenting the law as a workable and universalizable whole that while *The Rights of War and Peace* runs to more than two thousand pages, the rules for conducting war—the quintessence in his view of the law of nations—took up no more than three. "Two things then are requisite to make a War solemn by the Law of Nations," Grotius wrote. "First, that it be made on both Sides, by the Authority of those that have the Sovereign Power in the State: And then, that it be accompanied by some Formalitie."[49] What Grotius wanted to avoid more than anything, it seemed, was a confusion between wars "made by a Prince against his own Subjects"—a civil war, in other words—and wars that arose legitimately between and among countries in the world.[50] Only the latter were to be regulated by the law of nations, and only the latter could be evaluated for justness according to the rules he laid out.

One of the most significant outcomes of Grotius's innovations in this regard was making peace the result not of a moral adjudication or of blameworthiness but of a formal end to hostilities. Later law of nations theorists, including Emerich Vattel and Christian Wolff, referred to this idea as "lawful war in due form," stressing the Grotian notion that the law did not depend on evaluations of intrinsic justice but only on whether there was adherence to the rules. Whether the concerned parties had made a formal declaration of war, moreover, was to be determined not by moral but empirical authority. Either there was a declaration of war or there wasn't. For Grotius justness lay not in substantive claims but in the positivity of the law and its process. "We have already mentioned," he wrote in Book III of *The Rights of War and Peace*, "that according to the Opinion of the best

Authors, a War is often said to be Just, not from the Cause of whence it arises, nor as elsewhere from the great Actions done in it, but from some peculiar Effects of Right."[51]

Grotius's reference to "some peculiar Effects of Rights" reminds us of just how committed he was to replacing the moral sphere with a legal one. The rights to which Grotius refers clearly stem from a preexisting notion of justice, but they remain procedural rather than substantive and aim to avoid the messiness of moral deliberation. This translation of the moral into the legal has been a challenge for all law of nations theorists since Grotius's time and has caused problems for cosmopolitan theorists as well. The difficulty, as most cosmopolitan theorists see it, is that in articulating a law for the cosmopolis, as the seventeenth-century law of nations aimed to do, one is essentially offering laws for the use of the world without the help of a moral consensus to enforce them. As the contemporary cosmopolitan theorist Seyla Benhabib notes, questions remain about "how to create quasi-legally binding obligations through voluntary commitments."[52] Such questions are of particular concern to theorists who wrestle with the possibility of a legal cosmopolitanism, a project that is related to the law of nations but not entirely consonant with it. If we acknowledge that "[w]e have ethical and moral responsibilities to citizens of other countries who live far away and whose lives barely interact with ours," Noah Feldman writes, does that also mean that we "have legal duties to those people?"[53] In other words, in the absence of a morally informed sovereign authority, such as the pope, what binds the people of any one place to act in accordance with a law intended for everyone?

This question reveals the conditions it assumes: there can be no law, not even a law of nations, without the existence of a political association from which it issues. This assumption is what ultimately motivated eighteenth- to twentieth-century international law theorists to think about and form such associations, from Kant's global federation to the League of Nations in 1919 to the United Nations and the International Court at The Hague in 1945 and the Universal Declaration of Human Rights in 1948. In the seventeenth century, however, there were no such institutional counterparts, no supranational entity to which all or most nations belonged. Several virtual institutions asserting a partial universality did emerge, preeminent among them the Protestant International, a group of loosely affiliated Protestant sects, which came together for international purposes in the early modern Atlantic world. Although its reach was bound by the faith of its members, the unity made possible by the Protestant International operated in a fashion parallel to that of the cosmopolitan sphere. Like the cosmopolis, the unity assumed by the Protestant International depended not on the face-to-face encounters that had been essential to the gathered church and the congregational way but rather to the individual's ability to internalize the few rules and beliefs that served the community as laws, and to imagine and, when necessary, act on a sense of larger belonging.

Even in the face of only partial institutions, however, Gentili, Grotius, and Selden persevered, positing an all-encompassing sphere that would justify the creation of a universal law and that would serve as an admittedly imperfect enforcement mechanism for it. The basis on which the cosmopolitan sphere would legally bind its participants under the law of nations was, they reasoned, the law itself—the process of agreement among sovereign entities and the minimalism with which that process was articulated. The positivity of the law allowed for the creation of obligations that would be independent of political institutions. The idea behind Grotius's two rules for war was that the formal declaration of war would precede the identification of the authority waging the war, not the other way around. Far from being beholden to a sovereign in any traditional sense, the communities waging war looked to the textual declarations of war and peace for sovereignty. This was the triumph of formal law.

The Individual

One of the reasons the Grotian version of the law of nations offered a plausible model for the legal obligations of people all around the world was in part because it moved away from the sovereign or state as the primary unit of legal address for the individual. It is important to put this focus on the individual into historical context, however. What was central to the law of nations as opposed to modern liberal theory, with which the concept of the individual and of individualism is traditionally associated, was not the individual as an independent agent or bearer of rights, but the individual as affectively disaggregated from the state. Individuals in the early modern iteration of the law of nations were legally bound by the state, but the state and the individual were not isomorphic.

This move toward disaggregation, like those toward greater inclusivity and formal law, allowed for the kind of varied affiliations to which cosmopolitanism aspires. While the state (or other sovereign entity) remained the primary agent of the law, individuals were sufficiently distinguished from them to form their own nonstate directed social and cultural bonds. In this way people could maintain the local and global connections that the newly reconfigured universalism inspired. Written with a post eighteenth-century sense of the nation in mind, Pheng Cheah's recent observation that cosmopolitanism needs "a style of practical consciousness that overcomes nationalist particularism" is nevertheless apt for the early modern period as well.[54] Not yet steeped in the kind of monolithic sympathies of nineteenth-century nationalism, early modern individuals would nevertheless have been prone to what current writers Sheldon Pollock and Homi Bhabha call "territorialized imaginations of identity" to which cosmopolitanism offers an alternative.[55]

That the seventeenth-century Puritans also put the individual at the center of their theology helps us identify yet another natural link between them and the developing law of nations. To the Puritans, the individual was the repository of grace and pious learning, as well as the conduit for godly communion. The Puritans' insistence on the primacy of the individual was at the forefront of their break with the Anglican Church, which in their opinion came dangerously close to papist practices in privileging the clergy and church over the individual. Countless sermons reminded Puritans of the importance of individual prayer and meditation, and numerous Puritan journals and diaries recorded the many long hours ministers and laypeople spent closeted in prayer. One Puritan text in particular—Increase Mather's "Preface" to John Corbett's "Self-Employment in Secret," published in 1684, the year the Bay Colony's charter was officially revoked by the Crown—suggests the shared intellectual inheritance of individual worship and the disaggregated individual of the law of nations better than any other. Mather's decision to reprint Corbett's original sermon, an exhortation to individual dissenters to examine themselves "according to [their] best understanding by the Marks thereof set down in God's Word," was itself a bold move in the face of the Crown's recent threats to suppress Puritan worship and to commandeer Puritan churches in New England for Anglican worship. The content of the preface is bolder still in directing its colonial readers to consider their individual devotions as more virtuous and productive than any other possible activity, reinforcing the power of the individual above all. In support of this point, Mather reported that he had known many great men who on their deathbeds expressed regret about how little time they had spent in personal prayer. These particular men remain nameless in the piece, but to bring the point home, Mather singled out one man, Hugo Grotius, as his most compelling example. "Grotius," he wrote, "who is esteemed as Learned a man as any the last Age did afford . . . professed that he would give all his Learning and Honours for the Piety" of a man who had spent more time in religious exercises. "The same Grotius," Mather continued, "said of himself, Vitam perdidi operose nihil agendo," which translates roughly as "I lost my life in doing nothing." While Grotius is cited in a number of Mather texts, the mention of him in a context that juxtaposes his immense learning, much of which was devoted to developing the law of nations, with the primacy of individual contemplation offers a possible way of understanding the importance Grotius placed on the individual as a site of cosmopolitanism as well as spiritual affiliation.

Additional examples of the importance the Puritans placed on individual affiliation strengthen this connection between the directives of Puritan faith and those of the law of nations. With respect to their understanding of the covenant, for example, Samuel Willard returned them to the example of the diasporic Jews for whom the theory of the disaggregated individual was central. The covenant given to the Jews at Sinai was initially associated with their taking up residence in Canaan, but it proved in the long run, after multiple exiles, to have been a source of affiliation above and beyond territorially defined jurisdictions, linking individual Jews everywhere to a shared law. That the law of nations' emphasized the individual's capacity to detach affectively from the state without undergoing the multiple exiles of the Jews, however, would have given the Puritans an additional basis—and one that more closely resembled their own—on which to ground their more flexible sense of cosmopolitan affiliations. Such a sense of disaggregation would also have informed the Puritans' sense of Pietism as a bond for individuals over and above the state. The worldwide community of Pietists, for example, would never have developed without the ability of individual members in one state to align themselves with other states or with no state at all. While in the past the Puritans had often compared the degree of devotion among the faithful in non-Protestant communities unfavorably with those in states that adhered to the Reformed religion, the notion of the disaggregated individual made it possible to envision a broader and more equitable Christian community made up of people from all over the world.

The disaggregation of the individual from the state began with Gentili's focus on individual harm. To Gentili, the rule that governed the private citizen in his or her own state began with an individual harm and grew to include all other citizens on the grounds that "society cannot be maintained except by the love and protection of those who compose it."[56] The emphasis on the individual as the primary unit of concern grew to new heights in the work of Gentili's successor, Grotius. Agreeing with both Vitoria and Gentili that humanity formed the basis for human fellowship, Grotius, anticipating Arendt, writes, "But tho' there were not other Obligations, it is enough that we are allied by common Humanity. For every Man ought to interest himself in what regards other Men."[57] That Grotius understood this shared humanity in individualistic terms is best captured by his statement about the individual's motivation for coming to another's aid. "The condition that calls us to help each other," he writes, depends "on certain Persons who act by their own Will, but yet so as that their Will depends on another, that sets it in Motion."[58]

Grotius applied his understanding of the individual and the state as separate entities to the major axis of his work on the law of nations, his theory of war. In Book II of *The Rights of War and Peace* he explains why any individual is potentially entitled to pursue war against another individual wrongdoer, with the caveat that this formulation would not be relevant when the state went to war under the direction of the sovereign. In the case of public war, Grotius reasoned, people fought each other not because they had committed wrongs against each other as individuals, but because they were affiliated with the state and bound to do so by internal, domestic obligations. This approach signaled a departure from the medieval notion of war in which the cause of war and the enmity associated with it was ascribed to every individual on the battlefield. The effect of Grotius's decoupling of enmity and the individual was to clarify the obligation the subject/citizen had to the sovereign and at the same time allow that individual to retain affiliations with others across the globe without internalizing the individualizing enmity assumed by the medieval system.

This separation of individuals from the state helps us understand the extent to which the seventeenth-century law of nations represented a more extensive cosmopolitanism than its earlier or later iterations. In Grotius's formulation, while the nation could compel the service of its subjects in the military, it could not swallow up their individuality in the name of war. Grotius reinforces the idea of the subordination of the state to its individual inhabitants rather than to a single sovereign by explaining that people retained their form as a people regardless of their geographical coordinates or political associations. "If a people leave a place," he explained, "through famine, misfortune, or force or voluntarily, they do not cease to be a people."[59] Nor does it matter what form of government they adopt, whether it be monarchical, absolutist, sovereign, or free, for "sovereignty," he writes, always "reverts to the People."[60]

The association of sovereignty with the people and the people with an identity that transcended place would have been of particular interest to the late seventeenth-century Puritans in New England as they struggled to redefine themselves under direct royal supervision. Among other things, it would have spoken to their paradoxical status as English subjects, who had taken their English identities with them to live in semi-exile. Grotius's work would have given the Puritans a way to think of themselves as English not by necessity but by choice—a move that also would have paralleled their status as God's chosen people. In his embrace of various forms of sovereignty, Grotius would also have paved the way for a Puritan sense of self that went beyond the constructs of colonialism and imperialism the royal governor had imposed.

More importantly, the cosmopolis that underwrote the law of nations—with its extended sense of universalism, its turn toward formality and minimalism in the law, and its new understanding of the individual within the state—made it possible for the Puritans to capitalize on their already existing theocratic leanings to develop a sense of multiple and flexible affiliations with people all around the world. The law of nations made it clear that there were two worlds, which when translated into Puritan terms included the Colony of Massachusetts under the supervision of the Crown and the larger world outside it. These two worlds provided the authority for a vacillating sense of identity or belonging, which would in turn have allowed the Puritans to assert their particularity without jeopardizing their sense of themselves as legal actors. If the Puritans were attached to England, as they firmly believed they were, they were also attached to humankind as a whole and were at liberty to move between these two legal identities.

If the law of nations allowed the Puritans to assert their particularity without losing their legal affiliations, the converse was also true; it allowed them to reconfigure themselves as universal without losing their particular identities. What the law of nations offered, in other words, was a way of understanding one's place within a larger, more inclusive world as one embodiment of difference in a multiplicity of embodied differences. The universal in this vision was about accommodation, existing in that imaginary cosmopolitan sphere in which all differences had a place. In this sphere the differences among people remained intact but at the same time were absorbed or displaced until the historic, geographic, religious, and ethnic became elements of a principle that rose above them.

This principle led to a new understanding of the law. No longer a unitary mechanism, the law under the aegis of the law of nations became a site of pluralism and of a multiply determined and shifting set of ideas that not only spoke to all people in universal ways but also lent themselves to being integrated into particular belief systems, altering the fundamental ideas of a people to make them no less particular but at the same time more inclusive. In the chapters that follow, we will see the cosmopolitan principles to which the law of nations gave voice move in and out of many concepts the Puritans valued. As the concepts of law, the world, and obligation underwent transformation, so too did the Puritans' parallel concepts of covenant, millennialism, evidence, and Pietism, all of which became more cosmopolitan as a result of the convergence of the law of nations and the cosmopolis in this period.

{2}

The Cosmopolitan Covenant

It is from Mistakes about the Covenant, that Men are carried away with deluding Opinions to the unspeakable Prejudice of their Children as well as of themselves.

—INCREASE MATHER

Taking Increase Mather's warning about covenant-related mistakes as a starting point, this chapter uncovers an alternative provenance and meaning for the Puritan covenant—the Puritans' principal concept of community—by returning it, as the Puritans did at the time, to its place in an early modern context of outward looking, cosmopolitan thought. The cosmopolis in this chapter inserts itself into the most essential building block of the Puritan social order and so serves as an appropriate opening for our reconsideration of the Puritans' cosmopolitanism overall.

Anxious about making mistakes about the covenant—as Mather ardently hoped they would be—members of New England's Puritan communities debated its various meanings and iterations at almost every turn during their nearly hundred-year-long existence in New England, from the covenant of Abraham or Adam (which was never explicitly called a covenant but was taken to be one by many Christians, including the Puritans) to the covenants of Noah and Christ.[1] A theology based on the covenant and modeled on the Sinaitic covenant between God and the Jews was at the heart of the New World Puritans' faith and social order. Styling themselves the "new Israel," the Puritans of New England believed that a covenant bound them to God at every level of their existence. They believed, for example, that there was a covenant between every individual and God (a belief they shared with Protestants in general); that there was also a covenant among members of a given congregation requiring ethical behavior and mutual aid; and finally, that there was a covenant that bound them as a social and political collectivity to each other and to

God—a belief that only the Jews had held before them. This last form of covenant created what has been called a federal or corporate theology that governed the Puritans' religious and secular lives.

This last level of belief ties the religious covenant that linked heaven and earth and was made between God and particular groups of people to the covenants made between and among particular groups of people on earth, or what we have come to think of as contracts and treaties, which lack the divine component. There are three ways of thinking about this transition from theological to political or from religious to secular. The first lies in the nature of the original covenant or Ten Commandments, five of which were given over to outlining the proper relationship between humans and God, the other five to the relationship between and among humans. The Jews to whom this original covenant was given understood the covenant in religious and political terms at the same time, and they used it to order their republican form of government. In the process of secularizing the covenant for the uses of other groups, which began in earnest in the seventeenth century and extended through the eighteenth century, the Protestant thinkers who gave it the most attention had in some ways to go no further than the Hebrew Bible. The second way to understand this transformation is simply to recognize the profound ways in which the metaphor of the covenant entered into the development of governments and social orders from the eighteenth century forward. Covenant, as Daniel Elazar explains, became the basis for forms of constitutionalism and federalism as those concepts developed in the West.[2] While the God-given nature of the original covenant remained an authorizing concept in theory, its divine source dropped away in practice; in his 1975 landmark book about the covenant in American culture, Robert Bellah used the words religious and secular almost interchangeably, speaking of the covenant as a secular concept and of the secular culture of America as a form of "civil religion."[3] The particularity of the Puritan perspective on the covenant as both a religious and secular concept is explored in detail in this chapter and makes the cosmopolitan covenant possible.

Managing the transition from religious to secular was further complicated by the different levels of covenantal belief, especially when the terms of the individual covenant came into conflict with the social, legal, and political ones. Not surprisingly, then, it is within the framework of covenantal concern that we can best make sense of the two biggest crises endured by the Puritans in their first thirty years or more of settlement in New England: the Antinomian crisis of 1636–1638 and the Halfway Covenant crisis of 1662, both of which were covenant induced.[4] Far less familiar to scholars of the period, however, is the crisis associated with what I call the Renewal Covenant, which had its first iteration in the years leading up to and immediately following King Philip's War in 1676, but experienced a resurgence and reiteration from the mid-1680s through the 1690s and into the first few years of the eighteenth century. This second Renewal Covenant distinguished itself from the earlier covenants and from the earlier versions of covenant renewal by shifting emphasis away from baptism, church membership, and general declension to issues of corporate membership in the cosmopolis at large.[5]

The Renewal Covenant under examination here was, like its earlier counterparts, determined in part by the specific historical circumstances to which it was tied. Precipitated by doctrinal instability in the early years of the Massachusetts Bay Colony, the Antinomian Covenant crisis inspired sermons that tried to clarify the stakes between a covenant of works and a covenant of grace—two different ways of understanding the individual's covenant with God. Responding to a declining number of church members in the middle of the seventeenth century, the Halfway Covenant, by contrast, led to sermons about loosening the requirements for participating in the Lord's Supper and ended by revising the terms for congregational belonging, among other things. The first iteration of the Renewal Covenant crisis, which followed in the wake of the Halfway Covenant, was tied to the tremendous loss of life experienced by the Puritans in their pyrrhic victory in King Philip's War.

The sermons and histories about covenant renewal that stemmed from this event tended, with some notable exceptions mentioned later, to see King Philip's War—the first really devastating war in New England—as a punishment from God for the Puritans' apostasy. Not surprisingly, the sermons associated with these covenant renewals tended to revolve around lamentations and excoriations that would, the Puritans believed in true jeremiadic fashion, encourage people to improve their behavior and reform their sinful ways. As late as 1677, even Increase Mather, who ultimately expressed an altered understanding of renewal in later years, emphasized the connection between covenant renewal and personal or social reformation by reminding his parishioners and extended reading audience that people have a duty to renew their covenant "in the case of eminent [*sic*] danger and distress" or "in case of Apostacy [*sic*] from God."[6] In sermons in which the war with the Indians was taken as a direct sign of spiritual declension, the call to renew the covenant was accompanied by images of a catastrophic end for the Puritans that could only be staved off by insulating and consolidating the Colony's identity and power without reference to the rest of the world.[7] Discussing William Hubbard's *A Narrative of the Troubles with the Indians*, written immediately after King Philip's War, for example, Harry Stout observes an example of this consolidation in Hubbard's characterization of the Indians not as a separate nation but "as God's instrument of correction" for the Puritans alone.[8]

This habit of interpreting the wages of King Philip's War in terms of the Puritans' larger spiritual mission as opposed to seeing the Native people as rivals on a political or legal scale can be traced back to an even earlier Puritan approach to land ownership and treaty making with the Indian tribes. Putting the sermons that issued in the wake of King Philip's War in this context should help us distinguish between the first version of covenant renewal and the covenant renewal at issue here. While Puritans and the Indians had regularly engaged in a version of treaty making, beginning with the charter between the Plymouth plantation and the Wampnaoags that was, as Jeffrey Glover argues, tied to some of the protocols in the law of nations, in general these treaties did not develop or function in the same way treaties with other nations did. Roger Williams first pointed to this problem as early as the 1630s in his no longer extant treatise challenging the terms by which Charles I first issued a patent to the white settlers in New England in 1629. Because the patent gave the land and treaty-making power over the land in New England to the Puritans through the divine right of kings, Williams believed it was invalid. While many have correctly read Williams's position as sympathetic to the Indians, his challenge to the patent and the treaties that issued from it was rooted not in sympathy but in his belief in the impropriety of applying divine law to earthly jurisdictions. For Williams the Indian treaties of the early to mid-seventeenth century were an example of the misuse of a religious covenant to make political peace.

The late century crisis of covenant renewal, by contrast, tells a story in which the covenant came to be seen as a semireligious, semilegal instrument suitable for handling political and legal threats to the

Puritan commonwealth. Perhaps because the sermons were tied not to King Philip's War but to the revocation of the colony's legal charter—a process that stretched from threats first leveled in 1682 to the implementation of revocation in 1686—they represent the notion of renewal less as a personal reformation inspired by apostasy than as an opportunity for its audience to look outward, past traditional Calvinist models, to see how one might turn enemies into potential legal partners. This then was a covenant steeped in a theory of coexistence, of difference within a larger cosmopolitan sphere of similarity.

Unsurprisingly, this covenant literature offers a less fearful and less insular picture of the Colony's religious and legal identity in this period—a picture whose roots can be directly traced to passages about renewal in the context of other nations in the Hebrew Bible. As such, these covenant sermons, which typically appeared in the same form as other occasional Puritan sermons, from Election Day sermons to Fast Day sermons to Artillery sermons, uncover new story lines in Puritan literature that emphasize corporate renewal in the context of multiple nations and multiple belongings in the context of the law of nations and its turn toward the Hebrew Bible.

It makes sense that the Puritans, who believed they were, like the Jews, chosen by God, were drawn to the Hebrew Bible and the law of nations to recast their covenant—the centerpiece of their religious and legal identity—as they struggled to understand how the geopolitical space of their world was being transformed. In the spirit of the law of nations, the Puritans invoked a covenant that was inextricably linked to the ancient Near Eastern provenance of the Jewish covenant and to biblical passages that addressed the interconnectivity of the Jews with their neighbors. Put another way, if the goal of the Puritans' discourse about the covenant in the first three to four decades of their settlements in New England was to clarify the relationship between the reformation of the Puritans as individual members of the church and community, the goal of the later discourse was to remind audiences how profoundly their covenantal form of community was indebted to and dependent on communities across the globe.[9]

The Covenant and the Law of Nations

Typically, Christian sources have provided moral and religious imperatives for cross-cultural connection, but just as typically these have been met with strong legal prohibitions that have made these connections difficult, if not impossible, to enforce. Christian law, for example, prohibited making treaties with the "infidel," a prohibition Grotius rejected out of hand. Thus if the law of nations hoped to set in motion a cosmopolis that encompassed countries outside of Christendom, it had to look beyond Christendom for models of foreign partnership. As I discuss in chapter 3, Ottoman models based on an expanded understanding of diplomacy provided one possibility for integrating the foreign into the domestic legal and social order, but another and arguably more assimilable source for the West was to be found in the Hebrew Bible. Seen as the Old Law, which had, according to Christian doctrine, received its perfect expression in the New Law of Christ, the Hebrew Bible had been neglected for centuries as a source of political and social thought. With the Protestant Reformation and its theory of *sola scriptura,* however—of relying on the Scriptures alone without priestly mediation—people began to take a keener interest in the Hebrew Bible, its covenants, and the experience of the Jews overall as a model for Reformed religion.[10]

Recent scholarship on the early modern period reveals an intense Hebraism at work in the seventeenth century. The major focus of the Christian Hebraists—Christian scholars who were immersed in Hebrew scholarship—was on the Hebrew republic as a source for the civil republic in England. Much has been written about the importance of the Christian Hebraists and their Jewish contemporaries, such as Baruch Spinoza and Menasseh Ben Israel, with the result that paradigms for understanding the early modern period in a strictly Christian context are on the wane.[11] In fact, so pervasive was the influence of Jewish sources on early modern republican thought that Eric Nelson, among others, suggests we rethink our sense of the early modern period as an increasingly secular one in the first place.[12]

Less remarked on but no less influential was the use of Hebrew and Jewish sources for the concurrent development of the law of nations. Of the law of nations theorists, Grotius and Selden were among the most dedicated to these sources; they frequently cited the Hebrew Bible, the Talmud, Maimonides's *Mishneh Torah*, and a variety of rabbinic commentaries. Both men were also drawn to passages in Leviticus (on the toleration of strangers) and Deuteronomy (on the rules for approaching an enemy in the field and concluding terms of peace).[13] Most significantly, both found in the Noahide laws (as mentioned, the laws given to Noah and all humankind after the flood) the grounds for the law of nations.[14]

Grotius extensively quotes Genesis and Maimonides on the Noahide laws and accepts them as universal. He wrote:

> For a law obliges only those to whom it is given... and we read every where that the Covenant was made with them [the Jews] and that they were chosen to be the peculiar People of GOD, which Maimonides owns to be true, and proves it from Deut. xxxiii, 4. But among the Hebrews themselves there always lived some Strangers, Pious Persons, and such as feared GOD.... These, as the Hebrew Rabbis say, were obliged to keep the Precepts given to Adam and Noah... but not the Laws peculiar to the Israelites.[15]

Like Grotius, Selden also looks to the Noahide laws, but he takes their precepts one step further, devoting a separate book of his *Law of Nature and the Nations According to the Hebrews* to each of its seven laws.[16] For Selden the Noahide laws were, as Abraham Berkowitz writes, "the foundation of all human society."[17]

Altering the approach many countries took to global relations in general, the Jewish sources that informed the law of nations transformed Puritan thinking in many ways, most importantly by recharacterizing the covenant's corporatism. This new characterization was an obvious influence on the Puritans' *Body of Liberties,* published one year after Selden's work on the law of nations.[18] It was also an influence on Increase Mather, who started to refer to the Hebrew Bible as the covenant's primary source. Defending himself against contemporaries, who noted the absence of the covenant from the New Testament, Mather wrote, "And suppose it [the absence of a corporate covenant in the NT] were so indeed," he wrote. "Is the old Testament Apocrypha in these dayes?"[19]

Mather's recognition of the primacy of the Hebrew Bible with respect to the idea of covenant provides a glimpse into how the Puritans' view of covenant, Noahide and Sinaitic, was changing at this time. The Jewish covenant was a statement of God's particularism that juxtaposed the Jews with others. Although the Reformation gave Christians permission to refer to the Hebrew Bible in ways they had been loath to do before, Mather's choice to look to the corporate covenant of the Jews as a model for the Puritans was a risk that aligned him with the law of nations theorists rather than with Christian theorists. More specifically, his choice linked him to a cosmopolitan worldview of culturally specific entities united by the law as opposed to a worldview of geographically diverse entities united by religion. Christian universalism, as we saw in chapter 1, was a statement about the social order as a homogeneous whole at the expense of those who, like the Jews, resisted that theory of the universal. The social order captured by the covenant at Sinai, however, explicitly reinforced the singularity of the Jews.

Achsah Guibbory helps us understand the Puritans' predilection for the Hebrew Bible and the Hebrew covenant in particular by reminding us that Israel's history helped the Protestants distinguish themselves from the Catholics. To be the surrogate Israel, chosen by God, set the Protestants apart from Rome. But, as Guibbory points out, to be chosen in this context was highly ambiguous. "Disagreements about the Church raised crucial questions," Guibbory writes, "What did it mean to be Israel? Who was to be included in it, and who excluded?"[20] To these questions, it would appear, the Puritans gave a cosmopolitan answer: to be chosen in this context was to be keenly aware of one's own particularity and of the potential particularity of everybody else. To invoke the Hebrew covenant then was not an unadulterated expression of Jewish particularity but a kind of compromise between Christian universalism and Jewish particularity as it was understood by the Jews themselves. The Puritans felt singled out by God but were attentive to those parts of the Hebrew covenant that had reminded the Jews of their competitors.

Adopting a particularity that allowed one to fit into a larger sphere more generally made a big difference in Puritan thought. Formerly thought to be a covenant that provided guidelines for a community's internal, domestic policies and laws, the covenant given to the Jews, like that given to Noah, could scarcely be invoked by the Puritans or the law of nations theorists in this period without an awareness of its meaning for the rest of the world. The Sinaitic covenant was, after all, a more evolved version of the Noahide covenant itself. As David Novak writes, "one could arguably assert that the Sinaitic covenant presupposes the Noahide covenant.... That is, if Israel had not considered itself bound by the universal law of God perpetuated by the Noahide covenant with humankind on earth, it would have been in no position to conscientiously accept the more singular law of God revealed at Sinai."[21] A more specific commentary on the Sinaitic covenant suggests that the inclusivity and cosmopolitanism of the

Noahide covenant was part of its original meaning as well. As Bernard Levinson remarks, "The [Sinaitic] covenant creates the neighbor just as it creates the self." Invoking the covenant's cosmopolitan meaning, Levinson continues, "Adherence to the covenant brings into being a community of moral agents."[22]

Levinson's interpretation of the covenant can best be understood within the explicitly spatial framework captured by Bruce Robbins's metaphor of "attachment at a distance."[23] Focused anew on the cosmopolitan context in which God's choice of the Jews as "his treasured possession" was made, law of nations theorists offered a reading of the covenant that subordinated the internal coherence of the community to the community's relations with political and legal entities outside itself. As David Armitage explains, international relations theorists have long pondered the provenance of thinking about the world in terms of these two domains, tracing it variously to Hobbes, Bentham, or to later twentieth-century thinkers such as Carl Schmitt.[24] These options, however, overlook the prominence of the law of nations and the Puritans' adaptation of the covenant in its wake. It was after all Gentili and Grotius who produced the first popularly codified source books on the difference between sovereign state law and law among the states and thus made the discourse of internal and external available to political theorists in the first place. It was also under the auspices of the law of nations that the Sinaitic covenant received a rereading that made it clear how externally oriented it was.

A law of nations induced reading of the covenant depicted it less as a compact that created or aspired to create a society ex nihilo—as did its successor, the social contract—and more as a limited purpose pact or treaty between an already existing people and a sovereign, who pledged to serve his people largely by tending to their always changing and contingent relations with others. Early modern efforts to think through a parallel to the social compact on the global level would have reinforced the distinction between the social contract and the treaty-covenant for the Puritans. According to Locke, for example, the social compact pertained only to the state within because only the state possessed the power to offer something in exchange for the consent of the people. The question of whether the global order operated in a parallel fashion with some version of positive law and some source of overarching political power continued to interest political philosophers from Samuel Pufendorf to John Rawls, who as late as the second half of the twentieth century was still struggling with the question of how to theorize a social contract for the world.[25] That the law of nations came very close to doing just that is part of my argument here. That it did so by invoking the treaty as opposed to the social contract, moreover, tells us something about the similarity between the treaty and the covenant and the greater suitability of both for a cosmopolitan order scattered spatially across the globe.

This spatial reconceptualization of the covenant was accompanied by a covenantally inspired reconceptualization of time. The result of a refocusing within the law of nations on the Hebrew covenant's many ruptures and renewals in both the biblical and early modern periods, the covenant became a more temporally contingent phenomenon than it had been before. Like the treaties between and among discrete sovereign entities, as Grotius and Selden were quick to note, the covenant was constantly being broken and renewed. This feature suggested a provisionality that stood in contrast to the permanence that Locke or Rousseau later ascribed to the social contract. To be sure, neither Locke nor Rousseau believed the social contract was inviolable; Rousseau openly acknowledged that states based on the social contract were subject to decline, and Locke acknowledged that there were times when people might be justified withdrawing their consent from it. For both philosophers, however, the level of consent required for the covenant was minimal, and the ends of government—to pursue the public good—were always open to debate. These qualities made the social contract relatively easy to sustain.

The renewal covenant under examination by the Puritans in the last two decades of the seventeenth century, by contrast, was both more rigorous and less durable. This sense of the covenant, which corresponded more precisely to the form of a treaty than a social compact, was most visible in the ministers' repeated calls for the covenant to be renewed. This call for renewal, voiced by the Mathers, Samuel Willard, and Joseph Rowlandson, among other ministers, did not mean that the covenant had necessarily been broken; it served rather as an acknowledgment that a covenant made in the course of history, as the Sinaitic covenant was, would require updating from time to time.

Among other things, the Hebrew covenant invoked the notion of renewal though the perpetuation of the covenant relationship through time. Following the model of the ancient Near Eastern treaties on which it was based, the Hebrew covenant provided structurally for a succession of kings or leaders, who would inherit the covenant's obligations and ensure that the people adhered to them. The final sections of Deuteronomy, for example, a book of the Hebrew Bible that retells the story of the covenant and closely resembles the form of ancient Near Eastern treaties, speak to the issue of succession as Moses, who received the covenant directly from God, passes it on to Joshua, who, because Moses is too old to do so himself, will take the Jewish people beyond the Jordan River and into Canaan.[26] "Then Moses called Joshua and said to him in the sight of all Israel: 'Be strong and resolute, for it is you who shall go with this people into the land that the Lord swore to their fathers to give them" (Deut. 31:7). At the heart of this transition from Moses to Joshua, moreover, is an awareness that runs throughout the Hebrew Bible that future generations, who will inevitably be at a greater remove from biblical events, will require a roadmap for keeping their covenantal promises. "Their children, too," Moses instructs Joshua, "Who have not had the experience, shall hear and learn to revere the Lord your God" (Deut. 31:13). In a process that does not explicitly refer to itself as a renewal, provisions for future leaders pave the way for a sense of a covenant that needs to adapt to the times.

By the 1680s, to update the covenant through renewal was to recognize that new covenantal affiliations would also be made. In this way, covenant renewability made visible what Robbins calls "the reality of (re) attachment [and] multiple attachment," features of cosmopolitanism that along with "attachment at a distance" acknowledge the many different affiliations people tend to cultivate in worlds where technologies for cultural transmission abound.[27] These spatial and temporal transformations in the covenant serve as the major axes around which the discussion of the Puritans' sermon literature on the cosmopolitan covenant unfolds.

The Covenant and Cosmopolitan Space

General anxiety about the covenantal bond dominated the Puritans' sermons in the second half of the seventeenth century, but the language of their renewal sermons suggests the specifically spatial nature of this concern. It did not, for example, escape the Puritans' attention that if God had rejected the Jews for failing to hold up their end of the covenantal bargain—a story to which all Christians adhered—he could easily do the same with them. Having taken up residence in a contested part of the world, the Puritans were especially sensitive to the geopolitical implications of God's displeasure. "But we are very stupid," Cotton Mather wrote, "if we do not read an *Admonition* to our selves, in this Ancient and Famous Providence. Indeed I am not without my lively and grounded Hopes, that our *Good God* will not ever (or at least, *as yet*) Remove the People which is now enriching this part of the New World, for *Another Nation* to succeed in the room thereof."[28] The covenantal bond, as Mather's statement suggests, was intimately tied to the Puritans' sense of themselves as only one of many people vying for the same space.

In reading the uncertainty surrounding God's covenantal choice in terms of a possible removal from New England "for Another Nation," Mather also articulates how profoundly the spatial features of the discourse on war informed his covenantal imagination in the late seventeenth century and by extension that of many Puritans. Scarcely surprising for an approach to the covenant that was developed in the context of the law of nations, it is significant that war in this period—the mechanism by which Mather imagines being replaced in New England "by Another Nation"—departs from a tradition of covenantal curses and the earlier Puritan tendency to treat war as one of them. Of these traditional curses or punishments for breaking the covenant the Puritans were well aware. Their earlier covenant sermons, as well as their diary and journal entries, invoke curses such as disease or natural disasters as obvious scourges of God and ultimately incorporate war into this pattern as late as the first iterations of covenant renewal at the time of King Philip's War.

The distinction between war seen as a natural disaster and war seen as a man-made event is telling. Natural disasters foretell the destruction of a people from within. To fall ill or to suffer the consequence of fires, floods, or in some cases war, as the Puritans so often did, invokes a world in which the only relationship that matters is that between the people in question and God. The people sin, and the people are punished. No third party is involved. To suffer removal or destruction as a result of a politically motivated war, by contrast, was a far more public event for it involved God, the people bound by the ruptured covenant and, in a new covenantal configuration, the non-covenanted or newly covenanted people, who were to benefit directly depending on the outcome of the war. This vision of the covenant was interdependent and cosmopolitan.

In the sermons that filled the churches and provided reading matter throughout the colonies in the late seventeenth century, the Puritans often spoke of their interdependence with countries and peoples across the globe as a matter of covenant-inspired defense. An early glimpse into this discourse, although without the cosmopolitan overtones that accompanied the acknowledgment of God's ability to change his mind, was "Nehemiah on the Wall," a biblical story made famous by Jonathan Mitchel's well-known and widely read 1671 sermon of that name. For Mitchel, Nehemiah (governor of Judah in the fifth century BCE) became a model of the good ruler because he understood that keeping the covenant was largely a matter of looking to conditions in the outside world and of building a wall to keep hostile forces out. "When Nehemiah came to seek the welfare of the children of Israel," Mitchel wrote, his "great business was to build the Wall of Jerusalem, in which principal Concernments, both of Religion and Government, were laid up."[29]

Defining the covenant more explicitly in terms of the uncertainty war might introduce, Joseph Rowlandson, minister in Lancaster, Massachusetts, opened the subject up in ways that are even more explicitly cosmopolitan. In "The Possibility of God Forsaking a People," delivered in 1678 and published in 1682 as an appendix to his wife's far better-known *Narrative of the Captivity of Mrs. Mary Rowlandson*, Rowlandson explained that when God forsook a people in covenant, he did not necessarily destroy them; he simply removed himself from "their side." Rowlandson took pains to ensure that his audience appreciated the difference between these two outcomes. "There are two aspects of God's presence," Rowlandson wrote. "He is everywhere [the first] and his especial presence [the second], which is of a covenantal nature."[30] In *The Chosen Peoples*, Todd Gitlin and Liel Leibovitz describe a similar way of being in covenant with God as consonant with "the Bible's either/or way of thinking," but where for Gitlin and Leibovitz this explains the historical rivalry between Christians and Muslims for chosen status after the Jews had, according to Christian doctrine, been abandoned, for the New England Puritans in the late seventeenth century, it described a potential rivalry among all political entities and an existence in a politically and legally interconnected world.[31] When God forsook a people in covenant, he "was not gone from the world"; he simply left one place to emerge in another.

The action epitomized by God's disappearance from one place and reappearance in another was a form of spatial displacement that, according to the late century Puritan sermons on covenant renewal, pertained specifically to covenanted places in time of war. When God was gone from a covenanted place, that place became vulnerable to attack by others. This process was known to the Puritans as discovenanting and is to be distinguished from the fate of places in the Bible that were uncovenanted, meaning that they were never covenanted in the first place.[32] Such places, Sodom and Gomorrah, for example, were typically destroyed by divine fiat, without undergoing the struggle caused by God's shifting attentions. To make the fate of the discovenanted clear, Rowlandson lists numerous examples of what happened to cities that lost their gap men—those stalwart defenders who stood in the gaps between a city's defensive walls, literal and figurative. He starts with the attack on Jerusalem by Rome. "When the Lord had forsaken Jerusalem," he writes, "the Romans quickly made a prey of it. When they were destitute of God, their habitation became desolate. There is not Protection to a People, whom the Lord forsakes, but they are perplexed on every side."[33]

Surprising as it may seem, the idea that the federality of the covenant came to be expressed in terms of which side God was on, or whether he was on a side at all, made a good deal of sense in cosmopolitan terms since the conditions that led to a broken covenant boded ill for everyone, not only for those involved in the immediate dispute. Giving voice to this insight some time later in "Perpetual Peace," his outline of a law of nations for his time, Kant observed, "a violation of right in one place of the earth is felt in all."[34] Following their version of this belief, the Puritans came to understand that to keep the covenant was a way to keep the peace not only at home but also in the extended neighborhood. "Behold an effectual way to Do it [keep the covenant]," Cotton Mather wrote in "The Serviceable Man" (1690). "When a mans [*sic*] Ways please the Lord, He makes even his Enemies to be at peace with Him."[35]

One result of this new cosmopolitan understanding of the covenant was to emphasize the resemblance between the covenant and the treaties that had proliferated in the wake of the law of nations.[36] Most familiar to modern readers was the Treaty of Westphalia (actually a combination of several different treaties), which ended the Thirty Years' War (1618–1648) in the Holy Roman Empire and the Eighty Years' War (1568–1648) between Spain and the Dutch Republic. There were many other treaties concluded in quick succession after Westphalia that were also made widely available in print for an eager readership that included the Puritans.[37] More relevant in the context of the Puritans' late century covenant, however, are the pre-Westphalian treaties made between England and Scotland in 1638 and 1643. The first, known as the Scottish National Covenant, sent a clear signal to the English that the Scots were not to be cowed into giving up their Reformed religion. Incorporating the assertions made in the first Scottish covenant, the second, known as the Solemn League and Covenant, not only further unified the Scots but also forged an alliance between them and Charles I during the English Civil War. When as king in exile in the Treaty of Breda in 1650, Charles II adopted the Solemn League and Covenant and agreed to uphold the covenanters' terms, the treaty-like force of the original covenant was reaffirmed.[38]

Bringing these contemporary precedents to bear in the last decades of the seventeenth century, the Puritans began to refer to the peacekeeping function of the covenant in more explicitly contemporary terms, revealing their growing application of cosmopolitan principles to events in their day. Many of Mather's examples of the virtues of heeding the covenant are taken directly from contemporary politics. "A Prince in Germany hearing that a Neighbour Prince intended a War upon him," he wrote in a sermon devoted to the covenant, "immediately set himself upon the Reforming of the people under his Government; but this Adversary of his within a while after enquired, What Preparation his Neighbour was making to oppose him, and being informed, That his chief Preparation was Reformation [shorthand for keeping the covenant], He Reply'd, Nay, then, let the Devil fight him for all me, if he be at that, he'll be too hard for me to meddle with him."[39] That the Puritans saw themselves in the terms Mather used to describe the situation between a German prince and his neighbor became increasingly obvious as England's wars with its European neighbors extended to North American theaters. The most immediate threat to the Puritans took the form of skirmishes with their closest neighbors, the Indians, but there could be no doubt in the colonists' minds that the Indians in this war, as opposed to those in King Philip's War, were acting as allies of England's enemies, rendering them the locus of an external rather than a domestic threat.[40] Making it absolutely clear that keeping the covenant was to be considered a part of the Colony's foreign rather than domestic policy, Mather went on to ask his audience to recognize the primacy of such a strategy. "Believe it," he wrote, "we don't begin at the right End, if here [in keeping the covenant] be not the Beginning of our Services for our Countrey," where the word "Countrey" rather than colony or commonwealth, for example, conjured images of the outside rather than internal world.

The Covenant and Cosmopolitan Time

Working in concert with the revised sense of covenantal space in the Puritans' sermons from this period was a temporal reorientation that put an emphasis on the covenant's provisionality as opposed to its permanence.[41] This had the effect of acknowledging the detachment and reattachment of bonds between and among the inhabitants of various parts of the world that was as central to a vision of cosmopolitanism as the idea of attachment at a distance. This additional understanding of the covenant—as a way to separate and reunite or, to put it in even starker terms, to fail and recommit—was as significant a measure of the early modern cosmopolis as it is of the cosmopolis under examination today. Aihwa Ong refers to a modern corollary of the kind of detachment and reattachment implicit in the cosmopolitan covenant as a form of "flexible citizenship," an "alternative sociality" that encompasses transnational forms of belonging.[42] Not yet formulated as such, the early modern understanding of shifting forms of membership was nevertheless driven by a similar impulse: acknowledging the unrealistic nature of confining people to a single affiliation—be it national, regional, or municipal—when previously far-flung places had become newly accessible to all.

No strangers to the idea of mixed and changing affiliations, the Puritans seemed to embrace the idea of provisional affiliations as it applied to their status within a global context as well. Never rising to the level of an explicit rule or policy, the cosmopolitan nature of changing affiliations and legal reorganizations was nevertheless seen by the Puritans as a liberating alternative to the increasing constraints imposed upon them by England. With each covenant renewal that acknowledged the temporariness of the covenantal bond, the Puritans were able not only to reaffirm the virtues of their old, distant relationship with the mother country but also to reimagine themselves and announce a new legal and political identity vis-à-vis the rest of the world.

In "The Duty of a People who have Renewed their Covenant," which bears the unmistakable marks of a sermon written in anticipation of the threat of charter revocation, Samuel Willard makes the strength of rebranding by way of covenant renewal plain. In answer to the question, "What is done by a People in their Renewing of Covenant?" Willard explains: "[T]hey doe deliberately chuse God and strongly oblige themselves to serve him."[43] Choice on the part of the people was a central feature of the covenant from the start. Yet choice in the context of renewal involved far more than a memory of what was in its original context a momentary manifestation of voluntariness. In a sermon only ten pages long, Willard devotes a full five pages to an analysis of choice, explaining that to choose *again*, to renew one's loyalty to the covenant, puts one firmly in the path of history and entails a recommitment and reidentification far stronger than the first. He wrote:

> Now if choise itself be so obliging, then a renewed chusing of the same thing or an after asserting of a former choice, adds yet strength to the obligation. And this is the very thing that you have been this day doing: you have formerly... openly professed that you made God your Choice... this was a great engagement, but what you have now done, is a great deal more: That which you now tell the world... That after you have had the trial of God so many years... you have found him so good... and your selves so happy in your choice, that you have had no cause all this while to repent of it, but having experienced every whit as good as his word.[44]

One of the more stunning implications of thinking about covenant renewal as a means of reattachment and reidentification was that it helped the Puritans shift the burden for the charter-revocation crisis from their shoulders, where King James II had put it, back on the monarch. By casting their dissatisfaction with the revocation as a desire to demonstrate their identity through covenant renewal, the Puritans were able to represent themselves as even more devoted to the Crown—the original source of their charter—than the Crown was. Renewal soon became a preferred mode of self-presentation for the Puritans because it not only helped them normalize the period of the people's "revolution" described in chapter 4 (when the colonists, led by Cotton Mather, jailed Andros and reinstalled Simon Bradstreet as governor), but also because it reminded England of the longevity and legality of the Puritans' previous administrations. Holding Andros in jail for ten months despite strong protestations from the Crown, the Puritans persisted in governing themselves even after Andros returned to England on the logic that while their agents were negotiating for a new charter with the king, their old charter, which they felt certain would be reinstated through renewal, was still the law of the land.

Deploying the reversal of terms made possible by covenant renewal, whereby old became new and resistance a sign of loyalty, Cotton Mather set about rewriting the Colony's history with a cosmopolitan sense of renewal in mind. Reminding the crowd in "The Serviceable Man" that they were "this Day Assembled for a *Re*vival & a *Re*newal of your Anniversary Elections," he impressed upon them the simultaneously singular and duplicative nature of their duty to vote again for their governors as they had in the past. That he explicitly aligned the occasion and their duty to vote with the fate of the Colony's charter makes the practical relevance of their "renewal" more obvious still. This renewal, he explained:

> Is intended by you as no less a part of your Obedience to their Majesties, who upon the Address of our Convention to Them, Declaring, That they accepted Government of this People according to the Rules of the Charter, did in answer thereunto, Order a Continuance in the Administration thereof... [and] that the Invasion of our Charters was Illegal and a Grievance and that they ought to be restored unto us.[45]

Eliding covenant renewal with the "renewal of your Anniversary Elections," Mather further links renewal with "Obedience to their Majesties," who because they had previously "accepted... the Rules of the Charter," were bound, on his account, to see the Puritans' continued adherence to those rules as an expression of their newly reconfigured identity as a potential threat and an expression of their loyalty to the Crown at the same time.

To support the validity of the provisional attachments that allowed the Puritan community to reattach to an older model of identity and governance while at the same time articulate a new, stronger, more variable identity in the process, the Puritans drew heavily on the various covenant renewals in the Hebrew Bible. As was true of the expanded sense of covenantal space, the provisional sense of time embedded in the concept of covenant renewal drew on biblical sources as they were read by the Puritans on their own and through the lens of the law of nations. Among other things, a return to the Hebrew Bible revealed the intimate connection between detachment and reattachment that accompanied the covenantal bond in the first place. As Daniel Elazar explains, the idea of the covenant can be traced to the Hebrew word *brit*, which means both separation and binding and is related to the word for "cut" of the sort performed during male circumcision.[46] Thus the covenant, Elazar writes, "involves both—the separation of things and their reunification through binding in such a way that they will preserve their respective integrities within the new bond."[47]

Bible stories of covenant renewal would have reinforced the cosmopolitan significance of these etymological roots. The originary scene in Exodus, in which Moses receives the corporate covenant on behalf of the Israelites, tells the story of a covenant initially offered (Exod. 20–31), immediately broken (Exod. 32:19–31), and then immediately renewed (Exod. 32:32–40), integrating rupture and repair into the structure of the covenant from the start. Notable covenant renewals in the Hebrew Bible occur again in Joshua 24, 2 Samuel 5, Nehemiah 10:1, and as Elazar notes, "after every major political change or reform in the biblical period."[48] What Elazar does not emphasize, but what is nevertheless present in each covenant renewal, are the records of these political changes and reforms, which suggest how inextricably bound up covenant renewal was with the treaty-like documentation and memorialization of change itself. Sometimes taking the form of a written pact or contract, as in 2 Samuel, or an orally delivered prayer, as in Nehemiah 10, the records of covenant renewal in the Hebrew Bible could also be highly unconventional. The record in Joshua 24, for example, takes the form of a stone that served "as a witness against us, for it heard all the words that the Lord spoke to us" (Josh. 24:27).

In addition to creating a faithful record of the covenant at the time of renewal, covenant renewals were often marked by a recitation of poems and songs. At the end of Deuteronomy, for example, as Moses hands the covenant to Joshua, he calls the people together and recites a long poem, which is recorded in the Hebrew Bible. This poem, which describes God's power and exhorts the crowd to keep the covenant with him in the future, serves as a covenant addendum, a way to keep the covenant current and associate it with other forms of communication to which people might respond over time. In this way, the covenant becomes renewable though a variety of means, all bound up with the medium that best serves the particular moment of memorialization. Regardless of the form they took, the memorialization of the covenant's renewal for the Israelites, Puritans, and other early modern people was intrinsic to the process of reattachment. Accompanied by a record at every turn, beginning with the second set of tablets written by Moses at Sinai, covenant renewal simultaneously reaffirmed the old covenant and marked an occasion for collective reidentification, opening identity up to the cosmopolitan contingencies of affiliation over time.

It is also significant for the purposes of renewal that the covenant itself, like the treaty, was expressed through language in a way that self-consciously ascribed to the words of the document the power of the bond to which it aspired. "These are the words that Moses addressed to all Israel on the other side of the Jordan," Deuteronomy begins (1:1). By recalling Moses's words, the covenant that is recreated in Deuteronomy recovers the past and propels itself forward into revision, bridging the past, present, and future at the same time. That the words of Moses are being recalled is sufficient to suggest that they no longer issue from Moses himself but rather live on in the repeated utterances of his successors. To begin the substantive account of the covenant by attributing the words of the story to Moses—that is, to make the attribution of the words the story's starting point—keeps the focus on the mnemonic gap between the addressee and his audience. To be reminded that these were Moses's words is to acknowledge that that they have for a time been lost to memory and must be recalled and renewed to live on.

Willard engages with all of these aspects of renewal by citing not only Exodus but also Joshua and Nehemiah.[49] In "The Duty of a People that have Renewed their Covenant," a sermon devoted in its entirety to a reading of the renewal in Joshua, Willard remarks on the importance of making "a declaration of this [the renewal] to amount to an entering into Covenant" and of the "register made, and a monument erected of this Engagement . . . to be kept on File."[50] With this notation, Willard transforms the unwritten record of renewal in Joshua into a written document "to be kept on File." An even more telling statement about the importance of the commemoration at the heart of renewal comes not in Willard's focus on the transaction—"a register made"—but in his recognition that renewal served not only to repair internal mistakes but also to mark and broadcast moments of communal strength. "It [the renewal in Joshua],"

Willard writes, "was while the People were yet standing in good estate [and so it] instructs us: That there are other occasions of Renewing of Covenant besides Apostacy: It may be done for keeping out as well as thrusting out Sin... And it may be done to oblige our selves to a grateful acknowledgement of Gods [*sic*] faithfulness to us, & to be an engaging boon on us to be faithful to him: as this was here."[51]

The turn in this passage from thinking about covenant renewal as inspired by a people's strengths rather than their weaknesses exemplifies perhaps more visibly than any other moment in Puritan sermon literature how covenant renewal reflected the principles of the law of nations and of cosmopolitanism. We recall the 1677 sermon in which Increase Mather urged covenant renewal to ward off fear and to redress wrongs caused by apostasy. In redeploying renewal for the purposes of affirming a strong political and legal identity and in looking to Joshua for that example, Willard identifies a different form of covenant renewal, one that departs from the model associated with the sacrament of renewal that had been familiar to the Puritans as a ritualized way to ask for forgiveness. The renewal in Willard becomes an expression not of a people's backsliding but of their legal agency and development over time. To renew the covenant was not only to commemorate but also to celebrate one's journey from one point in time to another. It was also to acknowledge the contingencies of one's role in a collective history; a history to which the Puritans clearly belonged that was unfolding alongside others in a cosmopolitan context.

Contemporary treaties informed by the law of nations influenced the Puritans' sense of covenantal time as well, demonstrating the many ways—through misunderstanding, accident, ignorance, neglect, or insincerity—in which a treaty might be broken and stand in need of repair. The idea that one would not simply work to repair or renew a treaty once it was broken, but that one could and should anticipate such an eventuality made the temporal provisions of treaties, like the idea of covenantal commitment, truly provisional. Many treaties spoke openly of what to do if hostilities broke out again. The Treaty of Aix-la-Chapelle, for example, openly acknowledged the possibility of rupture by taking future violations of the treaty into account. "And in case the said Cessation [of hostilities] should happen to be contraven'd," the treaty read, "by the taking of one or more Places, either by Attack, Surprize, or secret Correspondence... Reparation shall faithfully be made on each side for any such Contravention, without any delay or difficulty."[52]

In part, these stipulations about rupture were no different from the other stipulations that made up the early modern treaty. War was no longer an instrument of justice; the law was. Thus stipulations about possible ruptures of the treaty in the future merely followed from the juridical nature of the treaty overall. Since there was for the first time under the rules Grotius had laid out a formal declaration of war, it made sense that there would also be a formal declaration of its cessation. As Randall Lesaffer points out, treaties in the early modern period were made up of countless clauses, among them clauses dealing with outstanding issues between the parties, making an end to the state of war, and pertaining to the restoration of peace in the future.[53]

The larger context for the stipulations about rupture, however, can be traced to a sense of the world's increasing fragility. In the absence of a universal authority, such as the one Christianity had long provided, it was incumbent on treaty makers to ensure that minor infractions of a clause here or stipulation there did not provoke a full-blown war in the future. For one thing, more was at stake in war than ever before. Unlike the limited wars of the medieval period, the sovereign states of the early modern period could devastate entire territories. For another, there were more people involved and more dissent among them. The interdependence of the otherwise sovereign entities of the world made treaties more susceptible to rupture. If war was a sovereign matter, so too was peace, and under the law of nations no one individual or group of individuals would have the power to determine the way a treaty was enforced.

The Puritans' sense of covenant renewal mirrored this attention to a more provisional temporality to an astonishing degree. The "promise and threatenings of covenant which are ratified to them," Samuel Willard reminds his parishioners in "Israel's True Safety," "are Temporary, and do refer to this World, and the blessing and evils that are to be withal here."[54] Any "distributions to men in another life," Willard explains, would be administered to men "personally," not as a people. The covenant, in other words, was of its time and as the Puritans came to understand it, the vows on which it was based could only be fulfilled in ways that would acknowledge the cosmopolitanism of flexible and temporally responsive ties.

Lest his audience forget the lesson, Willard wrote a sermon in which he explained the provisionality and conditionality of the covenant in more detail. "Now the People of God have an Argument, and an evidence, and clear manifestation of the particular love of God to them," he wrote in "Covenant-Keeping." "Now all this is done in the way of a Covenant, in which there are Termes, Propositions, and Conditions."[55] Although Willard speaks in terms of the positive duties that accompany the covenantal obligation, the vast majority of the lengthy sermon is devoted to the acceptance of conditionality as the essence of covenanting itself. "If he [the covenant keeper] have a grounded and apprehended assurance of his Title to the Promise [the covenant]," Willard writes, "he hath gained, and doth keep it by discerning and apprehending of the Condition [of the covenant] wrought in him." "To make the Promise itself [is]," he goes on to say, "to be an evidence of our interest in the Promise... if it be known, it must be known by the Condition."[56] "To make the promise," in other words, or to enter into the covenant was secondary to the expression of an interest in the Promise, as if this—the expression of interest—were all a supremely conditional covenant could entail.

The covenant described in "Covenant-Keeping" is relational—an expression of one's changing and uncertain ontological status in an increasingly cosmopolitan world. When considered from a spiritual and individual point of view, the covenant was a way to express one's aspiration for salvation; from a secular and corporate point of view, it was a way to express one's political and legal identity as a function of the contingent relations of the early modern world. In this sense, to keep the covenant, which as Willard suggests involved a constant awareness of how conditions might change over time, had more in common with diplomacy than with piety, demanding flexibility and adaptability rather than steadfastness.

A real-life corollary to this acceptance of the inevitability of covenant rupture and renewal was to be found in the growth of permanent resident ambassadors after Westphalia, who not only negotiated the terms of the treaties in question but worked diligently during periods of ostensible peace as well. As Jeremy Black observes, it was less the consequence of Westphalia than "the need to address current and new issues in the second half of the seventeenth century that encouraged the use of diplomats for reporting and negotiation."[57] Black's assertion is significant for it reveals the coincidence of the rise of treaties, whose ostensible purpose was, like that of the covenant, to create permanent bonds among people in different places, and the rise of "current and new issues" that would inevitably alter the terms of the treaties in time. To honor the treaty in place diplomats worked to "keep" the treaty as one would keep a covenant, renewing and rewriting it as circumstances demanded.

Two years after Cotton Mather argued that their charter "ought to be restored unto us [the New England Puritans]" his father, Increase, returned to the colonies with a new charter in hand. Celebrating as if it were the very renewal they were hoping for, the Puritans appeared content, but everyone, including the Mathers, would have known the truth: the new charter was simply another restrictive piece of royal legislation, scarcely a renewal or restoration of any kind. Under its terms the Puritans regained a few of their lawmaking capacities, but there was little about it that resembled the old. Once again the Puritans were put under the direct supervision of a royal governor, the adventurer William Phipps, whose policies, though more sympathetic to the Puritans than those of his predecessor, were nevertheless made in the interest not of the colonists but of the Crown.

Because of the restrictive new charter, the years under examination here—from 1680 to the end of the century—are traditionally read as a period of disappointment and failure, the beginning of the end for the Puritans who, faced with this final rebuke from the king, lost their lifeline and began to harbor the resentment that would fuel the revolution some eighty years later. Internal policies and laws, especially as the seat of decision-making shifted back to the king, may have justified such a view. It is at this moment that the story of the covenant as a central piece of modern American constitutionalism begins. According to this story, by this point in the late seventeenth century, the colonists had only two choices: they could succumb to the power of the Crown or resist it by reasserting their own. Choosing the latter (although not right away), allowed the covenant at the heart of their legal order to reassert itself. In this context the covenant was seen as the instrument of self-knowledge, separation, and independence it has remained ever since.

The view *from* the covenant, however, which under the influence of the law of nations fostered a cosmopolitan identity for the Puritans, tells another story. Moving us away from the isolationist and declensionist narratives that still dominate the field of Puritan studies in many ways, this story reveals a new form of legal agency on the Puritans' part at a time otherwise thought to be devoid of it. More importantly, the legal agency in question concerned itself less with independence from England or incipient nationhood than with a welcome dependence on the world. The Puritan covenant—the one that looked outward for its definition—relied on the need for every new generation to redefine itself covenantally; this was central to the Puritans' renewal literature. Renewal was an act of public commemoration, an updating and recommitment that simultaneously strengthened the internal bonds of the social order and called the community into being as a part of a larger order. To covenant in this sense was to internalize the external aspects of what it meant to live in a world of cultural, religious, and political difference.

Given voice by the Puritans as an alternative source of political and legal expression, the cosmopolitanism that emerged within the Puritan debates over the corporate covenant and covenant renewal in the second half of the seventeenth century can now be seen as a driving force within the life of the Puritans. Incorporating theological readings of the Bible informed by the law of nations, as well as precepts from treaties and treatises on the law of nations, the Puritans moved from a reading of the corporate covenant that in the first half of the seventeenth century underwrote their community's isolationism to a reading that in the second half of the seventeenth century underwrote their relationship to the rest of the world.

{3}

The Manufactured Millennium

It is not already the case that an already existing peaceful union has been savagely shattered. We have merely been reminded that unity has to be made; it is not simply observed.

—BRUNO LATOUR

Once a concept buried in Bible passages waiting only to be discovered and applied, the newly reinterpreted millennium also required the kind of human effort specified in early modern legal treaties in which peace—the major topic of such treaties—was carefully reconstructed and maintained.

We begin our discussion of the geopolitical links between the cosmopolis and the millennium by returning the millennium, which is most commonly understood in terms of time, to the later seventeenth-century debate about where it would be located. While the Puritans, like Christians everywhere, spent a good deal of time calculating the exact moment the millennium would arrive, they turned increasingly at the end of the seventeenth century to thinking about the millennium as another world, a "new earth" placed like the cosmopolis above and beyond any particular earthly location. Typically described as heavenly, but not a part of heaven per se, the millennium in late seventeenth-century Puritan sermons, which like all the sermons explored in this volume, appeared in a variety of sermonic genres including the Artillery sermon and the Election Day sermon, became a battleground of cosmopolitan proportions as the New England Puritans debated with their transatlantic counterparts about where in the world or possibly beyond it the millennium would take root. Many millennialists believed that the millennium would take the form of a City of God with "corporeal inhabitants."[1] Some millennialists, however, argued that Europe, and in particular Rome, would be the site of the new millennium, while others, most prominently the Puritans under scrutiny here, held that America would either be the locus of the millennium or at the very least not be excluded from it. Providing a sense of how diverse some of these opinions were, the always singular Samuel Sewall argued that the millennium would take root in Mexico.

For scholars focused on Puritan millennialist theology, such as Reiner Smolinski, the multiplicity of millennialist locations invites a confusion that strict attention to Puritan doctrine can readily clear up. Smolinksi argues that while many places seemed to hold an interest for the Puritans looking for millennialist real estate, their sights remained trained on Judea as the millennialist location par excellence.[2] From a cosmopolitan point of view, however, the multiplicity of places reveals the contours of yet another discursive domain in which a larger second sphere of unknown but developing proportions, such as that described by Seneca in his vision of the cosmopolis and later fueled by the law of nations, enters into Puritan thought and writings in the late seventeenth century. Toggling back and forth between architectural, spatial, and geopolitical terms such as city, kingdom, nation, new earth, earthly church, earthly capital, and the New Jerusalem, the Puritans in their late seventeenth-century millennialist sermons seemed to associate the millennium with a place somewhere between heaven and earth in a sphere large enough to encompass all the peoples of the earth without whom the elusive goal of a millennial peace would not occur.

Central to this new vision of the millennium as a kind of cosmopolis was a new interpretive assumption that drew on the law of nations' understanding of peace and the practice of treaty making that enabled the Puritans to associate the creation of the millennium with places, such as the Ottoman Empire, previously thought to be outside its bounds. While many conceptualizations of the millennium from earlier in the seventeenth century envisioned the millennium in utopian terms in which the processes of implementation and realization were ignored, later seventeenth-century representations seemed more concerned with how that world would come about.[3] Among other things, peace under the influence of the law of nations became more inclusive and practical; it grew to include places, such as the Ottoman Empire, which had for centuries been beyond its compass, and for the first time it entered into a discourse about peace not as a distant and ephemeral goal—a role peace had largely played in the past—but as an empirical and verifiable product of negotiation and hard work.

Peace, millennial or otherwise, as Gentili and Grotius explained, was not something for which one should idly wait; it was to be cultivated. Gentili spoke directly to this issue when he identified three methods of establishing peace. In the first, war would simply peter out, a prospect Gentili considered a continuation of war by another name. In the second, one side would surrender, which was less like peace than a form of warlike subjugation. And in the third, both sides would negotiate a settlement, far and away the best solution in Gentili's mind and, not coincidentally, the way the vast majority of wars actually ended.[4] By the middle of the seventeenth century, negotiated peace treaties providing for the cessation of military hostilities were standard in most European states. In the hands of Gentili and Grotius peace emerged not as an unattainable dream but as the result of rigorous diplomacy and treaty making.

Not everyone within the Puritan elite gave voice to this vision of a millennium that altered the concept of millennial peace and extended the geopolitical bounds of the millennium past the Christian world. Urian Oakes's 1673 sermon "New-England pleaded with, and pressed to consider the things which concern her peace, at least in this day," for example, tends to view peace more traditionally, as a dispensation from God rather than a product of human agency. Similarly, in his highly idiosyncratic *Phaenomena auaedam apocalytpica ad aspectum novi orbus configurata*, or, *Some Few Lines Towards a Description the New Heaven* (1697), Samuel Sewall seems largely focused on the constraints imposed by biblical interpretation on the notion of the millennium rather than contemplating a sphere like the cosmopolis above the earth and coterminous with it. In both of these sermons, however, there are hints of a move toward a more cosmopolitan millennium. There is a sense in Oakes's sermon that peace must be earned in ways that grace formerly had to be, and in Sewall's that the new heaven could be anywhere, including in North America. Thus there appears to be a shift in Christic cosmology that was arguably facilitated by the reach of the cosmopolis in this period.

A clearer sign that a cosmopolitan millennium was in the making geopolitically and hermeneutically can be found, not surprisingly, in one of the most far-reaching Puritan thinkers, Cotton Mather. Mather, as we have seen, was often more experimental than many of his colleagues, though it was typically not long before his more experimental notions found purchase in the works of other ministers with congregations outside the metropolitan parishes of Boston and

Cambridge, who looked to Mather for inspiration for their sermons at home.[5] Signs of Mather's millennial revisionism are especially salient in three works: the book-length sermon, *Things to Be Look'd For (*1691), the epistolary essay, *Problema theologicum* (1703), and his magnum millennialist opus, running to some three hundred pages, *Triparadisus* (1712/1726/1737). A small fraction of his numerous sermons, lectures, and pamphlets on the millennium as a whole, these compositions are among Mather's best known. Here we see him working out many thoughts about the millennium in overtly political and legal terms and frequently confessing to having changed his mind about them over time. Circling back to previous ideas, revising earlier positions, and reaffirming others, Mather does not offer a coherent image of the millennium in these works. Even in *Triparadisus*, a synoptic work completed at the end of his life, Mather falls short of presenting a summary view.

What we see instead in all three texts are discursive breakthroughs and recontextualizations that signal, without departing from the traditional link between the millennium and Christ's Second Coming, a new paradigm for thinking about the millennium in terms of cosmopolitan peacemaking. "There is," Mather writes in *Things to Be Look'd For*, "a Wonderful STATE of PEACE, which the God of Heaven will make His people upon Earth, to be the Joyful Partakers of."[6] This peace, he goes on to explain, is not to be confused with a purely internal peace but is rather "external" and so "lyes not merely in the Blessed Settlement and Composure of the Spirit, which Believers in all Ages, are the Subjects of." That internal, spiritual peace, he is careful to suggest, is still possible. "When our Lord Jesus went away to Heaven, He left us that legacy, peace I leave you with, my Peace I give unto you." Yet, Mather observes, this is not to be confused with the peace of the millennium. "[But] such a spiritual peace is not that we are to Be Looking for. The Peace promised unto us, is that External, as well as Internal, harmony, Amity & Unity."[7] Lest there be any lingering doubt about the legal and political nature of the peace to come, Mather explains that the millennium he envisions involves the acts of politically recognized entities. "It is foretold concerning this [millennial] Time," he writes, "the wolf shall dwell with the Lamb. Which whether or not it shall . . . be fulfill'd in a Natural Sense, will doubtless be fulfill'd in a Political Sense."[8]

The "Political Sense" is largely geopolitical and finds expression in Mather's concern about the age-old problem of where the millennium would be located and how far it would extend. As a result of recent discoveries by adventurers, merchants, and imperialists, the world as seen from the West had been changing shape for some time. The changes to which Mather's millennial vision is sensitive, however, are legally and cartographically inspired. Mather's millennium takes on the political and legal attributes of the cosmopolis not only because it extends to newly discovered territories like the New World but also because it encompasses territories—most significantly, the Ottoman Empire—which had long been on the map but were excluded from the mantle of Christendom. Being excluded from Christendom meant that the Ottomans were typically not seen as potential military enemies, but it also meant that if the West should find itself at war with the Ottomans, which as the Puritans knew well had already come to pass, they did not need to think about making peace with them in the wake of it. For centuries wars had torn Christendom apart, but as the ceaseless nature of the wars themselves proved, war was at best a partial solution; war might hobble enemies, but it did not obliterate them. It followed that when it came to the Ottomans, the only major power outside the Christian confessional sphere, war alone would not suffice, and this is why representations of total annihilation, typically in the midst of apocalyptically inspired flames, dominated Christian narratives about them. In the late seventeenth-century millennialist works examined here, however, the Ottomans form a vital part of the Western world; still considered an enemy, the Ottomans are brought back from the brink of total destruction to emerge in Mather's work as potential peacemakers as well—an innovation, I argue, that owed a debt to the law of nations.

The interpretive thread in Mather's work about the millennium concerns the Puritan approach to biblical prophecies, specifically those concerned with fixing the date of the millennium's arrival. Grounded in the providential history of the Bible, especially in Daniel and Revelation, the problem of figuring out when the millennium would arrive had long been a matter of lining up dates with prophecies. To this end, millennialists developed complex ways of calculating the days of creation, the ages of the world, the length of generations, and the duration of empires, all of which were outlined in the prophecies. Armed with these calculations, millennialists then turned signs in the contemporaneous world, including wars, famines, and earthquakes, into the fulfillment of scriptural promises. Rejecting an interpretive framework that grew less plausible as the year of each millennialist prediction came and went without incident, Mather offers an alternative that imagines the millennium's advent as a product not of prophetic alignment but of hard work and negotiation as underscored by the law of nations. Surrounded by the numerous treaty agreements that defined diplomacy and embodied the law of nations in the seventeenth century, Mather brings the acts of compromise and negotiation into the millennial sphere and the realm of the millennium into cosmopolitan view. Put another way, if Increase Mather believed "the millennial state, like salvation, must come from heaven in a divine dispensation," his son came to believe it would issue from human manufacture and hard work. "Paradise," Cotton Mather writes in *Triparadisus*, "is what we have under cultivation."[9] In the following sections a fuller account of these two millennium-based aspects of cosmopolitanism is explored.

The Geopolitical Millennium

The geopolitical embrace of non-Christian lands in Cotton Mather's millennium paralleled the shift from territorially defined to cosmopolitan, world encompassing thought among law of nations theorists. Starting as an ephemeral concept, located somewhere in the ether between heaven and earth, the millennium had, by the early seventeenth century, a recognizably material shape, with various territories vying for an association with it. Traditional millennialists had long connected the millennium with Israel, based on a reading of Romans 11:26, which stated that the punishment of the Jews would last only "until the fullness of the Gentiles should come in, and that then all Israel should be saved." Identifying the saving of Israel with its literal restoration, theologians located the millennium in Judea or Jerusalem where the Jews had formerly built their temples and grown to glory. Given the biblical history associated with the Jews, however, Israel was thought to be both material and spiritual at the same time. As the century wore on, however, Israel took a back seat to more specific, secular locations, including England, the American colonies, and South America. While Smolinski argues convincingly that these new locations may not have displaced the literal Jerusalem as the site of the New Jerusalem in the minds of many Puritans, later seventeenth-century millennialist sermons took an undeniable turn toward the inclusion of newly discovered territories and newly established polities in a redesign of the process by which the Christic millennium would achieve its geopolitical goals.[10]

Embracing already existing countries or their colonies in this newly redesigned millennial kingdom helped authorize those countries' spiritual election and legal sovereignty. England was quick to recognize this potential, especially during the Puritan interregnum when, with Cromwell, a coreligionist, finally in a position of power, many millennialists believed they had achieved a heaven on earth.[11] Newly confident and still clinging to the belief that before the millennium could be ushered in, "all Israel would be saved," many English millennialists looked beyond the verse in Romans to Isaiah 11:12, which foretold that before a millennium in which the Jews would return to Palestine, the Jews would first have to be scattered to the four corners of the earth. "And he shall set up an ensign for the nations," Isaiah declared, "and shall assemble the outcasts of Israel, and gather together the dispersed of Judah from the four corners of the earth." Reports from New England that the native tribes were descended from the Jews seemed to confirm the diasporic prophecy in Isaiah, reinforcing New England's role in bringing the millennium about. Additional reports from seventeenth-century travelers that Indians living in the Andes had been heard reciting the Jewish prayer, the "Shema," also went a long way toward convincing millennialists that the Jews were very nearly dispersed to the requisite four corners of the earth. All that remained, according to English millennialists, was for the Jews to be readmitted to England, whose coordinates, they argued, placed it firmly in the fourth corner.

Cromwell's achievements in England did not go unnoticed in America and gave New England's Puritans all the more reason to tout the virtues of their heaven on earth above those of the mother country. The New England Puritans after all had established their settlements long before Cromwell had come to power and did so with an energy and spiritual zeal that merited inclusion in the millennium. New Englanders writing back to England in the first years of settlement often drew obvious comparisons between their home and a heavenly, millennial kingdom. In works as diverse as Edward Johnson's *Wonder Working Providence* (1628–1651), John Cotton's "God's Promise to his Plantations" (1630), John Winthrop's "Model of Christian Charity" (1630), William Wood's *New England's Prospect* (1634), and John Eliot's *The Christian Commonwealth* (1659), Puritan authors described their experience of the climate and soil of the New World as a kind of proto-millennial experiment.

At the beginning of the last third of the century, however, it looked as if these millennially compatible visions of the New World in America were on the wane. Wracked by the Antinomian controversy, in which leading Puritan ministers were attacked for preaching a doctrine of works instead of a doctrine of grace, and then again by the controversy over admission standards for church members that ended in the Halfway Covenant of 1662, the Massachusetts Bay Colony, long the jewel in the crown of the New England colonies, found itself an unlikely source of or location for millennial visions. New World critics began to complain that the Puritans' legal and social order fell short as a precursor to the millennium. There were many from the first generation of settlers who held the second and third generations responsible for destroying the opportunities for an ideal society they had set in place. In addition to these internal rifts, the Colony suffered from stricter oversight by the Crown. Moved by rumors that the Puritans were violating conditions of the Navigation Acts, Charles II sent an agent to revoke their charter and divest them of their ability to govern themselves. Making the most of these problems, many Englishmen, including well-known biblical scholars Joseph Mede and Nicholas Fuller believed that the American colonies were not assimilable within the millennialist narrative. "These nations & c.," Mede wrote, "which are spiritually called Gog and Magog [the mythical enemies of God first mentioned in the Book of Ezekiel] live in the Hemisphere opposite to us, which God had excluded from the call of the Christian Gospel."[12]

This anti-Americanism galvanized a new generation of Puritan millennialists, who defended America's millennialist role against attacks.[13] With publications like Urian Oakes's "New England Pleaded With" (1673), Increase Mather's "The Doctrine of Divine Providence" (1684), Nicholas Noyes's "New-England's Duty and Interest" (1698), and Samuel Sewall's *Phaenomena quaedam apocalyptica ad aspectum novi orbis configurata*, or, *Some Few Lines Towards a Description of the New Heaven* (1697), the eschatological belief that America was worthy of millennial inclusion underwent a resurgence. While often read as a cover for the Puritans' persistent sense of disappointment in themselves, these late century sermons reflected that peculiar combination of isolation and self-aggrandizement to which the colonists were prone. Robert Middlekauf and Kenneth Silverman, the two most prominent Mather biographers, tie the millennialism of both Mathers, father and son, to the increasing isolation the Puritans felt as both God and England seemed to have abandoned them.[14]

Accurate as far as it goes, Middlekauf and Silverman's view of millennially inspired isolationism overlooks the strain of millennialism in Cotton Mather's late century sermons that pulls in an opposite, anti-isolationist direction. Admittedly vexed by America's detractors, Mather devoted himself in part to refuting the association of America with hell. "I that am an American must needs be Lothe to allow all America still unto the Devil's possession, when our Lord shall possess all the rest of the World," Mather writes in *Problema theologicum*.[15] It is clear from this statement that Mather did not accept the idea of an American hell, but it does not, as Smolinksi points out, suggest that he claimed for America the geography of the new Zion. Even in his most self-congratulatory piece about America, *Theopolis Americana*, Mather only went so far as to counter those who thought America would have no share in the millennium at all. "They that are of the [millennial] City," Mather wrote, "shall have something to do here for Him. *O* NEW-ENGLAND, There is Room to hope, That thou also shalt belong to the CITY."[16] What is curious about the statement from *Problema* is that Mather's defense of a potential place for America within the millennium rests on his understanding of the world as a whole. According to Mather the question to ask was not why America was evil but why it would be singled out for possession by the devil when the rest of the world was given to God. Important here is that America's place within the millennium seems contingent on the looming legal configuration of the world as cosmopolis made available by the law of nations.

Throughout his millennialist writings from this period, Mather proved sensitive to the world as the product of an ever-growing cartography. "It was never intended," he writes, "that the church of our lord, should be confined always within the dimensions of Strabo's cloak; and that, all the world, should always be no more, than it was, when Augustus taxed it."[17] An ancient geographer, Strabo believed that the habitable portion of the earth was no more than an island (which looked to him like a military cloak), a theory Mather, as his reference to Strabo suggests, disavowed. Legally, Mather also made important revisions to the millennium, bringing it into line with the law of nations. In *Triparadisus*, for example, roughly half of the third section, devoted to what Mather called the Third Paradise, describes a total, premillennial conflagration of the world. This is significant because just a few years earlier, Mather adhered to the more widespread belief that the conflagration preceding the millennium would be only partial. This belief about the partial conflagration was borne from logistical questions about how in the midst of a total conflagration the remnant of true believers, who were destined for the millennium, would be saved. Scholars have long puzzled over Mather's turn toward a belief in total conflagration, with Smolinski providing something of a final word by attributing the change to Mather's discovery of a sermon that resolved the theologically sticky problem of the remnant in a way Mather deemed satisfactory.[18]

Working toward a theory of total conflagration, however, must be seen not simply as the effect on Mather of theological persuasion alone. It was also a way of bringing the idea of the millennium into line with theories of the legal sphere. The conflagration that was to destroy the world in premillennial flames had to be total because the world that was to be remade for the millennium, like the world administered by the law of nations, had to be total as well. Mather's language about this world bears a strong resemblance to the idea put forward by Seneca of two worlds—the city-state and then somewhere outside and above it the cosmopolis. Of this cosmopolitan millennium Mather writes, "The Earth is to be CREATED over again, into an entire PARADISE; and, no doubt, the Second Edition will be, Auctior et Emendatior, and the World will be Recovered into a Better Condition, than it had before."[19] Here we note the consonance of the earth and paradise, but in a gesture reminiscent of the covenant renewals of chapter 2, themselves inspired by the opportunity the law provided for do-overs, this earth will be different. More specifically, it will be "better" because it will be "entire," suggesting the virtues of a world encompassing, cosmopolitan reform. More significantly, perhaps, Mather describes the second edition of the world as existing in a realm all its own; it is of the earth in that it will contain a "restoration of all things," but it is also, like the cosmopolis, above and beyond it. "The situation of the New Jerusalem," he writes, "will be in a Part of the Atmosphere, which will be neare to the Earth, where the nations are to Walk in the Light of it, than as yet it is, and it will be conspicuous to the Nations."[20]

In trying to describe the reach of the new millennium, Mather speaks in ways reminiscent of the law of nations theorists as they struggled to describe the law of nations' jurisdiction. The difficulty law of nations theorists faced was how to think about a legal domain beyond the territorially defined unit that organized much political and millennialist thought in the fifteenth and sixteenth centuries. The process of thinking of the world in terms other than territorial began with a reading of Roman law and its applicability to natural law by the early modern law of nations theorists. Alberico Gentili was the first to posit an extension of Roman law beyond the Roman Empire itself. "The law which is written in the books of Justinian," Gentili wrote, "is not merely that of the state, but also that of the nations and of nature."[21] In specifying that such a law existed to handle affairs among territories, as well as those that emanated from and applied to a sphere beyond the territorial, Gentili went even further. "If the empire were destroyed," Gentili explained, "the law itself, although long buried, would yet rise again and diffuse itself among all the nations of mankind."[22] The law, it would seem from Gentili's formulation, occupied its own "atmosphere," with many of the same abstract, ethereal attributes Mather ascribed to the millennium.

General theories of a geopolitically responsive millennium extending beyond the boundaries of any one territory provided the backdrop to a far more specific change in the cosmopolitan vision of the law of nations as well as in Mather's millennium: the inclusion of the Ottoman Empire. No longer defined exclusively as a space outside Christendom, the Ottoman Empire became in Grotius's work of a piece with all other sovereign entities, both subject to and maker of world encompassing laws. Grotius, we recall, parted ways with Gentili by endorsing treaty making with the so-called infidel, and in doing so opened up the world to a previously unseen legal partner. The legal confrontation with and material inclusion of the Ottoman Empire in the law of nations should not be underestimated, for it demonstrates how far the law of nations moved away from Christian universalism and toward a sense of non-Christians as something other than colonial subalterns or hostile parties.

The model of a world that encompassed Ottomans and Europeans alike would have been highly legible to the Puritans in the New World as it was to the reading public all over Europe, for the possibility of partnering in peace with the Ottomans issued in a glut of printed material about them. Among the most popular books and pamphlets were Richard Knolles's *History of the Turks* (1603) and Paul Rycaut's *Present State of the Ottoman Empire* (1665), both of which were in the Mathers' library. For the most part, however, scholarship on Mather and the millennium has not taken this emphasis on the Ottoman Empire into account. According to most scholars, the Puritans thought about the Ottomans and the Eastern world the way most Christians did, as a threat not to be contained politically or legally but to be obliterated in a conflagration of millennialist proportions. For religious writers in particular, the threat posed by the Turk was easily accommodated by the story of the opening of the sixth vial from Revelation, which foretold the drying up of the Euphrates, a geographical indicator that was taken to refer to the Ottoman world. Occupying a position formerly held by the pope, the Turk in most millennialist sermons is typically figured as the new Antichrist, leading an Eastern enemy to ultimate destruction by Christianity. Tucked neatly into the millennialist paradigm, the destruction of the Eastern Antichrist was generally acknowledged to be a sign of the millennium and thus worked, as Timothy Marr explains, to "contain the transgressive threat of Islam within a comforting realm."[23] Marr points to the work of several Puritans, including John Cotton and both Mathers, to support this belief.[24] On the strength of this conviction Marr contends that "[e]arly American understandings of Islam emerged . . . neither from substantial comparative dialogue with Muslims nor from engaged scholarly study of Islamic texts, but largely from investigation into what the Bible seemed to reveal prophetically about its existence and duration as a worldly challenge to the Christian Church."[25]

Other scholars, including scholars of Puritan millennialist texts, have made similar claims. For Smolinski, for example, Cotton Mather's interest in the figure of the Turk as the Eastern Antichrist was obsessive and unchanging.[26] To be sure, Mather more than once associated the Turk with the Antichrist in *Things to Be Look'd For*. In one particular passage he explicitly holds out the hope that the Antichrist's destruction will bring on the millennium. "There seem to be some Symptoms upon the Turkish Empire," Mather writes, "that speak hopefully about our Blessed State of Peace, and say, it will come quickly."[27] On the whole, however, Mather seems to turn in this sermon from a view of the Turks as the Antichrist to a conciliatory, even respectful view of them as potential partners in the millennium.[28] Central to this partnership were questions about how to find common ground and foster reciprocity between such drastically different cultures and how to maintain peace in between wars with people who continued to be viewed as the enemy. These efforts demanded that law of nations theorists come up with new ideas about amity and unity and recast what seemed to be impassable borders between religions, creeds, and ethnicities into bridges.

Responding to these and other changes in the law of nations discourse, the millennium of Cotton Mather followed suit. In *Problema theologicum*, for example, Mather describes the millennium as a place no longer divided by ethnic or religious borders. "There shall no longer be such an unhappy Division of Mankind, as we see at present," Mather writes, "when Mahometism is extended farther than Christendome, and paganism farther than either of them, and Christendom itself, is in many parts of it, little better than a revived paganism, and the very Empire of Antichrist."[29] Not yet a statement of ecumenism as such, the divided world Mather saw "at present" bespeaks a more inclusive vision of the millennium than had been articulated before. The divisions Mather bemoans include those within Christendom and those beyond it, and render the differences within and among "Mahometism," "Christendom," and "paganism" equally problematic. In Mather's formulation, the millennium must extend far beyond Christendom if it is to be appropriately millennial in scope.

Thinking in terms of total peace as opposed to total destruction, Mather carried forward his law of nations inspired view of the Ottomans in *Problema theologicum*. In a passage in which he associates the Turk with the Antichrist, he also introduces a new term for imagining the end of the Ottoman Empire that falls far short of annihilation. "At the Expiration of this term," Mather writes, by which he means the years between the destruction of the Roman Empire and the destruction of the Eastern Antichrist, "the second Wo is to pass away; which (to me) does not necessarily imply a Total Ruine of the Turkish Empire; but only a ceasing of its Hostilities; with a Peace or Truce."[30]

Mather's reference here to "a peace or truce" with the Ottomans introduces terms central to the law of nations that altered the geopolitical scope of the millennium and signaled an interpretive reversal in his millennialist thought. As the title of Mather's sermon, *Things to Be Look'd for* suggests, the Puritans were accustomed to "looking for" the millennium in Scripture. Like most millennialists, Mather devoted much of his earlier thought about the millennium to a hermeneutics of calculation and discovery that involved lining up prophecies from Scripture with natural and man-made events to predict the millennium's onset. In particular, Mather followed the narrative in Revelation in which the Antichrist is given power for "a thousand two hundred and threescore dayes" (Rev. 11:2–3, 13:5). According to Mather, if one counted these days as years and then equated them with Ezekiel's prophetic scheme, one would arrive at the conclusion that the 1260 years in Revelation was to be multiplied three and a half times which, not coincidentally, positioned the onset of the millennium within reach of people living in Mather's day.[31] In thinking about a peace or truce, by contrast, Mather turns from *looking for* signs to *manufacturing* them by engaging in dialogue with otherwise hostile parties.

The New Interpretation

To some degree the engine driving this turn from the hermeneutics of calculation and discovery to the hermeneutics of manufacture was the simple observation that all past efforts to align prophecy with history and to calculate the millennium's arrival had been met with disappointment. Many predictions of the date and time of the millennium came and went without the occurrence of anything even vaguely apocalyptic. Satisfied that the prophecies were correct, most millennialists chose to recalculate, but their methods were increasingly subject to ridicule. Many people, including one of Mather's contemporaries, James Franklin, brother of Benjamin Franklin and publisher of the influential *New England Courant*, were known to deride this kind of millennialism. Such "misguided prognostications," Franklin writes, "may serve to remind them [people who predicted the millennium with precision], that is it not for them to know the Times and Seasons, which the ETERNAL has reserv'd in his own Power."[32] Eventually even Mather saw the truth of Franklin's critique. Targeting the many millennialist readings that traced contemporary events to biblical forecasts of the Apocalypse in *Things to Be Look'd For*, Mather noted, "you may almost everywhere, after some digging, throw up some unsuspected Intimations of this kind, whereas you will find impossible to forbear crying out, with some Transport of Soul, I have found! I have found!" To read in this way, Mather cautions, is to engage in "very unsafe computations, to which, and by which, many have expos'd themselves. It ha's been Ridiculous to see," he writes, "by what Chronology, by what Cabala, and with what Temerity, some have Steered."[33]

Because of these frequent disappointments, some precedent for dissociating prophecies and millennial calculations had developed in the theological community as well. This development took the form of a belief that the signs of the millennium had been fulfilled in the past, making it pointless to look for them in the present. This belief, known to millennialists as preterism, had its origins with Grotius, who was, in addition to his law of nations work, responsible for a number of significant theological and specifically millennialist opinions. Legal and religious views of peace were completely intertwined for Grotius, as they came to be for Mather as well. Thus according to Grotius the Apocalypse was not intended to be read as prophecy since all of its predictions had already come to pass. One of the most significant implications of this view had to do with the Beast of the Apocalypse because according to Grotius this did not refer to the pope, as almost all Christians believed, but to the Emperor Domitian.[34] Perhaps even more chillingly, Grotius also believed that the Hebrew Bible's prophecies referred not to Christ but to the Israelites alone.[35]

Not surprisingly, Grotius's preterist approach to the millennium had legal and political implications that dovetailed with the law of nations. In contending that the millennium had already come and gone, for example, Grotius relieved Protestants of the burden of distinguishing the saved from the damned, a process that had generated much political and religious divisiveness. More specifically, Grotius's refusal to associate the pope with the Antichrist allowed him to further the peacemaking agenda that lay at the heart of the law of nations by considerably improving the relationships among Holland, his own country, and the Roman Catholic countries of Spain, Italy, and France.

Nevertheless, most millennialists, with Increase Mather preeminent among them, found Grotius's stand on the millennium alarming. For one thing, Grotius's interpretation of the apocalyptic past robbed Protestants of their claim of superiority over Catholics. It was, after all, the pope's corruption and tyranny that had fostered the association between him and the Beast of the Apocalypse and removing that taint was tantamount to endorsing him. For another, it implied that the events in the Bible were to be taken allegorically, which was anathema to millennialists such as Increase Mather, who read the Scriptures literally. To read the Bible allegorically threatened to equate it with other forms of literature and thus fracture the foundations of Christianity.

For most of his life, Cotton Mather had agreed with his father and the vast majority of millennialists in this regard. By the end of the seventeenth century, however, under the influence of the law of nations, he had begun to change his mind. What ultimately emerged as an about-face occurred with his rejection, after 1724, of the hope he had shared with his father that the Jews would be converted to Christianity as a prerequisite to the millennium. Millennialists of all persuasions believed that the Jews would be converted, and like all other aspects of the millennium, they looked for signs, pinning their hopes on the discovery of Jews among the indigenous tribes of North and South America and in the movements to return the Jews to England from which they had been banished at the end of the thirteenth century.

Under the influence of Grotius and other preterists, Mather, however, finally came to believe that most Jews had already been converted and that waiting for future conversion for the remnant was futile. Christians were no closer to converting Jews by the beginning of the eighteenth century than they had been before, and the Jews themselves were flourishing in places where no one expected, including the Ottoman Empire. Even Mather's father seemed to recognize this when he observed that "Salonica [then Ottoman, now Greek] is full of none but Jews, where they do (and no where else in the world do they so) if reports of Travellers may be credited, speak Hebrew as their natural language. And there are [those?] that affirm that in those Cities of Salonica . . . and Constantinople there have inhabited fifteen hundred thousand Israelites."[36] To this observation, Cotton Mather added his own astonishment in *Problema theologicum*: "The Israelitish Nation is a Numerous Nation, even at this Day; when to our Surprize we find near Ten Thousand of them, even at Prague, and more then [*sic*] Ten Thousand of them even at Rome, in the very midst of their Popish Persecutors!"[37] It was thus more convenient to believe that the vast majority of Jews had been converted at the time of Christ's First Coming and that despite their apparently large numbers, those who remained were merely a small fraction of the whole.

Scholars of Puritan millennialism have typically acknowledged this shift in Cotton Mather's views about Jewish conversion, but they have not taken his more general acceptance of preterist practices into account or related them to his understanding of the law of nations. Smolinksi, for example, believes that Mather's adoption of the preterite view of the Jews was "inadvertent," while Jeffrey Mares observes that Mather accepted certain preterite principles in "alliance against the greater threats of deism and skepticism."[38] The millennialist sermons examined here, however, in particular *Triparadisus*, suggest that Mather's preterism had interpretive implications that went beyond the threats to theology posed by deism and skepticism. So pervasive had Mather's general sense of preterism become that he raises a question in *Triparadisus* about the validity of looking for signs of the future as an interpretive method in the first place. "Yea, Quare," he writes, "whether the Signs are not all giv'n, and past; so that there is no more to be look'd for." Expressing an almost complete rejection of the hermeneutic of discovery, Mather went on to incorporate preterism into his millennialist vision in an effort to release the millennium from its dependence on the conversion of the Jews—a single event that seemed to have little chance of occurring—and bring the millennial vision of peace in line with the legal vision of peace Grotius had forged. Thus in place of the interpretive framework of looking *for* signs in the scriptural past, he looks, as the law itself was wont to do, *to* political and legal events of his day, including peace treaties and truces.

Among other things, Mather's preterism would have been reinforced by the preterism that characterized the intertextuality of treaties. For one thing, treaty negotiations were conducted with a view to the conditions that prevailed before and after the hostilities. This reliance on past conditions, or more accurately the alteration of past conditions, determined the present in treaty terms. The present peace was thus a direct response to the past. For another, the currency of any one treaty might determine the future of all others. Article II of the Treaty of Nimeguen concluded between the Holy Roman emperor and the king of France in 1678, for example, openly declared "the Treaty of Munster shall be the foundation of this treaty," while Nimeguen was said to "have full effect" in the Treaty of Ryswick concluded between England and France in 1697.[39] This created a cascade of treaties that reinforced the contingency of any one treaty in the process, and this contingency became the model for bringing the peace of the millennium about as well.

By the time Mather was writing his late century eschatological lectures and sermons, treaties were regular reading for a large audience, making the language of treaties pervasive. Copies of the Peace of Westphalia were popular, but after Westphalia, news of diplomatic efforts flooded the printing presses and newspapers of Europe, and negotiations were on everyone's minds, including those in the far-flung American colonies. In 1659, for example, public demand for the peace of the Pyrenees was such that copies were printed for collective and individual purchase. Soon after printers started publishing treaties in compilations, such as Leibniz's *Codex juris gentium diplomaticus* in 1693.

From the multiple diary entries and correspondence that mention the treaties of his day, we know that Mather was an avid treaty reader. So focused is Mather in *Things to Be Look'd For* on the imminence of a possible treaty with the Ottomans that he seems to be in conversation with the negotiations in real time. Driven by a hope that no one country or sovereign entity would hold more than its fair share of power—a principle that later became known as the balance of power—King William was preoccupied with brokering a peace between the Hapsburg emperor, Leopold, and the Ottomans, also known as the Sublime Porte, so that Leopold would be free to help England defeat France, a goal close to William's heart. Since 1689, England's ambassador to the Porte, William Trumbull, had been working toward this end.[40] Integrating this into his millennialist vision, Mather writes, "If we should shortly hear of a general Peace or Truce with him [the Ottomans], it would add unto our probabilities."[41] The probabilities to which Mather refers are those of the coming millennium, but the fact that he includes the possibility of a peace with the Ottomans among the signs of that probability suggest how altered his sense of the millennium has become. "A general peace or truce with the Ottomans" is a feature of the law of nations that in Mather's hands becomes a prophetic sign on a par with the vials and trumpets of Revelation.

In a letter to his friend, Samuel Penhallow, during the peace negotiation at Utrecht in 1712, Mather gives us an even clearer sense of how focused he was on the hard work and manufacture of peace. "The Negotiation of Peace, is going on," Mather begins:

> and all Things conspire to give us a strong Expectation, that it will speedily be accomplished.... The French King makes an Explanation of his offers for a general peace; wherein he acknowledges the Q[ueen] of Great Britain, and the Succession according to the present Settlement. He demolishes Dunkirk, for an Equivalent that will not be much disputed about.... He consents to a Treaty of Commerce on the most agreeable Terms. He allowes the Dutch, the Barrier they desire in the Netherlands. He brings the Spanish Indies, into the Condition wherein it was before the Death of Charles II.... He consents to have things in Portugal and Germany, as they were before the War, and Contents the Duke of Savoy.[42]

Under the spell of a promised peace, Mather is hopeful, yet the emphasis in this passage is on the labor of negotiating peace, which was variously, in his words, "accomplished," "offered," "acknowledged," "agreed upon," "settled," "consented to," "not much disputed about," and "allowed." With this medley of verbs, Mather attends to the myriad ways in which peace could be brought about and resorts to a variety of verbal expressions to articulate his new consciousness of the terms and conditions to which the parties had agreed, including how contested pieces of land were to be divided, how prisoners were to be transferred, and how the formerly warring governments would interact.

These terms demonstrated how difficult the work of peacemaking could be and how easily a peace could be broken. It is no wonder then that Grotius paid almost as much attention to how peace might be broken as to how it might be made. "There are three ways," Grotius wrote, "in which a peace may be broken—either by doing something contrary to the very essence of all peace—or something in violation of the express terms of a particular peace—or something contrary to the effects, which are intended to arise from every peace."[43] The peace that issued from the midst of war, in other words, rested on terms specified by the parties. Portions of many peace treaties prescribed what measures should be taken in case the treaty was violated, anticipating the undoing of the document even as it was being signed.

In emphasizing the impermanence of peace, Mather followed the lead of treaties from this period that outlined the specific outcomes of war and tried to resolve many of the issues that led to war with less of an interest in preventing war in the future than in cementing admittedly fragile and time-limited bonds in the present. Of course, the idea of a perpetual peace was often reaffirmed in the preambles to treaties, many of which specified a peace that would be "perpetual and universal," but the detailed provisions of these same treaties—ranging from new arrangements about border patrols, the repatriation of goods and territory, or the order of succession within a royal house—made a literal interpretation of terms like perpetual and universal impossible.[44] In addition, conditions in these treaties often provided explicitly for a limited number of years of peace or set out exactly what should happen if the peace were violated.

Mather's millennialist timetable reflects this sense of temporality by directly accepting the possibility that peace might take a long time to be realized and that there might be a gap between cause and effect. Referring to the chronology by which prophecies were to be fulfilled, Mather writes, "When a period [marked off by prophecy] is up, there is not always a Necessity that there should be no pause, between, the Thing that has been done, and the Next Thing to be done. . . . What I mean, is, That Some Space of Preparation for the Following Event, may sometimes be well enough supposed."[45] Between the instigation of one act toward the fulfillment of peace and the onset of the millennium, there might, in other words, be gaps or reversals.

In place of a millennialist projection that guaranteed peace's perpetuity or the precise moment of arrival, Mather offers a vision of contingency that borrows from the language of the law of nations and the peace treaties of his day. He begins by acknowledging biblical history in asserting the importance of truces in making peace. "The Pagan Historian," he writes, "related concerning the Time of our Lords First coming, that there was then, Totius Orbis aut Pax aut pacis; a Peace, or at least a Truce among all the nations; but a far greater thing of the kind will be bought about, at the day."[46] The invocation of a truce here, however, for the sake of comparison to a millennial peace, which will be like it but "far greater," could not have failed to put Mather's audience in mind of the frequent truces then being made between the European and Ottoman powers, among others.

The shift from a belief in the millennium as a function of prophecy to that of hard work and negotiation also took the form of an explicit acknowledgment on Mather's part of the tenuousness of peace in his day. Without directly addressing the possibility that the millennium—that blessed thousand-year-long peace—might be interrupted, Mather makes reference in the three millennialist sermons under examination here of how short-lived any given peace might be. At one point, Mather deliberately pulls back from the traditional understanding of the relationship between peace and the destruction of the Antichrist when he cautions against thinking of peace as coming on suddenly in the wake of it. "Tis not unlikely," he writes, "that after the next fatal Blowes upon Antichrist the Perfect peace of the Church may Require some Time for the settling of it. But yet, be of Good Cheer, It comes on apace," where "apace" seems to hint at the kind of gradual progress made by negotiators.[47] The negotiations required to make the peace of the millennium, like those of the peace of nations, depended on time and unlike the time of Revelation so often rendered in precise temporal projections, this time remained vague and ultimately incalculable.

Millennial Diplomacy

Preoccupied with the act of negotiating peace, Cotton Mather also turned in his late century millennial sermons to the negotiators themselves, representing them as models for ushering in the new cosmopolitan millennium. This first became visible in Mather's shift from representing rulers as the primary peacemakers to showing diplomats in that role. Mather offers a parable about the biblical Jeroboam to this end. "Who are they that breake the Peace of the World," Mather asked, "more than the bad Rulers of it, they are the Jereboams of the world, that corrupt and poison their Subjects with such evil manners as bring the Vengeance of War upon them."[48] One of the kings of Israel in the tenth century BCE, Jereboam was a biblical figure of ill repute, known largely for leading the ten northern tribes of Israelites into unnecessary war with the remaining two tribes of the southern Kingdom of Judah. For making war, but more importantly for driving a wedge between people of the same nation, Jereboam has been widely reviled by Jewish and Christian interpreters alike, but Mather's use of him is notable not for its excoriation, but for the distinction he draws between bad rulers and rulers like Jereboam who in his words "corrupt and poison their Subjects." For Mather bad rulers were not optimal, but unlike Jereboam, they could still make and keep the peace, a vision sustained for the first time by a formalism introduced by the law of nations. Having arrived under the law of nations at a point where the justness of war could be verified empirically and where diplomats worked the terms of conflict resolution, peace was no longer the sole province of good rulers and war no longer the sole province of bad ones. This was a new world for the Puritans, a world in which the lingua franca was diplomacy among countries rather than internal domestic rule by divine fiat or by wise rulers, and the millennium reflected these changes as well.

That diplomats took the lead in negotiating peace with relative autonomy in the early modern period was perhaps nowhere more visible than in the fiction of diplomatic immunity, which underwrote the law of nations and the cosmopolis itself. Gentili, who was the first to speak of diplomatic law as a coherent whole, believed that the ambassador should be immune from domestic law proceedings. Asked to consult on the case of Bernadino de Mendoza, the sixteenth-century Spanish ambassador to England accused of plotting against the queen, Gentili brought his theory to bear on a practical situation by suggesting that even a charge of conspiracy should not subject the diplomat to the host country's laws. If an ambassador were to be punished, Gentili argued, he should be expelled from the host country, not put to death inside it. Following Gentili, Grotius framed a more general rule, which included an explicit reference to the legal fiction of extraterritoriality. "Embassadors," he wrote, "who are . . . by a sort of Fiction, taken for the very Persons whom they represent . . . so may they by the same kind of Fiction be imagined to be out of the Territories of the Potentate, to whom they are sent."[49] This was, as Abraham de Wicquefort noted in his 1681 text, *The Embassador and His Function*, crucial to understanding the law of nations. "The necessity of Embassies makes the Security of Embassadors, by the universal consent of all the Nations of the Earth," he wrote. "And it is in this general Consent that constitutes what is called the Law of Nations."[50]

Diplomats under the law of nations, it was believed, needed immunity from prosecution by the host country's laws because they were engaging for the first time in serious negotiations with territories vastly different from their own, such as the Ottoman Empire. Diplomacy between the Ottomans and the West began as early as the fifteenth century with delegations from Genoa and Venice. Although England did not send its first consul to the Porte until 1583, its understanding of diplomacy, like that of all other Western European countries, was permanently altered by Ottoman culture, by its inassimilable nature and its openness to foreigners. As Daniel Goffman and Virginia Aksan point out, the Ottomans had a very different view of the foreigner—as someone who might be absorbed into the empire and continue to live there in peace.[51] To this end, they devised "capitulations," or the terms that governed the duties and privileges of foreigners living in Ottoman lands.

Though they were imposed on subjects of the sultan, the capitulations effectively served as peace treaties with foreign countries. Goffman argues it was the Ottomans who introduced or at least influenced what is now called the new diplomacy.[52] Others have gone so far to argue that the new diplomacy between Europe and the Ottomans was a joint enterprise where we "find many common methods and techniques of establishing interstate relations, which belong neither to the Islamic nor to the European law of nations."[53] Authorized to make treaties with the Ottomans and not simply to spy on them, as was the norm in many other places, ambassadors to the Porte fostered a new mode of negotiation in which they had to do more and work harder than they had with partners within Christendom with whom they shared religious values and secular legal forms.

Soon the model for the Ottomans became the model for the rest of the world as well. As global agreements became increasingly routine, Jeremy Black argues, the importance of sending negotiators who understood the culture in question and who could speak the language became more pressing.[54] The new resident diplomacy also favored ambassadors who knew more about peace than they did about war. They were expected to have a facility with the language and a familiarity with the culture that would naturally lead to fuller and more detailed descriptions of what a peace potentially agreeable to all parties might look like.

Mather draws his final inspiration for his new vision of the millennium from the new diplomacy's emphasis on learning peace—by way of cultural immersion and education—rather than on learning war. Among other things, this explains why one of Mather's greatest sermons about millennial peace is addressed to a group of soldiers. In *Things to Be Look'd For*, which Mather delivered to the artillery corps, an elite branch of the Massachusetts militia, he argues that preparing for peace is just as important to a soldier's training as preparing for war. Addressing the soldiers of the 1691 artillery corps, Mather acknowledges their role as men of battle who "maintain by stronger Arms against all Foreign Injuries."[55] He does not, however, leave the artillery company with the idea that swords alone will bring peace about. He stresses the soldiers' role as protectors of the peace above all. "Tis to you under God, that we owe the many Comforts of our Lives. We should soon be Rob'd of all that is dear unto us, in the World. If it were not known that there were such as You to set the Price of all."[56] Nor is it only personal comforts that the soldiers protect. The sermon goes on to suggest that the very essence of peace—the "Lives, Liberties, [and] Properties" that make life worth living—are in their care.

To protect these features of peace, soldiers also needed a broad education. Like the new diplomats, Mather suggests that soldiers needed to cultivate relations within the domestic sphere in order to project a different, more global identity abroad. "The soldier," Mather writes, "should wake up and study."[57] War, more specifically, was no longer confined to a series of victories on the ground but was a way of understanding the world and the mixed approaches to peace among communities and nations. So it is not to war, Mather writes, but to the "*Learning of War*, to which I must now for a while Encourage you," for there were many contingent and unpredictable things about war that in a millennial vision informed by the law of nations needed to be studied to bring peace into being.

Nor was peace the mere antithesis of war. The subject was, as the diplomats then conducting negotiations demonstrated, capacious. Thus Mather suggested a broad, interdisciplinary program of study for soldiers that would include military training and the humanities.[58] The soldier "should indeed have some Insight into all the Liberal Arts," he noted. "They that Learn War, had need Learn something else, and they that handle Swords & Spears ought at the same time to be furnished with Qualifications that shall be truly Extraordinary."[59] Adhering to such a mandate, Mather's soldier emerges as the mirror image of the diplomat, learning about other cultures and bringing a well-rounded education to the discipline of peace.

Mather's insistence that soldiers learn the liberal arts in order to advance peace reminds us of how far he has come from the interpretive framework in which one anticipates peace by looking for external signs of it. The millennium in Mather's hands is no longer a product of passive absorption or spiritual speculation. It is made and embodied by humans, physically and mentally. The soldier like the diplomat carries peace around in his mind. In figuring the soldier as a diplomat of millennial peace, Mather incorporates the script of contemporaneous peace treaties. Peace is achieved in the Treaty of Westphalia, for example, as a result of people forming thoughts about peace. "It has at last happened," the treaty reads, "that the one side, and the other . . . have formed Thoughts of an Universal peace; and for this purpose, [sign] . . . a mutual Agreement and Covenant of both Parties, in the Year of our Lord, 1641."[60]

The thoughts of peace central to the Treaty of Westphalia are also central to the legal imaginary from which the law of nations and its vision of a cosmopolis sprang. And it is to thought that Mather turns in his new understanding of the millennium. In Mather's late century sermons on the topic, the millennium becomes a larger, more inclusive place, but also, more importantly, a place susceptible to human interaction and refashioning. Like the concept of peace in contemporaneous treaties, the peace of the millennium remained one part universal and perpetual—universal and perpetual being words that often appeared in treaty preambles—and one part devoted to the often tedious and labored-over details of how such a peace could be achieved. Mather's millennium thus became cosmopolitan through its integration of the legal machinery that had been put into place to bring secular peace into being. It was no longer a matter of looking for signs of the millennium's imminence in texts written long ago, but of actively thinking that world into existence through the legal imagination.

That the law of nations became the inspiration for and bedrock of a newly cosmopolitan millennium also reveals how inextricable the legal and religious imaginations of the Puritans had become by the late seventeenth century. Scholars have long observed that the Puritans, though adhering to a church-state divide in theory, bequeathed to us a system riddled with legal and religious interconnections, which under guidelines that required strict separation between church and state, have taken centuries to tease apart. The relevance of this problem, however, applies exclusively to the intersections between religion and Anglo-American common law. When we consider the connections between the religious or more specifically millennialist imagination of the Puritans and the law of nations, we see a far less problematic association. In this chapter the law of nations and the millennium emerge as a shared site for projecting into the future and suggest compatibility between the legal and religious imaginations that helps us recast the Puritan legacy and even revise our understanding of the separation of church and state. What this chapter makes clear above all else is how the concept of the cosmopolis, which belonged to both spheres—church and state—helped the Puritans bridge what has otherwise seemed to historians and theologians a peculiarly American gap. Looking beyond America to the cosmopolis provides a new perspective on how law and religion spoke to each other in the Puritans' expanding world.

{4}

Evidentiary Cosmopolitanism

A wise man proportions his belief to the evidence.

—DAVID HUME

The late seventeenth century, known for its many contributions to the new scientific method, also saw a number of shifts in the understanding of legal evidence. The most prominent charted a course away from faith-based claims about knowledge to claims based on ocular observation and eyewitness testimony. Less well-known but no less momentous was a complementary shift that occurred in legal evidence from the local to the global or from circumscribed to cosmopolitan witnessing. When John Locke argued that knowledge was the result of human interactions with the external world, the category of what counted as knowledge became geopolitically extensive, opening up to "facts," as they were beginning to be understood, in local and global contexts. This expansion of the sphere for available facts influenced the scope of truth. In an age when human interactions with the external world subtended the far more inclusive world encompassed by the law of nations, local truths were often insufficient. In this world, evidence—the legally ordained version of facts that constituted knowledge in Locke's formulation—could literally come from anywhere. This meant that truth claims from eyewitnesses, who had the potential to provide local and global affirmations of truth, were highly prized.

This preference for truths grounded in the facts of the larger world—what I call evidentiary cosmopolitanism—emerges in the writings of the late seventeenth-century New England Puritans as the centerpiece of their argument against royal oppression. Seeking witnesses to their oppression from a global community that was conspicuously outside England was central to the Puritans' efforts to oust their royal governor, regain control over their government, and further their connection to the law of nations and the cosmopolitan sphere. In the myriad documents that surround these late seventeenth-century events and that detail the colonists' grievances, the Puritans accuse the royal commissioners of lying in ways that tested the limits of belief not only of local eye witnesses but also of people all over the world. The only way to circumvent the global lies of the royal commissioners, the Puritans' discourse on truth-telling suggested, was to invoke the new protocols of evidence that, under a law of nations responsive to the new Lockean regime, could only be accomplished by looking for proof in the cosmopolis as a whole.

The new evidentiary cosmopolitanism that emerged from the Puritans' struggle with their royal governors explains a lot about how a legal standard imported from the colony's foreign policy affected their domestic political and legal lives as well. This overlap—between the local and the global—adds an important wrinkle to our understanding of the work being done by cosmopolitanism in this period. In integrating the mandate to be cosmopolitan into a revised understanding of legal evidence in their courtrooms, the Puritans were actively blurring the lines between the categories of internal and external or foreign and domestic. As colonists the Puritans had long been operating in a gray zone between these categories, implementing new laws to address New World circumstances and yet looking beyond their territorial borders for legal redress when necessary. Having exhausted their appeals in domestic courts, for example, many Puritans were allowed and sometimes even encouraged to seek remedies on the other side of the Atlantic in the courts of the Crown. If committing to the law of nations in their external affairs turned their transatlantic relationship with England into a relationship with the circumatlantic and beyond, it also cosmopolized their domestic sphere and affected the lives of Puritans from all walks of life, whether they were aware of it or not. In this way, evidentiary cosmopolitanism turned Puritans from all walks of life into cosmopolitans.

In folding the cosmopolitan objectives of the law of nations into their domestic evidentiary standards, the Puritans also opened new possibilities for thinking about the emergent categories of race and nationality in domestic terms. Enlarging the evidentiary sphere to include people from all over the world meant the Puritans were in part acknowledging the importance of people of different races and nationalities. When sovereign actions were in dispute, for example, the new evidentiary cosmopolitanism required that sovereigns from around the world weigh in on their veracity, bringing to bear their knowledge of the act in question in local and global contexts. Thus without making a diversity of voices an explicit part of their agenda, the Puritans of the late seventeenth century furthered their cosmopolitanism by demanding that legal evidence, at least in certain contexts, include these voices and by admitting that evidence from people all over the world was stronger than evidence without them.

The immediate impetus for the rise of the new evidentiary cosmopolitanism in New England was the revocation of the Puritans' charter in 1684 and the subsequent installation in 1686 of their first royal governor, Edmund Andros. Accustomed to receiving threats of charter revocation for decades for, among other things, violating one of the rules of their original charter, which required they refrain from making "laws that were contrary and repugnant to England," the Puritans had previously found success through evasion. When Charles II, for example, moved by rumors that the Puritans were violating conditions of the Navigation Acts, sent Edward Randolph in 1676 to warn the Puritans of his displeasure and again in 1684 to revoke their charter, the Puritans denied and dismissed his charges until Randolph was effectively worn down. By taking advantage of the lag before news of events in the colonies reached England, the Puritans managed to ignore Randolph and his colleague, Joseph Dudley, who was installed by the king as governor of the Bay Colony but had been largely ineffective in prosecuting the king's interests. By 1686, the new king, James, Charles's brother, sent Andros to rule over the newly named Dominion of New England, which included the Massachusetts Bay Colony, New Hampshire, Maine, the Narragansett territory and later Rhode Island, Connecticut, New York, and the Jerseys in his name.

Andros lost no time after his arrival in Boston in making himself unpopular with most Puritans. He commandeered space in the Puritan churches for Anglican services, voided land titles that the Puritans had upheld, abrogated laws passed by the Puritan Assembly, and started a war with the Indians that the Puritans believed could have been avoided. It was the first time the Puritans experienced the harsh reality of royal rule up close. In disorganized ways at first, the Puritans protested against Andros's rule, provoking Andros in one instance to imprison Increase and Cotton Mather for defamation and potential insurrection.[1] On April 18, 1689, however, what had previously been fairly small and intermittent protests grew in size until thousands of people swarmed Boston, and the colonists, led by the Mathers with several other self-appointed leaders, stormed the fort where Andros was hiding in the South End, demanding he surrender. Refusing at first, Andros later left the fort to see if he could reach a deal with the protestors peacefully, but he was quickly apprehended. Randolph, who had stayed on as Dominion secretary and assistant to Andros, and Dudley, who had stayed on as a member of Andros's council and judge of the superior court, were also arrested, and the three men spent nearly ten months in Boston's jail before they were sent back to England at the Crown's request.

Characterized as a "revolution" by the colonists and marked by claims of sedition and inequitable treatment by the royals, these events have traditionally been read as a dry run for the much larger revolution some eighty years later. The historian T. H. Breen has argued that the principles articulated in the grievances from this era "were to be repeated throughout the eighteenth century and were to have a profound influence on the politics of the American Revolution."[2] Championing this claim in reference to one of the central documents from the time, "The Declaration of the Gentlemen, Merchants, and Inhabitants of Boston and the Country Adjacent," Kenneth Silverman argues that the events of 1689 "launche[d] a New England revolutionary tradition that would culminate in 1776" in the Declaration of Independence, the earlier Declaration's namesake.[3] Reinforcing Silverman's view, David Levin argues that the language of the "Declaration of the Gentlemen" "resembles both in diction and parallel structure the charges laid to George III in the Declaration of Independence."[4] Even Jack Sosin's three-volume history of English America from the Restoration through 1715, which offers a subtle picture of the late seventeenth century, characterizes the years of the colony's charter revocation and reinstitution of royal rule as a prelude to autonomy and independence followed by a period of provincial disintegration that revolved entirely around the colony's relationship with England.[5]

These claims, dominant to this day in the historiography of late seventeenth-century New England, mark these events and the contemporaneous documents that describe them, including "The Declaration of the Gentlemen" (1689), "A Narrative of the Miseries of New-England, By Reason of an Arbitrary Government Erected There Under Sir Edmund Andros" (1688), Cotton Mather's three "Vindications" of colonial resistance to the governors (1689–1690),

"An Account of the Revolution in New England" (1689), and "The Humble Address of the Publicans of New-England" (1691), as primarily, if not exclusively, transatlantic. In this chapter, by contrast, the cosmopolitan aspects of these documents come to the fore as we follow the course of the Puritans' emphasis on the limitations of the royal commissioners' local and, speaking in evidentiary terms, uncorroborated views. In making their case against Andros, what occupies the Puritans has less to do with their own suffering—taken to be the catalyst for the revolution to come—than with Andros's inability to tell the truth about them or himself due to his lack of experience with and knowledge of the world.

The Cosmopolitanization of Evidence

Driven by a turn away from faith and toward experience as a source for evaluating the truth, the standards for assessing evidence were changing in England and across Western Europe at the time.[6] An increasing reliance on empiricism and sense-impressions in both legal and scientific circles caused a transformation from older, medieval models of truth and certainty, which were thought to inhere in the character of the witness, to a far more relativist approach, where knowledge was to be measured in terms not of absolute certainty but of varying degrees of certainty, otherwise known as probability.[7] Among other things, the crisis of evidence made it possible for the first time to take doubts about truth seriously, to evaluate witnesses for accuracy and reliability, and to implement measures to safeguard against lying. In scientific circles, these measures famously took the form of demonstrable and imitable models, while in legal circles they took the form of evidentiary rules that privileged eyewitness testimony and excluded various forms of hearsay that made people into unreliable witnesses.[8]

The Puritans saw their royal oppressors in just such evidentiary terms. To the Puritans the royal appointees were "violent," "unreasonable," and "unworthy,", but above all they were liars. Responding to accusations that they were engaging in unorthodox trade practices, promoting a lack of religious tolerance, and making laws that were "contrary and repugnant" to the laws of England, the Puritans called the reports of both Edward Randolph and Edmund Andros "one Loud lie (sounding from American to Europe.)"[9] They contained "not a little falsehood," as Increase Mather wrote in his first "Vindication of New-England," and were full of "matters," as he added in his second "New-England Vindicated," that were "fallaciously represented."[10] Responding directly to Edward Randolph's "Account of the Irregular Trade since the Revolution in New-England," which accused the colonists of violating the Navigation Acts, the Massachusetts agents then negotiating for a new charter in England decried the "many false Informations and misrepresentations of that Govermt [*sic*] exhibited by him [Randolph]." These "Informations," they went on to claim, were so "defective that the Jurys could not find for his [majesty]."[11] Lest the claim that the royal governor and his minions were making things up be lost on the growing audience for these rebuttals on both sides of the Atlantic, the subtitle of the widely distributed broadside "The Present State of the New-English Affairs" appeared in font almost as large as the title to announce: "This is published to prevent False Reports."[12]

Many scholars have noted the impact of the new insistence on eyewitness testimony in the early modern period. Sarah Rivett points out that this emphasis on empiricism found its way into the Puritans' spiritual practices, merging religious with scientific methodology. The new "science of the soul," as Rivett calls it, required a version of empirical and verifiable proof of grace on the one hand and sin or evil on the other, resulting, as Rivett explains, in the application of science in an area long thought to be devoid of it.[13] Others have examined the impact this empirical emphasis had on the law as it played out in courtrooms across Europe. Andrea Frisch, for example, traces the rise of the "epistemic witness" in travel literature in early modern France and its implications for the juridical process throughout Europe.[14] Few, if any, however, have noted the extent to which this emerging empiricism intersected with the law of nations and the growing legal focus on the global sphere. Though never explicitly adopted as a tenet within the law of nations, the new focus on eyewitness testimony was nevertheless consonant with the law of nations' wider geopolitical compass and its emphasis on arriving at legal standards that would elicit agreement from people all around the world. The more one observed how things were done in different countries, the more reliable one's testimony about a contested fact might be. To be present at a given event made one's access to the truth more likely, yet to be present at similar events over time and in different places increased that likelihood immeasurably. Thus in generating skepticism from various heads of state around the world about the truth of the governor's complaints against them, the Puritans, as this chapter shows, made some headway against the Crown in evidentiary terms.

The idea was that observing events in foreign countries made a domestic witness more trustworthy at home. This meant foreign witnesses who had observed domestic events in a domestic courtroom also became valuable. As Harold Berman points out, one of the most reliable ways to increase the probability that a fact was true in science and the law was to increase the number of witnesses to it. "If the experience of it [the event in question] can be extended to many persons," Berman writes, "and in principle to all, then the result may be treated as a fact, that is, as a truth having the highest degree of probability."[15] The effect of this increase was well known in the law: the "two-witness rule," as its name suggests, called initially for two eyewitnesses to ensure the veracity of an event, but the credibility offered by witnesses around the world, especially in telling the truth about governance and sovereignty, was an added bonus.

Calling Edmund Andros a liar, among the many other accusations that were leveled against him in the Andros tracts, brought the issues of evidence, eyewitness observation, the desirability of similarly situated witnesses, and sovereignty to the fore. The claim that tied these concepts together was that Andros's observations and the conclusions he drew from them lacked corroboration. Although his observations about the Puritans were not initially aired in a juridical context, both parties—the Puritans and the king—treated them as juridical matters and offered legal responses to them. Andros's unfavorable view of the Puritans only reinforced the king's impulse to keep a closer eye on them and to hem in their autonomy. For the Puritans, Andros's claims raised red flags about his use of evidence, which gave them the legal grounds on which to object to his rule.

The Puritans launched an evidentiary attack against Andros that culminated in the claim that he violated the unofficial principle of evidentiary cosmopolitanism. It began, however, with the much more traditional claim that Andros and his minions had no corroborating evidence for their accusations against the Puritans because they were not eyewitnesses. The Puritans' argument moves from this claim to a second claim that occupies an intermediate status with respect to the new evidentiary standards, namely that Andros could not testify truthfully about New England because he had no basis for comparison, having never been anywhere else in the world. Responding to these charges, Andros claimed that he had no need of corroboration because he spoke with the authority of a sovereign (or in his case an agent of the sovereign) whose truth, as everybody knew, was unimpeachable. But as the Puritans pointed out, the two features that had made the testimony of sovereigns reliable in the past—that they had good reputations and generally spoke in uncontested terms—were now the very things that made them suspect. In leveling this allegation, the Puritans were no doubt influenced by the rise of sovereign impostors around the globe.

The suspicions of an oppressed people were one thing, but the Puritans needed evidence to prove their case. How, the Puritans wondered, could they discredit a sovereign impostor and what would that evidence look like? In a world where, as the law of nations showed, all sovereign entities were seen as interdependent, the most logical answer was to look for evidence all over. After all, to govern under false pretenses was to lie to people who were not only under your control but also scattered in far-flung places whose participation in the larger cosmopolitan sphere depended on the truth of sovereign representations. The genius of this particular innovation was that the required counter-evidence involved the acknowledgment on the part of people around the world that the king and his appointed governor were lying. This kind of evidence would position the Puritans as more authentic Englishmen than the English back home.

To "Know New England"

The Puritans' first claim was that Andros could not know what kind of royal subjects they were because before 1684 he had not been in the colonies for any length of time and therefore had no firsthand knowledge of their behavior in the 1670s and early 1680s—the very time period about which he complained so loudly to the king. The figure of the witness at the center of this claim was of paramount importance to the changing standards for truth-telling in the law, even more than in science where the act of witnessing could theoretically be replicated under the proper laboratory conditions. "The natural realm," Barbara Shapiro writes, "could claim a unique capacity for achieving... certainty because some of its observed facts and many of its experimentally created ones could be replicated before multiple, impartial, skilled, and often instrument-employing witnesses."[16] In the law, by contrast, the "fact" in question was often fleeting or one of a kind—a theft, a murder, an accident—and certainty about it could only be achieved by ensuring the witness's firsthand observation and by barring certain forms of witness testimony (such as hearsay) and material evidence (such as copies) from the court. The further one got from ocular observation, jurists agreed, the weaker the testimony would be. As Locke wrote: "a credible Man vouching his Knowledge of it [a contested fact], is a good proof; But if another equally credible fellow witnesses it from his [the first man's] report, the Testimony is weaker; and a third that attests the Hearsay of an Hearsay, is yet less considerable."[17]

Asserting this point in the Andros tracts, the Puritans deployed a memorable phrase: Andros and his men did not "know New-England."[18] To be sure, similar claims about other newcomers had surfaced among the Puritans during the half-century of their rule in the colonies, but they lacked the evidentiary overtones of this claim. To distance themselves from the renegade Thomas Morton, for example, who had come to New England long before the settlement of the Massachusetts Bay Colony, but who did not share the Puritans' religious views, the Puritans referred to him and his followers as strangers and intruders. They also used these terms to describe the many English Quakers, who were interested in visiting or residing in the colony in the middle of the seventeenth century. By accusing the royal governors of not "know[ing] New England," however, the Puritans stressed the royal appointees' distance not from their religious agenda, as the term "stranger" might suggest, but from the kind of knowledge that might pass for trustworthy in a courtroom.

To highlight this lack of eyewitness knowledge on the part of the royal governor and his appointees, the Puritans responded with eyewitness testimony of their own. History, a series of facts like any others, was newly subject to the skeptic's cautions in this period. To write a history was tantamount to testifying in court: one should ideally have been "an eye or ear witness" to the events in question, as the contemporaneous critic, Seth Ward, wrote.[19] While other types of histories were not entirely discredited, the best kind was the result of firsthand observation. "Although documentary proof was familiar to courts," Shapiro reminds us, "it was not immediately clear whether documents should be treated as evidence for historical 'matters of fact' or whether they were in some sense 'facts' themselves."[20] The Puritans capitalized on this new approach to history, and in their earliest attempts to address royal complaints, they referred to their own histories as authoritative. In a letter to Charles II, for example, who sent a commission in 1664 to investigate charges of fraud, boundary disputes, and violations of the Navigation Acts, the Puritans assume the tone of eyewitness historians. "Wee shall not largely repeate," the letter reads, "how that the first undertakers for this plantation, having by considerable summes purchased the right thereof, granted to the counsel established at Plymouth by King James, your royal grandfather . . . plant this colony with great labour, hazards, costs & difficulties."[21]

Sensitive to the passing of time since those early years and to the passing of critical eyewitnesses along with it, the Puritans responded to the late seventeenth-century misrepresentations by Andros and his men by privileging the voices of the elderly, who had lived through the events in question and whose memories were long. To this end, they submitted a series of individual petitions to the king with testimonials from a variety of people, including John Gibson, "aged about 87," and George Willow, "aged about 86 years." Inserted into otherwise official reports, the testimony of such eyewitnesses, the Puritans hoped, would remind the king how "with much hard labour and great Disbursements, have [the Puritans] . . . subdued a Wilderness, built our Houses, and planted Orchards before the Quo Warranto was issued by which their charter was revoked."[22] These older inhabitants, who were present for the unfolding of the colony's history, proved invaluable additions to the new evidentiary hierarchy in which eyewitness accounts reigned supreme.

In addition to demonstrating their privileged position as eyewitnesses of their own history, the Puritans also invoked their evidentiary privilege with respect to current events. They wrote many reports countering the evidentiary impact of Andros's representations, including several about the "revolution" in which Andros and Randolph were imprisoned. Perhaps the most decisive document in this regard was a tract written by an author known only as A.B., entitled "An Account of the Late Revolutions in New-England." In this piece, the author specifically takes it upon himself to refute and supplement Andros's characterization of the leaders of the "revolution" as unrepresentative and unpopular by retelling the story as a series of events that gained more followers as new evidence became available. "The first work," he wrote of Andros's jailing, "was done by small parties here and there about the Town," but soon the army "got well together," and as soon as the news of the action spread, "all sorts of people were presently inspired with the most unanimous Resolution."[23] Soon, A.B. notes, not only was the "whole town . . . up in arms," but "all the Country round now began to flock in, and by the next day some Thousands of Horse and Foot were come in from the Towns Adjacent" to express a consent that was so unanimous, A.B. notes in a triumphal flourish, that "there was no bloodshed, nor so much as any Plunder committed in all the Action."[24]

Describing the revolution as an ongoing process that grew more inclusive and more popular as time went by gave A.B. an evidentiary authority that the royal commissioners could never have. The facts of the revolution, A.B. implies, were so complex and multifaceted that they defied description by anyone who did not actively participate in them. Even eyewitnesses who were on the sidelines of the protests were at a disadvantage. To tell the truth about the excitement, the growing consensus, and the sequence of inextricably linked events, A.B. suggests, one had to be a member of the swelling crowd, which put a new spin on what it meant to be an eyewitness.

Proximity to the ongoing event becomes in A.B.'s hands an additional source of evidentiary privilege as he ascribes to the participants sensory forms of witness to which others outside the crowd were not privy. Whether or not such testimony would have made sense in the context of an official trial, A.B. reinforces the truth of his account of the "current event" by including evidence not only about what was seen and observed in the moment but also about what was *felt*. In this way, he appeals to the entire range of sense impressions on which the new evidentiary standards relied. "Sir," A.B. began, "I own, that we *Argue simply* about the Affairs of Government, but we *Feel True*. I have sometimes challenged any man to mention so much as *One Thing* done by our Late Superiors for the welfare of the Country; a thousand things we all *Felt* every day for the Ruine of it."[25] By adding evidence about what the colonists felt in addition to what they saw, A.B. elevates the nature of eyewitness testimony to a new level by supplementing the proof provided by eyewitnesses with the feelings that inevitably accompanied it, bringing his readers that much closer to the truth of what happened during Andros's reign.

Promising as it may have seemed to the Puritans, the argument discrediting Andros and others because they had not been eyewitnesses to the colony's successes in the past was scarcely enough to convince the world that they were right and the royal commissioners wrong. For one thing, Andros and his minions countered the colonists' counter-evidence. They contended, for example, that even if they had not been not in the colony from the beginning, they had been there long enough to see the havoc the colonists had wreaked on the royal agenda. Edward Randolph, who actually had been in the colony for short stints since 1676, was meticulous about listing the abuses he had seen the Puritans perpetrate, including coining money without his majesty's permission, trading contrary to the Navigation Acts, failing to enforce acts of Parliament that had not yet been voted on in the Puritans' General Assembly, and punishing his majesty's subjects on the basis of their religion via fines, whippings, banishment, and execution. John Palmer, a Dominion official, was as vociferous as Randolph in his counter-complaints against the colonists. Palmer's pamphlet, "The State of New England Impartially Considered," was largely devoted to a blow-by-blow defense of Andros against many of the accusations. Among other things, Palmer refuted Puritan claims that Andros brought on the French war with the Indians, prevented the Puritans from making their own laws, failed to let them know what new laws Parliament had made, and referred to the people of New England as slaves.

Palmer's most important contribution to the underlying evidentiary debate between Andros and the Puritans, however, was his response to the accusation leveled by the colonists that he and certain others who agreed with Andros's conditions did not "know New England." "I must confess I cannot easily comprehend [how they did not know New England], unless to inhabit fourteen or fifteen Years within the territory will make a Man such," Palmer writes.[26] Palmer also points to the fact that there were several long-standing members of the Bay Colony community, including Simon Bradstreet and Joseph Dudley, who held relatively moderate views about the royal governor. Although the vast majority of colonists sided with A.B. against Andros, Palmer's reminder that there were divisions within seemed to motivate the Puritans to new heights in their evidentiary campaign against Andros.

The next step for the Puritans involved the epistemological claim that knowledge, once the exclusive province of internal belief, was now also, if not primarily, a matter of one's interactions with the external world. To this end, the Puritans called once again on the discourse of eyewitness testimony. Even if the royals could rightly claim that they had seen some of the colonists' offenses with their own eyes, they had, the Puritans argued, not seen enough of the world to make their claims about New England reliable. Significant here were the connections Locke had made among sense impressions, the external world, and the rules of evidence. "Our observations employed . . . about external sensible objects, or about the internal operations of our minds perceived and reflected on by ourselves, is that which supplies our understandings with all the materials of thinking," Locke explained.[27] Central to Locke's understanding about how people came to acquire knowledge was a claim about the world, which had implications for cosmopolitanism. If fully half or more of one's knowledge came from "observations employed about external sensible objects," then attending to the external world in all its expansiveness was imperative.

International maritime commerce has long been recognized as a source for cosmopolitanism, but the important contribution this commerce made to evidentiary cosmopolitanism has been overlooked. The inclusivity that had long been the standard for evaluating truth claims in the context of maritime trade links the law, commerce, and cosmopolitanism. The connection between an individual's knowledge of how things were done "abroad" and that individual's ability to speak truthfully about trade was deeply embedded within the English laws about commerce. Perhaps more than any other area of the law, trade was regulated by practices that were common to the people engaged in the activity, which encompassed people and practices in various parts of the world. The law of trade demanded an acquaintance with practices abroad, for its operation made the link between trade and the value of empirical evidence from around the world clear. This in turn made the link between trade and the law of nations indissoluble.[28] Commerce, as Arthur Nussbaum points out, in particular the mercantilist policies of England, the Netherlands, and France, served as the source for some of the earliest treaties (about protective tariffs and exported goods) between nations and thus set the stage for the growing law of nations.[29] By the time Immanuel Kant was writing in the late eighteenth century, the links between the law of nations, evidence and the shared culture of fine arts and sciences that fueled early modern cosmopolitanism were clear.[30]

The Puritans made use of both trade standards—the older more restricted standard, and the newer more inclusive standard—which encompassed more international facts and practices than ever before. Accounts of these new facts and practices from around the world in the form of travel narratives, diplomatic dispatches, and foreign histories formed a large part of what was beginning to be considered evidence in legal terms.[31] It was in the spirit of this greatly expanded evidentiary sphere that the Puritans claimed that to "know New England" one had to know the world. Yet Andros and his royal advisors, they noted, remained ignorant in this regard. "The most they have done for Trade," the Puritans wrote, "has been upon the Projects of Persons who have never been abroad, nor seen any thing; and who only hatch their Inventions out of the warmth of their Brains, without any other helps."[32] The implication of this statement made by the anonymous author of "The Humble Address of the Publicans," perhaps the most vicious and satirical of all the Puritan pamphlets about Andros, was that Andros could not possibly know New England because he did not know how people in the rest of the world behaved. Of the world and its various trading practices, the Puritans maintained, Andros had no knowledge.

The epistemological knot at the center of this statement is key. The argument was not simply that Andros could not evaluate the Puritans' practices without knowledge of other people; it was the far more radical proposition that Andros could not even "know" the Puritans (and therefore could not submit any evidence about them) without knowledge of the world abroad. Without knowledge from abroad, the commissioners' claims were pure fancy. Pinpointing this deficiency in Andros's evidentiary case, the pamphlet's author goes on to link the governor's ignorance about trade to the colonists' general dissatisfaction with the royal government.[33] "One of our great Unhappinesses," he writes, "is that most of the Persons in our Government understand little or nothing of Trade, *and so they leave it always at uncertainties*, or if they do any thing for its Interest, *it's commonly by chance*, and not from Knowledge or Experience of the thing."[34] This statement extends the epistemological argument even further. The implication here is that to lack knowledge about how trade operates in other parts of the world—to lack knowledge of the cosmopolis—is to rule haphazardly and without expertise. This logic suggests how deeply implicated New Englanders felt in the world and how cosmopolitan their sense of good government was.

"A Frenchman and Four More"

Claims that the royal commissioners had limited "knowledge or experience" of trade practices abroad helped further the Puritans' cosmopolitan evidentiary agenda with respect to the royal commissioners, but their most devastating attack was yet to come: the royal governor, they claimed, was giving false testimony about the colonists because he was an impostor. The accusation of imposture revolved around the most obvious requirement of the evidentiary scheme, old and new: there could be no claim to truth unless the person telling the truth could prove his or her identity. Alain Badiou observes, "no discourse can lay claim to truth if it does not contain an explicit answer to the question: Who speaks?"[35] This requirement—that we know who speaks—is not to be confused with the older evidentiary tendency to associate trustworthiness only with people who had good reputations. Rather it entails the far more existential claim that as a threshold requirement for telling the truth about an event in the world, people must first tell the truth about themselves.

Part of this accusation against Andros was no doubt due to the widespread presence of impostors in the middle to late seventeenth century. Just as the colonists were making their "declarations" and publishing their screeds against the royal governor, numerous accounts of large-scale religious and political impostors were finding their way into print. These pamphlets included histories of Mahomet; a treatise of unknown provenance about the imposture of the two additional leaders of the major world religions, Jesus and Moses; the story of the Jewish messiah, Sabbatai Sevi (which proved particularly popular with the Puritans in New England); and the stories of the Russian Dmitris—I, II, and III—each of whom claimed to be the son of Ivan the Terrible and in rapid succession became the czar of Russia for brief periods.

The early modern period was rampant with stories of deceit, including forgeries, shams, and hoaxes, but the impostor held a unique position within them.[36] Of course imposture was in vogue long before the early modern period. There had been famous impostors since the dawn of time, including various Nero impostors in ancient Rome and various Joan of Arc impostors in medieval Europe. The middle to the late seventeenth century, however, spawned an unprecedented rash of them, and in England, imposture was intimately tied to the threat of a Catholic takeover.[37] Since the reign of Henry VIII, who had famously converted to Protestantism after the Catholic Church had refused to grant him a divorce, there was arguably a suspicion among Protestants about the sovereign's fidelity to the faith. Several sovereigns, in particular Henry's daughter, Queen Elizabeth, managed to work free of this suspicion, but others were less successful. Although not directly a matter of imposture, the gunpowder plot of 1605, in which Catholic dissenters tried to overthrow James I, kept this lingering suspicion alive. And with the ascension of James II, whose policies increasingly favored the Catholics of the realm, suspicion was rekindled. The question of sovereign imposture came to a climax on the tenth of June in 1688, with the birth of James's son, James Francis Edward, known as the Pretender.

The reason James's son was known as the Pretender had to with the mysterious circumstances under which he was born. For one thing, it was widely related that the queen had never looked pregnant. Neither had any "protestant lady," as the author of a popular tract about the Pretender complained, "ever felt her belly."[38] It was also said that no one other than those employed by the king had witnessed the delivery of the child. There were, as the author of yet another popular tract wrote, "no witnesses who saw the child come from the queen's belly."[39] Bizarre even under normal circumstances, these oversights were especially suspect in the case of the birth of a royal heir whose delivery was customarily attended by multiple witnesses. Even more significant were the mysteries about the chamber in which the birth had occurred and in which no search had been conducted "of all the doors etc.," such as was required by law "when a princess or queen Is lying in heat."[40] The absence of such a search led many people to suspect that deceptive practices had been at work throughout the pregnancy, including "stuffing the queen's dress with pillows," and using a "back staircase" to usher in another person's infant at the time of the delivery.[41]

The story of the Pretender was of particular interest to the Puritans in New England, for on it hinged the future of their faith and political survival. At issue was the question of who would succeed King James: his infant son, James Francis Edward, who would, it was widely believed, carry on his father's crypto-Catholic practices and turn England over to the pope, or Mary, James's daughter and a devout Protestant then living in the Low Countries with her husband, William, who was poised to attack James's armies and depose him. Not surprisingly, the Puritans' sympathies were with William and Mary, who assumed the throne in the Glorious Revolution in 1688. That King James fled to the court of Louis XIV in France after being deposed only reinforced the suspicion that James and his son were impostors.

From an evidentiary point of view, imposture was rife with problems relating to sovereignty and the relativity of judgment. As a lie, imposture was in a class by itself for it concerned the facts in question and the status of the truth-tellers. To engage in imposture, in other words, was to lie not as an average liar—about a fact or an event in the observable world—but to lie about everything—the kind of lying as it turns out that was much more difficult to disprove. In his essay on liars, Michel de Montaigne makes the difference between these two sorts of lies and their vulnerabilities clear. "Now liars either invent the whole thing, or they disguise and alter an actual fact. If they disguise and alter, it is hard for them not to get mixed up when they refer to the same story again and again because, the real facts having been the first to lodge in the memory... they will hardly fail to spring into the mind and dislodge the false version, which cannot have as firm or assured a foothold." Liars who "make a complete invention," however, "have much less reason to be afraid of tripping up, inasmuch as there is no contrary impression to clash with their fiction."[42] These liars are more difficult to expose because their lies are of such magnitude that they subsume all the relevant evidence around them, making it unavailable to witnesses to confirm or deny while remaining in absolute, one might even say, sovereign control of it. Sovereigns were particularly prone to making "complete inventions." The divine right of kings encouraged it for centuries. Under the legal presumption of divinity, corroboration of the sovereign's "truth" was deemed unnecessary.

Just as it was no longer possible for the average witness in the early modern period to rely entirely or even partially on faith or reputation to assert the truth of his or her testimony, it was no longer possible for the sovereign to put forward his reputation as incontrovertible proof. Under the new evidentiary regime of the mid-seventeenth century, the sovereign's testimony was as susceptible to testing, revision, and skepticism as anyone else's. Joseph Glanvill wrote in his *Essays on Several Important Subjects in Philosophy and Religion* in 1678, in "things of Fact, the people are as much to be believ'd as the most subtile philosopher and Speculators; sincere Sense is the Judge."[43] The democratization of witnessing to which Glanvill's statement gives voice implies an increased suspicion of the "most subtle philosophers and speculators," not to mention the sovereign whose testimony was, precisely because it was rarely if ever questioned, potentially more prone than that of others to deceit. In the case of the Pretender, the consensus was clear. "We must say with all due reverence, and most humble Submission," the author of the widely circulated pamphlet, "The Pretender an Impostor," wrote, "that our Laws will not allow that the Declaration; or Testimony of his Majesty, or the Queen, should be accepted, and believed in this case as lawful proof, that this pretended Prince was born of the Queen."[44]

The real problem with sovereign testimony, however, as the author of the pretender pamphlet goes on to say, had less to do with the reputation of the witness than with the self-corroborating nature of the evidence. "But there is abundant reasons also from natural Equity and civil Justice," the author explains, "that the Kingdom should not receive and rely upon the King's Affirmation about the Birth of this supposed Prince," for "none on earth, Kings or Subjects, may justly expect, or be suffered to supply the Place of witnesses in their own case." If sovereigns were allowed to testify on their own behalf, the author warns, the consequences could be dire: "If they might lawfully be their own proof for their cause, they might as justly be Judges of their own proofs, which . . . would turn up the Foundations of Civil Government."[45] Here at last is the clarification for which readers would have been waiting. Sovereign testimony was not permissible because it could disrupt the workings of the civil government. To have the sovereign serving as judge and jury would undermine the justice system and propel early modern England, which had worked so diligently to constitute itself as a parliamentary government, backward in time. "Our Law," the author explained, "requires that the Birth of this pretended Prince of Wales should have been proved by a greater number of Witnesses than ever was needful heretofore . . . that it might have been manifest to all that had heard it, that the Eyes of so many Witnesses of such Condition, Knowledg [*sic*] and Judgment, could not have been deceived."[46] To tell the truth in the early modern period, especially the truth about who was in charge, multiple eyes and multiple voices were required.

The pretender crisis would surely have loomed large for the Puritans in their claims about Andros's imposture. After all, the king who commissioned Andros was suspected to have French loyalties, and his escape to France after William and Mary took the throne confirmed that suspicion. It was their particular political situation, however, that spurred the Puritans in Andros's case, for the general fear of encroaching papal authority throughout the Reformed world was brought home to them by way of French incursions into the New World. The French had long allied themselves with certain Indian tribes, among them the Abenaki of Maine, and just months before the "revolution" against Andros, the Puritans heard that some of their own people had been killed in Indian skirmishes ostensibly organized by the French in Canada. To this news, the Puritans believed, Andros responded strangely. He called up the militia of many Bay Colony towns to press an attack on the Indians, leaving the towns themselves defenseless and open to a French assault. Based on these actions and other rumors of suspicious behavior, the Puritans began to believe that Andros might have orchestrated the Indian skirmishes, leading them to speak of the attacks as the "Intented Invasion of a foreign French design."[47] In this political climate, many Puritans came to believe that Andros, following James, had plans to destroy the English.

The stage was set for the Puritans to muster all the evidence they could to prove that Andros harbored French sympathies as well. To this end the focus shifted from the illegality of Andros's commission to his violation of it by ceding rule of the colonies to the French by way of the French-allied Indians. More specifically the Puritans charged Andros with sabotaging their militias to give the French a strategic advantage in what later became known as King William's War. Andros was accused of instigating the war by mounting a rigorous campaign to counter what seemed to the colonists to be no more than a few scattered Indian attacks in the summer of 1688. "A small body of our Eastern Indians had begun a War upon us," A.B. explained, emphasizing that the number of Indians was "small." In response to this "small" group of Indians, Andros overreacted, raising "[a]n army of near a Thousand English (and the flower of our Youth)."[48] A.B. went on to characterize the "Occasion" as well as the "whole management of it" as "mysterious."[49] According to A.B., there were reports from New York, where Andros had served as governor before assuming control in New England, that Andros had incited the Indians to attack the colonists and that the war that ensued had been manufactured to deplete the colonists' resources and to decimate their population. This charge led to widespread claims that Andros "had hired the Indians to kill the English," left their towns "defenceless," and let the armies "starve, freeze and perish there [on the eastern front]."[50]

Suspicious though Andros's conduct was during the Indian skirmishes in the summer of 1688, two subsequent acts more clearly revealed his betrayal of England as an agent of France: the first was to force Cotton Mather to read a proclamation welcoming the birth of the Pretender, and a few months later to keep from the colonists the news that William and Mary had arrived on the shores of England and were ready to take back the throne. "But Sir Edmond Andros took all imaginable care," A.B. wrote, "to keep us ignorant of the News, which yet he himself could not be unacquainted with."[51] For the colonists there was perhaps no more transparent evidence of Andros's imposture, for it suggested that Andros would fight to maintain his rule over the colonies even without the new king's authority, privileging James's Catholic agenda over William's Protestant one.

At this point, Andros's imposture was sufficiently obvious for the colonists to withdraw their allegiance from James openly and offer it to William. A representative Puritan petition from the time suggested "a Design to deliver that Countrey [England] into the hands of the French King" would have been accomplished had it not been for "his highness the prince of Orange whom a Divine Hand has raised up to deliver the Oppressed, shall happily and speedily prevent it."[52] Andros's "Frenchness," which some had gone so far to suggest was hereditary, made the struggle with him not simply a matter of ridding the colony of a hostile governor but of "rescuing the country out of the hands of the French," a phrase and sentiment that was repeated frequently.[53] Once William was safely enthroned, the language of the colonial texts became even more aggressive in calling for evidentiary cosmopolitanism. "As to New England in particular," Mather wrote, "it was a monstrous favour, to overturn that Government under which the Plantation had flourished some scores of years, and not one in Twenty but dreaded an alteration thereof, and in the Room of it to Establish a Government absolutely destructive to the England-Mans Magna Charta, empowering *a Frenchman with four more* to make laws, levy Taxes, and send all of them 2 or 3000 miles out of their Country when they pleased."[54] A question of sovereign misrepresentation, imposture had consequences for the national affiliation of England, and of this, the Puritans believed, the world would have to take notice.

Sovereignty and the Cosmopolitan Witness

Having established the groundwork in descriptions of Andros's military deployments for the claim that Andros was an impostor, the Puritans went on to make the connection between his evidentiary position and truth claims within a cosmopolitan context clear. Impostors, they explained, were impostors for a reason: not satisfied to lie in a normal way, as Montaigne put it, impostors took the risk of impersonating others to convince not one or two individuals but entire communities of their counterfeit status. One way to think about the distinction Montaigne drew between run-of-the-mill liars and liars "who make a complete invention" would be to point simultaneously to the suspicious nature of much sovereign testimony and the sovereign nature of much suspicious testimony, especially from people who made sweeping claims about who they were. Not only were many sovereigns prone to making up claims about who they were; almost all impostors lied in specifically sovereign ways. In the "Christian Commonwealth" section of *Leviathan*, for example, Hobbes points to the strange reciprocity between sovereignty and this deceptive form of self-evidence when he writes about people pretending to be angels or prophets: "For he that pretends to teach men the way of so great felicity, pretends to govern them," he wrote. "[T]hat is to say, to rule and reign over them which is a thing all men naturally desire, and is therefore worthy to be suspected of ambition and imposture."[55] Hobbes was not alone in linking pretense and the desire to rule. The author of a famous treatise on impostors, widely circulated at the time, observed that the impostor doesn't lie like other people but "upon his own Fund of *Confidence,* by personating *Another,* [and so] sets up for *Himself,* and a *Kingdom,*" making the association between sovereignty and imposture clearer still.[56] When Descartes later asserted that self-knowledge was the most reliable form of knowledge, he too implied that imposture—a form of falsified self-knowledge—had the capacity to tyrannize others through deceit.

This tendency of the impostor to set "up for himself, and a kingdom" would have been available to the Puritans, as mentioned, in the highly popular stories of the three Dmitris, Mahomet, and the Jewish Messiah, Sabbatai Sevi. Not born to sovereignty, these impostors set out to become sovereign and to alter the political and legal landscape in which they lived. In "The Devil of Delphos or the Prophets of

Baal," a popular tract on several impostors, the author remarks that among the more extraordinary tricks of impostors no less eminent than Mahomet, Christ, and Moses, was their ability to gain credit and "over-spread some of the most noble and beautiful parts of the world, where it obtains even at this day."[57] Sabbatai Sevi also comes in for his sharpest critique for this kind of sovereign behavior, which manifested itself in enticing Jews from all over the world to leave their homes, goods, and businesses, disturbing the normal course of business and government. "And here I leave you to consider," Sevi's biographer John Evelyn writes, "how strangely this Deceived People was Amused, when these Confident, and vain Reports, and Dreams of Power, and Kingdomes, had wholly transported them from the ordinary course of their Trade, and Interest."[58] For Evelyn and others, the most heinous consequence of Sevi's imposture was to disrupt governments as if he had had the sovereign power to do so, implicating the impostor within a domestic and a cosmopolitan context at the same time.

The argument that Andros was an impostor who invoked the sovereign evidentiary privilege and claimed an identity of sovereign proportions akin to that of Sabbatai Sevi is the centerpiece of "The Humble Address of the Publicans." Outraged by this attack, Andros showed the colonists papers that attested to his royal commission on his arrival. But the Puritans, whose suspicions of him ran deep, remained skeptical. Far from being a duly appointed governor of the Dominion of New England, they argued, Andros was not even an Englishman. He was a Frenchman working for Louis XIV and appointed by James II, whose French and Catholic allegiances were well known. More specifically, the "Address" attacks Andros and the royal commissioners for being "publicans"—a term used for tax collectors in ancient Rome and for pimps in the early modern period—whose behavior was characterized by "tricks" and "hocus pocus." That the royal commissioners were referred to as "publicans" was enough to cast doubt on their virtue, but the "Address" suggests that the term is used in the present instance to distinguish them from the "Re-publicans" or supporters of the colonial government. "[F]or your Republicans are clearly for keeping what they have," the Proem to the "Address" explains, "but your Publicans are for taking it away."[59] This claim went to the heart of Andros's potential to disrupt the social order.

That the publicans were capable of commanding the attention of sovereigns in other parts of the world made them menaces to sovereignty worldwide. Of the publicans, the author writes, "it's almost impossible for Princes and Great Men to shun them, for... they put a gloss upon every thing, and cast Mists before the Prince's Eyes." What confirms the status of such impostors as sovereign threats, however, was their tendency, like that of Sabbatai Sevi, to use their powers to upset governments and to draw people away from the social orders they had previously helped sustain. "Thus the Austrian Publicans," he writes, "have almost ruined Spain, Italy, a great part of Germany, and the Indies and yet not helpt themselves."[60] To demonstrate this capacity, the author ties the publicans in England and the colonies to those in other parts of the world and calls attention to their power to disturb individual kingdoms and relations among them.

As agents of the French king in New England, the publicans of the "Address" are accused of turning the colonial government against England and making the need for witnesses from other places more urgent. "Before our Publicans began their Projects among them," the author wrote, "New England had a Sweet, Easie, and Gentle Government, Made and Constituted by, as well as for the good of the People, a Government that knew no interest inconsistent with that of their Country and Charge."[61] Characterizing the publicans as enemies to England would naturally have helped curry favor among the Puritans with the new Protestant king, but it would also have served as a warning to the heads of state across Europe and beyond that they could no longer assume a stable, trustworthy government in the colonies. "These, and such as these are the Causes," the "Address" goes on to say, "that Foreigners can hardly find an honest man to Correspond with."[62] The most satirical aspect of the "Address" inheres in its dedicatory rhetoric, which offered it "to some King or other," or "To which King you please," alternatives that are, as the author repeatedly points out, ambiguous enough to refer to William and Mary, James II, or Louis XIV, depending on which of them appeared to be dominant at the time.[63]

What was needed to counter the publicans, who were making New Englanders into pariahs of cosmopolitan proportions, were cosmopolitan witnesses. This would solve the problem peculiar to sovereign testimony in two complementary ways: one, in providing more than one witness to fulfill the preference for multiple witnesses in the evidentiary rules, and two, in providing equally powerful witnesses to combat the testimony of a sovereign who was leading the people politically and legally astray. Sovereign witnesses were also called for in the case of England's Pretender when the issue of sovereign testimony about the infant's birth was under suspicion. In the first case, a representative pamphlet writer suggested, the witnesses to the infant's birth should have been representative of the country as a whole so that "amongst such a number some of them [the witnesses] might have been known in one part of the Kingdom, and others in another part." In such an urgent sovereign matter, however, it was imperative that the witnesses come from outside the country's borders. In the matter of "a counterfeit prince," the author explains, "the Ministers of Foreign Princes...ought to have been some of the witnesses."[64] This demonstrated the preference in the law for truths about sovereigns issuing from other sovereigns.

The Puritans' most explicit appeal for cosmopolitan witnesses comes in their turning the narrative of the royal governor from a domestic matter, in which an English colony was resisting direct royal rule, into a matter of domestically inflected global importance, in which England was under siege by France. The charge that Andros was an impostor posing as an agent of the English king but in reality working for the French king put Andros at the center of a global dispute over North America and paved the way for a story that was tailor-made for a cosmopolitan audience. It is no wonder that A.B. begins his account with a direct invocation of the global implications of New England's predicament. "Among the many matters of Discourse and Wonder at this day abroad in the World," A.B. writes, "the state of New-England cannot but be One."[65] In his "Vindication," Increase Mather further capitalizes on a rhetoric that calls attention to the circumstances in New England as a source of interest for the entire world. "The twelfth Article of New England," he writes, "is the Key of the New World America, if the French King had got it into his Possession, he might soon have made himself Master of America."[66] According to Mather, the Puritans deserved worldwide recognition because they were the only ones to intervene in a matter of cosmopolitan importance. "This [the conquest of America by the French] in all Probability would have been done, this Summer," Mather wrote, "if the New Englanders in and about Boston, penetrating into the Designes carrying on, had not risen as one Man and seized Sir E.A. [Edmund Andros] who is as of a French Extract, so in the French Interests, being sent to New England by the Late King James)."[67] That France was at war with England was already a matter of global importance from a military point of view. That France was acting under English cover to take over the Bay Colony was a matter of cosmopolitan importance from a foreign and domestic point of view, and this, as Mather and other Puritans knew, would make sovereigns the world over want to weigh in as witnesses to their travails.

The cosmopolitanizing of evidence that played out in the Andros tracts reinforced the Puritans' place in a cosmopolitan sphere and revealed their growing knowledge and application of the new evidentiary standards that brought the world into the modern age. Having characterized the Andros incident as an emblem of the new evidentiary cosmopolitanism among the Puritans in the late seventeenth century, however, it is necessary to square this characterization with another, seemingly more regressive use of evidence among the Puritans at roughly the same time, namely the Salem witchcraft trials. In the summer of 1692 in Salem, a campaign against a group of so-called witches culminated in a series of trials that ended with the execution of twenty people on the basis of nothing more than "things unseen." Known officially as spectral evidence, the "things unseen" that condemned these individuals to death and that served as the basis for scores of additional accusations rested on testimony by the afflicted about apparitions and spirits only they could see.

Traditionally viewed as a reversion to mystical, medieval thought, the spectral evidence invoked at Salem has recently been shown to be empirical in its own right. When seen as an effort to uncover the material grounds for an invisible world, the search for spectral evidence, Sarah Rivett writes, should be considered "an intensification of rather than a diversion from the more general epistemological quest for invisible evidence within the natural world."[68] While the belief in a spectral realm may have been a throwback to an earlier time, Rivett implies, the evidentiary methodology used to uncover it, although misapplied, was entirely modern, another effort like those of John Locke and Isaac Newton to uncover the mysteries of the unseen.

Putting the witchcraft trials in the context of the evidentiary cosmopolitanism of the Andros affair offers yet another way to think about the uses of spectral evidence in keeping with Rivett's revisionism. This comparison, however, focuses not on the trials' methodology but on the uses to which the spectral evidence at Salem was put. Previously seen in other witchcraft trials in the American colonies,

England, and Europe, as a way to uncover an invisible world inhabited by God and the devil, the search for the spectral in Salem aimed to uncover the visible but hidden. The difference between the invisible—a realm inaccessible to humans—and the hidden—a realm akin to imposture—is significant and depends on the legal difference made by confessions. As David Hall notes, the existence of a very large number of confessions—more than fifty out of a possible two hundred—set Salem apart from other venues in New England and elsewhere where witches were tried.[69] Of course, confessing to the crime of witchcraft did not make one any less a witch; it merely confirmed the judges' suspicions about the unseen world and invited their mercy. Unsurprisingly, then, the defendants who did not confess were seen as witches who, in contrast to their confessing counterparts, added insult to injury by lying about their exploits in the unseen world. With this assumption in mind, the pressing question for the judges was not whether these witches had consorted with the devil but how to uncover the lies and imposture behind their denials of the same. This legal supposition helps us make sense, among other things, of the repeated reminders issued to the accused by the lawyers and magistrates during interrogations to "tell the truth" when it was already clear that the law demanded nothing less. In the face of so many confessors and against a background of the imposture perpetrated by Andros and his men just a few years earlier, the spectral evidence of the Salem witchcraft trials begins to look like another form of evidentiary cosmopolitanism.

Owen Stanwood, whose theory about the witchcraft trials dovetails with my own, argues that the trials were mandated by the exigencies of domestic politics. Links to paranoia about France, he explains, led the colony to execute the witches so "the leaders of Massachusetts" could "show their subjects that they could act boldly against the colony's enemies at home, even if they could not abroad."[70] Putting the witches and Andros, as well as the uses of spectral and cosmopolitan evidence, on a legal and political continuum, however, allows us to draw out the implications of Stanwood's theory about domestic politics beyond the border of the colonies. If the Puritans couldn't succeed militarily against their enemies abroad, they could certainly send a message to their enemies through their legal system—a system they had come to see, as the evidence mustered against Andros shows, as a vehicle for worldwide communication. By means of the law of nations, the Puritans had come to view the law as a cosmopolitan tool that called the world to witness. In many ways the revolution against Andros in 1689 had a repeat performance in 1692 when the Puritans showed the world once again that they would not tolerate impostors and frauds from France or any other place in the visible or invisible world.

{5}

Cosmopolitan Communication and the Discourse of Pietism

Aware that there are no neutral procedures for adjudicating the differences among the stories told by various groups, the attention of cosmopolitan communicators turns to the possibility of coordinating among them.

—W. BARNETT PEARCE

As they went about laying the foundation for a legal cosmopolis in the seventeenth century, the law of nations theorists at the center of this study did so with a keen awareness of the differences between religious and legal communication in different cultural contexts and the need, as Pearce suggests in the epigraph, to coordinate rather than adjudicate among them. As they worked to overcome territorial boundaries in constructing a law that dealt with war and peace, they did not neglect the problems peculiar to communication across diverse cultures and regions. Gentili was the first law of nations theorist to reflect on matters of intercultural communication, but only Hugo Grotius and Samuel Pufendorf, the latter of whom seems to have influenced the Puritans in this regard alone (and so has not figured in the book until now), discussed these issues at length. Grotius devoted an entire book to the subject of language and communication in his *The Rights of War and Peace*, and Pufendorf, largely in response to Grotius, added a shorter but still significant section about language to his *Of the Law of Nature and Nations.*

These reflections on language in the midst of treatises otherwise devoted to legal and political matters suggest that it was one thing to imagine a model that would foster a cosmopolitan sense of belonging in people all over the world and another to think about how to communicate that model in meaningful ways across vast distances to different peoples. The most obvious outcome of these reflections on language by some of the law of nations theorists was the development of a lexicon and grammar common to legal treaties—a kind of treaty literacy. While the purpose and language of treaties underlie much of the Puritans' cosmopolitan thought, as previous chapters demonstrate, in this chapter the link between language theory, treaties, and the law of nations is brought to bear most explicitly in the context of Cotton Mather's version of late seventeenth-century Pietism which asked, along with the law of nations treatises on language, how to construct a cosmopolitan language practice that would serve a cosmopolis made up of far-flung and diverse populations in equal ways.

That we find this cosmopolitan language in the works of Cotton Mather, in particular, confirms what we know about Mather's work and stature over the course of his lifetime. Although he started out his career in the guise of Increase Mather's dutiful son, he soon grew to be one of the most prolific, broad-minded, and independent thinkers of the seventeenth century. More specifically, Mather's interest in the language of cosmopolitanism dovetails with his interest in softening the requirements for church membership, a movement that began in the middle of the seventeenth century (when Mather was born), but gained real momentum in the 1690s in Mather's full-throated endorsement of the *Heads of Agreement*, a church document that David Hall describes as a kind of "treaty" drawn up in 1691 "between English Congregationalists and Presbyterians" to promote denominational harmony.[1] Mather's experiments with a law of nations and treaty-inspired language in the context of an ecumenical pietism also corresponds to his most theological work, the *Biblia Americana*, a multivolume commentary on the Bible, which he began in 1693, advertised for the first time in 1706, and finished by necessity in 1728, the year of his death. As Jan Stieverman points out, the *Biblia Americana* was a thoroughly ecumenical work "preoccupied with the reasonableness of Christianity" and aimed at engaging the widest possible audience. In these two goals, it shared a cosmopolitan agenda.[2]

Pietism and Language

While one of the biggest impediments to a cosmopolitan language was that people in different places spoke different languages, Babel was only the beginning of the problem. In addition to the discovery of many previously unknown foreign languages in the sixteenth and seventeenth centuries, there were a variety of new theories about language itself. Older theories, which posited that words were of divine origin and that language was as much a part of nature as plants or animals, were being superseded by theories that language was, as John Locke argued in Book III of his *Essay on Human Understanding*, a convention that did not make meaning but enabled people to share meaning they had already acquired through their sense impressions. As a convention, language proved indispensable in this regard, but the shock of having to acknowledge language's imperfections (as a human convention rather than as a God-given gift) often overshadowed people's appreciation of its usefulness. In light of these new theories, language seemed capable only of approximating what people were thinking. As Hannah Dawson puts it, many in the early modern world were coming to realize that words bore "a fragile relation to the concepts and things to which they were supposed to be fixed" and thus had an "extraordinary power to disrupt truth and society."[3]

This semantic instability led to a number of mainstream solutions; the two most prominent were translation and universal language theories. Institutes for translation cropped up in many European capitals, and scholars set to work connecting people by translating works of fiction and nonfiction never translated before. The growing number of people who knew multiple languages and had honed their translating skills played a large role in the extensive communication networks among religious dissenters in the second half of the seventeenth century. Universal language schemes were also popular in England and France throughout the seventeenth century. Replete with diagrams of new alphabets and characters, treatise after treatise suggested ways to avoid the idiosyncrasies of written languages that were ostensibly keeping people from communicating with each other. Many universal language scholars turned to Egyptian hieroglyphs and Chinese ideograms in the hope that these pictograms would overcome the absence of an intrinsic connection between letters and meaning in the Roman alphabet, among others.

Marvels of Baconian learning, neither universal language nor translation schemes spoke to the real problems of cosmopolitan communication. These problems lay not in the Babel of languages that still mark our communication pathways, but in the ways we communicate with each other.[4] Translation and universal language schemes target only the most superficial aspects of linguistic exchange—the recognition of graphical markers. As Kwame Anthony Appiah suggests, even when shared, these markers prove limited since giving people the same vocabulary does not ensure they will say similar things or understand them in similar ways.[5] Additionally, although efforts made toward a universal language or lingua franca had many positive consequences in the seventeenth century and beyond, most were undermined by the same problems that undermined universal Christianity; universal languages represented artifacts of cultural imposition as opposed to organic ways of talking and thinking in cross-cultural terms. Cosmopolitan communication then as now required a language that allowed for the noncoercive and dialogical kinds of communication necessary to render meaning genuinely intercultural. It required modes of what communication specialists now call presentational writing, a form of one-way communication that does not allow for on-the-spot questions or clarifications. To overcome these limitations, presentational communication must be proficient and easy to understand from the start, and deployed only in interpretive communities where shared cultural assumptions make standard readings of texts possible.

With these goals in mind, Grotius and Pufendorf offered solutions that were located not in translation, universal languages, or the lexical or grammatical efforts of the language philosophers in England or elsewhere, but in theories that would build a contractual consensus of meaning around the world. For Grotius and Pufendorf, the relevant linguistic question was how to develop and promote presentational expression and interpretative practices that conveyed a vulnerability and openness to dialogue devoid of cultural imposition. These features of communication, it was thought, would surmount the peculiarities of cultural reception and the barriers of semantic misconstruction to facilitate cosmopolitan communication. In furthering such writing and interpretation, Grotius and Pufendorf offered ideas about how to create networks of communication that would render words in any language easily recognizable and allow people to communicate without loss of meaning, no matter how distant they were from each other.

These objectives figured prominently in the Puritans' discourse on Pietism. Not to be confused with earlier attempts in New England to renew faith and piety among the Puritans, including the mid seventeenth-century movement inspired by the Halfway Covenant, Pietism was a specifically late seventeenth-century phenomenon, which began in Germany with the work of Philipp Jakob Spener (1635–1705) and August Hermann Francke (1663–1727). Pietism spread to the American colonies and settlements in the late seventeenth century and across most of Europe by the early eighteenth century. Several scholars have discussed the link between German Pietism and the Puritans, contributing to our understanding of the transatlantic nature of the Puritans' late seventeenth-century lives.[6] A particular focus on the links between Pietism and language can be found in Patrick Erben's work on the Pietism that also took hold among the German immigrants in Pennsylvania, who interacted with the Quakers and the American Indian tribes. For Erben, the language of Moravian Christianity as preached by the German missionaries to the Native American tribes in Pennsylvania held a special capacity for bridging spiritual worlds. As Erben demonstrates, however, the linguistic debates engendered by Pietism in the Pennsylvania communities were focused not on the contractual expectations spurred by the law of nations theorists but rather on comparing the virtues of oral versus written expression and assessing which translations were best suited to convey God's truth.[7] In this regard, these debates were more reminiscent of the earlier pietistic controversies over language in New England than those under scrutiny here.

These earlier pietistic efforts, which had their own approaches to language reformation, included the efforts of John Eliot, who worked for decades starting in the 1640s to translate the Christian Bible into the native Wampanoag of the Algonkian Indians in New England.[8] For Eliot and others in the Spanish and French colonial traditions who were also bent on learning and translating from the native languages, the point of translation was to teach the Indians about Christianity and to make the native language, which they considered a fallen and primitive language, worthy of disseminating biblical truths.[9] Many of these efforts resulted in altering translation from the act of turning one Latinate word into another—common in European translations—to the act of turning native hieroglyphs or nonalphabetic symbols into Latinate words for the first time. As Kristina Bross, Hilary Wyss, Matt Cohen, Andrew Newman, Birgit Brander Rasmussen, and Sarah Rivett, among others, have shown, these transformations of aboriginal sign systems into the printed word had a sizeable and reciprocal impact on both language systems, the European and the native, frequently causing an epistemological shift that had its own effect on the late century system of pietistic communication as it developed in New England.

The work done by these earlier Pietists with native languages and grammars, however, did not share the particular focus of late century Pietism on encompassing, as per the law of nations, a cosmopolitan world. For the later Pietists, the point of communication was not to capture one person's phrase or concept in the language of another, but rather to craft a language, albeit for limited use, that would come to represent and bind together all its adherents, giving them another place to congregate, if not actually, then conceptually. The idea was to build a language that would transcend all cultural barriers and constitute a true cosmopolis. As the late seventeenth-century English Pietist Richard Baxter put it, "one must not live as if his neighbourhood were all the Land, or his Country, or his Party were all the Church, or all the World."[10] The ultimate assumption behind Baxter's statement was a cosmopolitan fellowship of Pietists, which became known as the Protestant International. According to Hartmut Lehmann, the Pietists "lived and operated with the consciousness that they were part of a trans-local, trans-regional, indeed a universal movement, and that they were co-laborers in the solutions of problems and in the mastery of projects that affected the fate of all humanity."[11]

Devoted to spreading the word of God across the Christian world and linking all sects of Protestantism to each other, late-century Puritan Pietism saw its task not only as the revival of a flagging religiosity at home (through an emphasis on Christian practice over doctrine), but also as the breaking down of sectarian, regional, and national barriers among the Protestant faithful across the globe. As such, Pietism provided a natural site for the kind of linguistic innovations that occupied the language philosophers and law of nations theorists in the seventeenth century. Based on the Pietists' efforts to reach people worldwide, many scholars have identified the Pietists' networks the Puritans joined in the late seventeenth and early eighteenth centuries as conspicuously cosmopolitan, bringing the otherwise isolated Puritans into contact with people in remote corners of the world. Mark Peterson, for example, has made us aware of the enormous attraction Pietism held as a conduit for international communication, intellectual, financial, and otherwise. For Peterson Pietism served the Puritans in "developing [a] vision of the ideal society that Boston could come to represent, a vision that was shaped by the transatlantic conversation with continental Pietism."[12]

The designation of Pietism as a cosmopolitan discourse in this chapter, however, stems from a different understanding of Pietism and its relationship to cosmopolitanism. The important point about Pietism here is not that it was globally disseminated, but rather that a certain aspect of its content, which revolved around the gospel of good works, enabled a mode of easily accessible presentation and cohesive and widespread interpretation that cosmopolitanism communication required. Though few, if any, have stopped to think about the formal, communicative features of Pietism's content, the radical turn in Pietism toward a doctrine of works will be familiar to those with a passing knowledge of Puritan theology. From the moment they established their communities in New England, the Puritans were caught up in a battle over the proper way to understand God's providence: on the one hand, there was the invisible acknowledgment of God's grace, which was according to Puritan doctrine known only to God; on the other, there was the visible manifestation of good works, which was anathema in theory but necessary in practice for Puritan society to thrive. Accusing the ministers of preaching a doctrine of good works in violation of Puritan belief, Anne Hutchinson first brought the issue to the fore six years after the Massachusetts Bay Colony was established. Although it was never raised as vociferously again, the works versus grace controversy continued to simmer over the subsequent five or six decades. By the end of the seventeenth century with the rise of Pietism, however, the rancor over the works-grace divide was on the wane, as demonstrated in part by the central goal of Pietism, which was, as it was practiced by the Germans who first gave it voice, to perform good deeds by building schools, orphanages, and other demonstrably visible institutions. In this way good works came to be accepted alongside grace as a Puritan aspiration.

The pietistic focus on spreading good works brought with it a new understanding of presentation and interpretation, which scholars, in their focus on the cosmopolitanism engendered by the international Pietists' networks, have overlooked. In addition to their early to mid-seventeenth-century pietistic work discussed earlier, the Puritans made other contributions to the development of language systems and language philosophies over the years, including their preference for literal over allegorical interpretations and a "plain style" of writing and preaching. Nothing has been said, however, of their specific contributions to a cosmopolitan language system that went beyond these concerns. In what follows we will see how the pietistic writings of Cotton Mather, including *Bonifacius* (1710), *Nuncia bona* (1715), and *Notitia Indiarum* (1721), and some of his relevant correspondence take up the challenge of cosmopolitan communication by engaging many of the presentational and interpretive methods Grotius and Pufendorf advanced.[13] That Mather was, like Grotius and Pufendorf, concerned with preserving cultural differences by working to minimize language while simultaneously enlarging the sphere of communication can be seen in part in his hope that piety would unite people of different sentiments and places. "It will be an Addition unto the pleasure, to see the Harmony which True, Right, Genuine PIETY will produce," he wrote, "in Persons that are in many Sentiments as well as Regions, distant from one another."[14]

The Language of the Law of Nations

To recognize Mather's debt to the cosmopolitan theory of language embedded in the law of nations, we need to understand more about what Grotius and Pufendorf actually said about language and its cosmopolitan reach. Like many language theorists of their day, both men hoped to bridge the communication gap among people in different places. Unlike other theorists, however, they proposed two distinct methods: the first was to simplify or minimize language for the purposes of presentation, and the second was to foster and disseminate the "right" interpretation of language to which everyone regulated by the law of nations would theoretically agree. To these ends, instead of looking to translation or to the universal language schemes that were popular in their day, Grotius and Pufendorf looked to the tools at their immediate disposal, namely the treaties that joined two or more otherwise sovereign countries in a bond that brought them into dialogue with the world.

The workhorses of the law of nations, treaties were contracts used to create consensus between or among different language communities by minimizing the number of words needed for any given formulation and by promoting shared interpretations among the signatories. This meant that treaties had to speak in ways that accounted for the differences intrinsic to the diverse cultural and interpretive regimens they addressed; it further meant that the diplomats who designed and implemented them had to acknowledge cultural differences while also building bridges across them. Thus Alberico Gentili, who was central to the development of the new diplomacy, spoke of the diplomat in his *Tres libri legationibus* as someone who understood the need to appreciate the differences between people while also finding grounds for consensus.[15]

The most important feature of treaties with respect to bridging distances between culturally or geographically remote countries, the contractual bond depended on a linguistic formula for achieving peace. In this contract, two or more parties agreed to abide by a number of relatively set phrases—"reciprocal Amity," "general Amnesty," and "disputes shall be terminated," to name a few—that in themselves indicated little but were understood to initiate a relationship where none had existed before.

In turning his attention to these linguistic formulas, Grotius acknowledged the need for law to use language in ways that departed from traditional rhetorical modes. In the past, the law, like almost all other forms of discourse, tended to use language persuasively. Even treaties, which were hardly among the most persuasive forms of rhetoric, relied during the period of the religious wars on subjective, moral, and theological determinations that required the use of persuasion. In the service of persuasion, the language used by one party was more or less independent of the language used by another. Each entity under the old model of rhetoric spoke in terms of its own understanding, typically making treaties into one-sided declarations of new terms of territorial ownership, the surrender of captives, the payment of taxes, and the like.

In addition to minimizing the number of words in which peace was to be signified, treaties implemented under the law of nations exhibited a tendency toward interpretive agreement rather than rhetorical persuasion, which signified a radical departure in understanding the ends to which communication could be put. No longer confined to persuasion, treaty writers and the law of nations theorists who made the promulgation of the modern treaty possible, emphasized the "right" interpretation—right not in the moral sense, but in terms of a consensus that was conducive to being understood and agreed upon, in most cases because it had already been divested of extraneous verbiage.

Under the newer model of treaty rhetoric, the presence of agreement solemnized by the treaty became the treaty's primary goal; more than a contract about the exchange of land, money, or captives, what the modern, law of nations inspired treaty represented was an agreement about the conditions of interpretation. This agreement followed the basic principle of the law of nations itself, which as Grotius wrote was "agreed on by common Consent, [and] which respect the Advantage not of one Body in particular, but of all in general."[16] The treaty, in other words, was an agreement to agree which led, to use Grotius's terminology, to the "right interpretation." "The Person to whom the Promise is given," Grotius wrote, "has a Power to force him who gave it, to do what the right Interpretation of the words of his Promise does require."[17] The logic here appears circuitous at first glance. We tend now to see a difference between agreeing voluntarily and being forced to agree to a certain interpretation, whereas Grotius, at least in this instance, did not. Yet for Grotius what was at stake in agreeing to the terms of a treaty was a promise to communicate relationally and dialogically. This is what modern contract theorists call "a meeting of the minds," and in its emphasis on forging a consensus about justice through an agreed upon interpretation of terms, it pointed to a departure from the medieval and Renaissance tendency to use treaties to impose a version of justice that favored one side over the other.

The language used to facilitate the "right interpretation" would have to be simple if it were to conform to the stripped-down principles of war and peace Grotius advanced.[18] Thus, according to the law of nations theorists, a minimal number of words and an avoidance of metaphor were crucial for the language of the law. It had certainly occurred to others that to facilitate communication, one should abbreviate where possible. Many seventeenth-century language theorists had worked to boil languages down to their core components by producing "short tables" and etymological keys that could aid in interlinguistic communication.[19] But these were more like mnemonic devices than linguistic reformations. Alberico Gentili set the stage for thinking about a language that would cater to the law of nations by promoting linguistic simplicity above all. The contract, Gentili wrote, "is in harmony with the simplicity of international law, to which agreements on truces, treaties, and peace belong. . . . and that nought enters into it which has not been expressly mentioned."[20] For Gentili, simplicity meant attending only to the explicit terms of the contract, but for Grotius and Pufendorf, who took Gentili's suggestion further, simplicity also meant that the terms themselves should be spare.

Using spare and simple words, treaty writers inevitably wrote in ways that were conducive to the right interpretation by avoiding linguistic excess. Yet Grotius had additional guidelines in mind as well. Aware of theories about semantic instability, Grotius also addressed the problem of interpretive community head on. It was not enough to write sparingly, he observed; one had to set words down as they were commonly set down and understood by most people in their vulgar use. "[B]ecause the inward Acts and Motions of the Mind are not in themselves discernible," Grotius wrote, "there would be no Obligation at all BY promises, if every Man were left to his Liberty [in interpretation]." Thus, the "right" interpretation would be the one dictated by "Right reason," a term that points in this linguistic context to the way words are commonly used. Interpretation should proceed "without any Trick or Collusion," Grotius wrote, "just as the words are now used and understood." Taking a page from the common law tradition, Grotius added, "Use is the Judge, the Law, and Rule of Speech."[21] If words were understood in their most commonly used sense, he explained, their inherent ambiguity and semantic instability would be reduced.

Common usage had long been a standard mode of interpretation among language philosophers and was especially familiar to the Puritans whose celebrated "plain style" already conformed to many of Grotius's requirements. We note that the Puritans' plain style, so-called, was not characterized in all or even most cases by a literal plainness of language—for many Puritan sermons display lengthy and complex explanations of Scripture—but rather by an implicit understanding that whatever language was being used was there to serve the common meaning and common usage of scriptural verse. Meredith Neuman refers to this aspect of plain style as "the self-authenticating revelation of the Word."[22] Yet Grotius did not leave the problem of interpretation there. His chapter on language includes a series of examples, which address the potential for specifically legal terms to be misunderstood. "So the word Arms sometimes signifies Instruments of War," he wrote in one example, while it "sometimes [means] armed Soldiers, and is to be interpreted either in this or that sense, as the Matter in hand requires."[23] To agree on the meaning of a given word according to "the matter in hand" created an interpretive community that was for Grotius the ultimate goal of treaty relations.

With this and similar examples, Grotius's method takes on a specifically legal focus and contributes to a body of rules about the way relations among political entities might be construed in terms above and beyond the specific cultural readings each state might be inclined to give them. In cases with more at stake than the meaning of a term such as "arms," Grotius favored the interpretation that was most common, where common indicated the community not of a single state but of the cosmopolis. The spatial reach of the community was an important linguistic variable for Grotius. "[W]e must understand the Words in their full extent," Grotius wrote, and "in the largest sense," where the goal is to apply them "universally."[24] With this goal in mind, Grotius folded into his theory of presentation and interpretation the original principles by which the law of nations operated. "Favourable" interpretations," he explained, "which carry in them an Equality," and thus augured well for humankind generally, took precedence over interpretations that were "odious, such as those that lay the Charge and Burden on one Party only."[25] The way to understand language that bore on the commonality of more than one country, therefore, was to assess its implications for the world as a whole and choose that understanding above all others.

Building on Grotius's roadmap for cosmopolitan communication, Pufendorf, whose *Law of Nature and of Nations* was first published in 1672, put even more emphasis on the relational or contractual nature of communication. Like Grotius, Pufendorf agreed that language was mere convention. "[T]he power of signifying determinately, thus, or thus" he wrote, "doth not belong to Words by nature, but ariseth purely from the Pleasure and the Imposition of Men."[26] Where others saw semantic chaos in this, however, Pufendorf saw an open field, which gave people the opportunity to agree on a given word's meaning. "All signs except those which we call natural, denote some determinate thing by virtue of Human Imposition, so this imposition is attended with a certain agreement, consent, or compact (pactum), to cite [tacit] or express," he wrote.[27] Pufendorf's explicit invocation of a compact here reinforces the legal sense in which he understood language, for it was by means of a compact that the law created the relation necessary for language to be understood. It was irrelevant whether language was found to be innate—a topic of great interest to the language philosophers and grammarians of his day—for what mattered to Pufendorf was that without an agreement about the meaning of words "this Faculty [of language] would not have obtain'd its proper End and Use."[28] For Pufendorf, as for Grotius, the law of nations depended for its efficacy on the communicative contract people made to agree on the meaning of certain words and phrases.

Many aspects of Grotius's and Pufendorf's understanding of the relational nature of treaties and of individual words within treaties found their way into the Puritans' cosmopolitan approach to pietistic discourse, but Pufendorf's particular awareness of varying spheres of communication had the greatest impact on the Puritans' Pietism. For Pufendorf there were two kinds of linguistic contracts: "general compacts" that brought people together in large groups that potentially included humankind, and "special compacts" that brought people together in far smaller groups united, for example, by a common profession and common terminology. "[I]f those Words or Marks rightly discover my Mind to those, with whom I have thus enter'd into a particular Covenant about their Use," Pufendorf explains, that would create a "Special Compact."[29] For an example of such a compact Pufendorf invokes the "Mechanicks," a guild whose members were accustomed to using "Terms of Art" few others would understand. Such terms of art, Pufendorf notes, "have been invested with a peculiar Signification, different from what they bear in Common Use, or which are utterly unknown to the Ordinary methods of Speech."[30] General compacts, however, involving much larger numbers of people, required a wider sphere and different rules of expression. Outside the various special compacts among known members, the "general Compact" obligated all people to "express our Minds by the clearest and plainest Signs, when if we do otherwise, we may bring some hurt or prejudice on Innocent persons."[31] This obligation—to speak in ways accessible to everyone—became a type of legal obligation determined by the universal mandate to keep the peace in the public sphere whenever possible. So important was the general compact that if there were a conflict between special and general compacts, the general compact would prevail. "[W]ords of publick Use," Pufendorf clarified, "derive all their force from Public Imposition, which Private Persons [such as Mechanicks] ought not, to its prejudice, to contradict."[32]

Pufendorf's recognition of smaller and larger spheres of communication has its pietistic counterpart in Cotton Mather's *Bonifacius*, where Mather addresses the challenge of cosmopolitan communication through the image of ever-widening discursive spheres. Mather's correspondence, *Nuncia bona*, and *India Christiana*, demonstrate the lexical minimalism that both Grotius and Pufendorf endorsed. In the next section, we look at the connection between Pietism and discourse generally and at Mather's efforts to develop a language system for conveying the pietistic message around the world. In the final section, we explore Mather's more complex notion of a cosmopolitan dialogue in depth.

Works and Words

In some ways Pietism—a movement that stretched from the end of the seventeenth century into the first third of the eighteenth century—was a natural site for the contemplation of language. On the wane for decades and newly threatened with extinction by the rapid spread of Catholicism to the New World, Protestants in Europe, England, and New England began to experiment with a looser construction of faith to enlarge the sphere for possible union among disparate and far-flung Protestant sects. For the denominationally strict Puritans in New England this was a particularly radical move, but once made, they pursued it with a zeal unusual even for them. Sermons from Puritan pulpits in these years touted the virtues of welcoming Lutherans, Anabaptists, and even Familists into the Reformed religion.

The ecumenical and cosmopolitan thrust of the Pietists' movement made translation into a variety of languages imperative, and so the Pietists became avid translators. Under the direction of August Francke, the German founder of Pietism, the town of Halle in Germany became a center of translation with both a Seminarium Orientale and an Englandishe Haus, where people flocked to study languages and produce translations. Francke championed the project of translation and was said to have had at least five hundred correspondents in almost as many countries, including Scandinavia, Switzerland, Holland, and North America. To these many correspondents Francke regularly sent pietistic brochures about his various successes in Halle—he had established an orphanage, school, and medical dispensary there in addition to translation institutes—in languages they could understand.

Missionary activities around the world also brought the skills of translators into play in a variety of denominational contexts. In one particularly memorable translation event, two translators turned the Latin exchanges between the Quakers William Penn and George Fox into Dutch in real time during a five-hour presentation in Amsterdam and then turned the questions of the Dutch-speaking audience into

English for the speakers.[33] One of the masterminds behind the translation project for missionaries in general was Anton Boehm, a polymath who had served as chaplain to Prince George of Denmark, the consort of the future Queen Anne. Boehm selected which German Pietists' writings would be translated and which would be sent to different countries for foreign consumption. It was also Boehm who, more often than not, wrote the prefaces and introductions for the translations. Under Boehm's direction, the Bible was also translated into dozens of new languages, including Arabic and Estonian. The most notable of the missionary translations and the most relevant for the Pietists' work with translation was the mission to Tranquebar in southern India where two German missionaries, Bartholomäu Ziegenbalgh and John Ernst Grundler, set up a printing press and paper mill of their own and translated Latin and German works into Portuguese and Damulick, also known as Malabar, the language spoken by the native population.

Learning about these and other Pietist accomplishments, Cotton Mather was visibly impressed. He wrote letters to various correspondents heaping praise on Francke and Boehm for translating, teaching others to translate, and establishing printing presses in exotic locations. In 1715 he published an essay devoted entirely to his fascination with and admiration for Francke's and Boehm's work, called *Nuncia Bona e Terra Longinqua: A Brief Account of Some Good & Great Things a Doing for the Kingdom of God, in the Midst of Europe.* Among the many Pietist accomplishments he celebrated were "the printing-presses [which] have brought forth Books, which have had an incredible Efficacy for the Producing of Piety, even in far distant Countrys."[34] Going on to name the many countries affected by the Pietist translation efforts, Mather marveled at the distance these books had bridged with some reaching "as far off, as even Siberia itself," and others "by Swedes carried into those remote regions."[35] Best of all, Mather noted, were the Bible translations that made "the Waters of Life to run into all Parts of the Earth."[36] Francke, he noted, had the Bible translated into the "Sclavonie Tongue, for the Use especially of the Poor Bohemians, and Hungarians," as well as into the "vulgar Greek" for the "Poor Greek Churches under the Mahometan Oppressions."[37]

Not a man to be outdone, Mather, a polymath who regularly read texts in Latin, Hebrew, Ancient Greek, Spanish, and German, also touted New England's contributions to the world of pietistic translation. In the *Magnalia Americana* he wrote hagiographically about his fellow Puritan and New Englander John Eliot, who translated the Bible from English into the Algonkian Wampanoag dialect and taught the Indians to write in Algonkian using Roman letters in *The Indian Grammar Begun*.

Mather's own translation efforts also formed a part of his correspondence with Francke and his missionaries. Inserted into his *India Christiania*—a text about the propagation of the gospel to the Native Americans written in 1721 and sent to the missionary Ziegenbalgh in Tranquebar—was a bilingual text, about five pages long, in English and Wampanoag, which laid out the "sum of the Christianity, Taught to the Indians."[38] The appearance of Wampanoag alternating with English text must have been of great interest to people who had never seen or heard an Indian language before. Mather inserted it, he wrote, so that "the more Curious may . . . have a Taste of the Language wherein their Instructors give it unto them." This bilingual text, Mather noted, "sets forth the spirit and doctrine of piety which all good men are united in." That Mather referred to the spirit and doctrine of piety in his own translation hints at his appreciation for the epistemological shifts attempted by Eliot and Williams in theirs. In what Philip Round calls the "unstable bicultural communicative field" of English-Algonkian translation, Eliot resorted to "a special discourse of the middle ground—using simple concepts, familiar metaphors, and exaggerated gesture" that constituted what we might today call a loose translation.[39] Round's description of these practices suggests an acknowledgment on the part of the translators that some concepts, especially those of the spirit, required a form of communication that went beyond literal translation, which later became part of Mather's toolkit. One cannot help but surmise, however, that Mather's purpose in sending *India Christiania* to Ziegenbalgh, who did not know the native tongue and therefore could not read the text for content, was to demonstrate graphically how serious the Americans' translation efforts had become.

Proud as Mather was of New England's efforts in translation, such a demonstration in which content was necessarily divorced from form begins to suggest his growing skepticism about the translation project overall. It may have been the recognition that although Eliot, together with Roger Williams before him and Experience Mayhew in Mather's own day, had made great strides toward translating the Indians' languages, the translation project in America had seen no real success. There were many Indians who had learned fluent English, to be sure, but there were very few Puritans who had bothered to learn any of the Algonkian dialects, which made discourse among the groups virtually impossible. Alternatively, it may have been that like contemporary cosmopolitan communication theorists, Mather found translation wanting because he knew on a deeper level that no matter how good the translation might be, there would always be territorial and cultural impediments to communication across large distances.

There is additional evidence that Mather was aware of deeper problems in the realm of communication. His correspondence with Francke, Boehm, and the missionaries in Tranquebar is riddled with a self-consciousness and anxiety about communication that belies a mistrust that went deeper than translation. Part of this was a lingering doubt that America, which so many of Mather's transatlantic counterparts had equated with the depths of hell, was an unlikely site for Pietism. In fact, one of the reasons Mather first touted Eliot's efforts was to dispel the age-old impression in Europe that America was the "outer darkness" of which the gospel of Matthew speaks.[40] The bulk of what Mather said in this correspondence, however, suggests he was thinking more about the association between language, individual territories, and the assumption on the part of many that Americans could not compete with their more sophisticated European counterparts when it came to expressing themselves.

When he first started corresponding with Ziegenbalgh, for example, Mather expressed considerable uneasiness about his own stature as a letter writer. "It pleased the Excellent Ziegenbalgh," he began, "to address his letters unto a Mean American who happened (I scarce know, how) to be known unto him, under an Undeserving Character; Expressing his Desires of an Epistolary Correspondence; and that he might have our Sentiments upon the ways of advancing the Kingdom of God."[41] A diary entry for 1715 expressed a similar sentiment. "Sir Such is the Candor to be found in Persons of a Superiour Character on the other side of the wide Atlantick, that they will admit us Obscure Americans into Correspondencies with them; from which our Informations of such Things, as are most worthy to be known, and perhaps also our Opportunities to do Good in the World, may be very much befriended, and enlarged."[42] In these dismissals of what a "mean" or "obscure" American might have to say on a matter as important as Pietism, we might sense a false humility on Mather's part. Aware of his growing international reputation, as well as his recent election to the Royal Society of London in 1713, Mather may have indulged in these disingenuous statements to make a point about the enduring national prejudices with which international correspondents would be met. Neither "mean" nor "obscure," Mather seemed to understand that he was nevertheless at the mercy of what many in Europe believed was a backwardness shared by all Americans about language. To form a cosmopolitan community through language, then, notions of cultural authority had to be dismantled, and to this end Mather set about creating a language for cosmopolitan communication devoid of territorially based literary markers and generally stripped of all but the lowest common denominators of meaning.

In moving toward this end, Mather followed the Grotian principles embodied in the treaty language of his day. Treaties had been central to Mather's appreciation of cosmopolitan thinking in earlier instances, but Grotius's and Pufendorf's presentational and interpretive methods—minimizing language, arriving at the "right" interpretation, and promoting intercultural dialogue within "special" and "general" spheres—had a special relevance for Mather's goal to speak to Christians across the world in diverse and remote places.

Mather's Cosmopolitan Pietism

Mather's first impulse in offering his own specifically American contribution to the Pietism movement was to reduce the pietist message by minimizing its content and with it the number of words needed to communicate in the first place. This way the presentational format of pietistic writing would be simpler and the interpretive community developing around the text would have fewer problems agreeing on its meaning. That Mather considered this a peculiarly American innovation is demonstrated in, among other places, a note he wrote in his diary on April 19, 1716. After having read all three volumes of Francke's *Pietas halliensis,* Francke's magnum opus on his own contribution to Pietism, Mather writes, "Quaere whether ye Marvellous Footsteps of ye Divine Providence, in what has been done in ye Lower Saxony, have not such a voice in ye World, that I may do well to think of some farther methods, to render it more sensible unto these American Colonists."[43] Presumably with such "farther" methods in mind, Mather would allow "these American Colonists" to join the global discourse about Pietism without anxiety about their literary prowess or cultural backwardness. It is curious that in his articulation of the global reach of Pietism, Mather tended to focus on those parts of the world that went far beyond Europe and included language speakers who would, ostensibly along with the Americans, not have been considered particularly sophisticated. "Will our Glorious Lord fetch His People, from one Circumcised Nation only!," Mather asked confidently in his *Terra beata* (1726). "NO, NO; This Blessed People shall be fetched out of Many Nations. Even, the Indians, and the Negro's."[44] Statements such as these hint at the impact of the translation efforts of people such as John Eliot on the English side and Don Felipe Guamon Poma de Ayala on the indigenous side, which were focused on translating native languages into written forms while relying on the structure and concepts of nonalphabetic systems of communication.[45] Later in his *Triparadisus*, the culminating work of his pietistic phase, Mather reinforced this focus on the outermost regions of communication by referring to Africa and India in the same breath as America. "Now, One found in the Sultry Regions of Africa, or, among the Tranquebarians in the Eastern India, or the Massachusettsians in the Western, is acceptable to God through faith in Christ." Not just the Protestant churches of New England and Europe but "All Nations do Desire a Reconciliation to GOD, or Good Terms with Heaven."[46]

Developing a language devoid of the cultural markers impeding better communication often meant dropping certain forms of address. Thus nowhere to be seen in the Pietists' language were the "thee"s and "thou"s of the Quakers or even the constant references to "godliness" that had earlier set the Puritans' discourse apart from other Protestant sects. In removing these identifying markers, Mather had a predecessor in Hugo Grotius, who formulated bare-bones rules for a cosmopolitan audience within the context of the law of nations. Where for Grotius the point of reducing and simplifying the rules was to increase the verifiability of justice in the context of war, for Mather the point was to streamline the threshold requirement for membership in the pietistic community. Thus in one fairly radical statement to Francke about the unity of American churches, Mather wrote: "Whoever is united with Christ, is admitted to all communities without any restriction. Thus the American churches kindly admit the adherents of all the different denominations to their communion and Eucharist, and grant them all ecclesiastical privileges."[47] Drawing a circle around "whoever is united with Christ" was an ambitious goal because with such a minimalist definition of community, countless numbers of people might qualify for membership.

Eliminating all "restrictions" to membership in the Pietist community would require stripping language down to its basics and simplifying content as well. To this end, Mather radically reduced the number of precepts one had to accept to be a Pietist. Thus in Mather's hands, Pietism became a site of religious and literary reductionism. In his first attempt at reduction, in his *Evangelicum aeternum*, Mather reduced from dozens to fourteen the number of precepts of Protestantism as they had been known and promulgated throughout the world. Detractors objected that this made a mockery of the faith, but as Ernst Benz remarks, Mather was "thoroughly convinced that his fourteen principles contained the true essence of Christianity, and are therefore capable of establishing unity among the different denominations."[48] The only truly meaningful precept, according to Mather, was the Golden Rule or, in Mather's words, the notion that "whatsoever you would have Men do unto you, do you even the same unto them."[49] Later, when discussing his missionary efforts with Francke, Mather decided to reduce the precepts even further, this time, unthinkably, from fourteen to three: (1) God was three people—the Father, Son, and Holy Ghost; (2) Christ was the redeemer; (3) Above all else was love, otherwise known as the Golden Rule.[50] Surely there was no one within the Protestant faithful, Mather believed, who would disagree with any of these.

Unsurprisingly, the people who had balked at the reduction of Christianity to fourteen principles were appalled by Mather's consolidation of them into three, but Mather persevered, knowing that this reduction would bring more people into the fold and increase the likelihood that the Pietist message would not be associated with any given nation's practices. These three precepts, Mather explained, were the only things one needed to know about Christianity to form the right kind of Christian community. "That all the servants of God who do and endure many things for the Evangelizing of the World," he wrote, "may Exhibit unto the whole World the Pure Maxims of the Everlasting Gospel, and would Preach unto the Nations, the Weightier Matters of the Gospel, and the Wheat well cleansed from the Chaff, and from those Less matters, whereabout Good Men, may and often do, carry on their Disputations."[51] It was probably no coincidence that Mather's three pietistic maxims were the subject of his translation from English into Wampanoag in *India notitia*, for in setting out the fewest number of pietistic principles in the most concise way, Mather ensured that where translation might fail, simplicity, of the type envisioned by Gentili, Grotius, and Pufendorf, would succeed.

A certain kind of literary reductionism also pervaded Francke's magnum opus, *Pietas halliensis*, even though it was three volumes long (1707). Identified by Mather as one of the "seeds" of his thinking about Pietism, Francke's work was unusual from a narrative point of view; billed as the story of his charitable undertakings, the volumes read more like a ledger in which Francke lays out his methods for receiving and distributing contributions for his various projects. In a passage characteristic of the work as a whole, Francke described how he set up a box in his house for donations, receiving the "value of Eighteen Shillings Sixpence English" one fateful day. After receiving this considerable sum, Francke noted, he "caused the same day as many Books to be bought as cost Eight shillings," and spent the rest in getting a "student to Teach the poor Children Two Hours a day."[52] Further instructions for raising and saving money populate all three volumes. Practical in the extreme, Francke's book tells the story of his charitable institutions—especially the orphan house—by focusing mainly on how much money was taken in and given out with sparse details about the people involved or the energy expended. Francke's solution was to avoid the pitfalls of language by essentially turning letters into numbers and narrative into sums, thus reducing language to symbols everyone could understand.

Although they followed different paths toward literary reductionism, Mather and Francke shared Pietism's focus on good works or good deeds. The whole point of language, it would seem, was to encourage good works, a view that reflected just how practical and material language had become. *Pietas halliensis* served as a blueprint for others to build the same kind of institutions Francke had, which, once constructed, would be, it was thought, the best way to communicate Pietism around the world. Even meditation, once thought to be a highly ethereal practice that inspired the kind of inward soul-searching that would make one's piety invisible, turned into a dialogue with oneself that was expected under the dictates of the Pietism movement to bear fruit in terms of deeds, rather than words or sentiment. "And why should not our meditation," Mather urged, "expire without some resolution! Devise now, and resolve something, to strengthen your walk with God."[53]

Extending this material approach to language, Mather instituted a preference for writing in short, pithy maxims that would be easy to remember and motivate people to do good things on their own. To this end in *Bonifacius*, as David Levin has argued, Mather tried to be utilitarian. "He worked hard to reduce his experience and knowledge to usable form," Levin observed.[54] Following Levin, the traditional approach to *Bonifacius* is to see it in this light, as a system to encourage the good works of Pietism through the creation of short and memorable phrases, or maxims of the sort to which Benjamin Franklin soon gave voice in his *Silence Dogood Papers*, written in direct imitation of *Bonifacius*. The preface to *Bonifacius*, however, makes it clear that Mather's contribution to language went beyond a mere preference for the maxim. In *Bonifacius*, Mather ascribed to language a kind of performativity, as if the right words, once found, might even substitute for the deeds they identified.

For Mather, words were useful for devising maxims that might lead to good deeds, but they also had the potential to function as deeds themselves. "To the title of Good Works there do belong," he wrote in the preface to *Bonifacius*, "those essays to do good, which are now urged for."[55] Here he clarified that essays about doing good should be classified as actual artifacts of good works in and of themselves. Mather gave voice to this new sense of language in multiple places, but above all in describing the whole of *Bonifacius* as an illustration of a particular sentence in which the conflation of words and deeds was self-evident. The sentence in question—"A capacity to do good, not only gives a title to it, but also makes the doing of it a duty"—essentially came to substitute for the book itself and demonstrated the process by which a verbal articulation—in this case the capacity to do good—became the imperative or duty that epitomized the action.

In performing the act or deed toward which it gestures, Mather's text is treaty-like, presenting its meaning in the most neutral form and moving its interpretive community, as Grotius suggested, toward agreement. For Mather, as for Grotius and Pufendorf, the goal of communication was to create the "right" interpretation through the mechanism of contract—an agreement to agree about the meaning of words that was so widely shared as to be not only unambiguous but also tantamount to the work the agreement proposed. Mather too had an understanding of the linguistic contract, which he exhibited in his sense of the materiality of words. On first hearing that Francke had built an orphanage in Halle, for example, an accomplishment others in various cities across Europe attempted to imitate and which George Whitefield would later use as a model for his own orphanage in Georgia, Mather sent Francke some gold to help defray the costs. He also sent his "Orphano-trophium," a lengthy essay written expressly for the orphanage in which he exhorts Francke's young charges and orphans all over the world to look on their orphanhood as one of God's blessings. His diary entry about the delivery of the text to Francke explained that he would be sending his "Orphano-trophium" for the "use" of the orphan house in lower Saxony.[56] Emphasizing the "use" to which the text was to be put was Mather's way of praising Francke and inducing gratitude in the beneficiaries of his charity. Far more significant, however, was the inescapable suggestion that Mather's essay, whose title was Latin for orphanage, was a kind of textual orphanage and no less a monument than the building itself.

The index of this text's monumentalism is tied to Mather's sense that texts are contracts that create the agreements necessary for interpretive communities. We find this demonstrated in the language Mather uses to talk about the delivery and receipt of texts within the Pietist network, where once again the materiality of texts is more important than their content. In his diary entry for December 9, 1709, for example, the earliest date for his correspondence with Francke, Mather notes he is sending two of his essays, "Heavenly Conversation," and "Dust and Ashes," "to lodge these treatises in ye Hands of many ministers, throughout the Country... and unto Dr. Franckius, in Saxony." The verb "to lodge," used here to describe the process of delivery, provides yet another clue that in sending texts, Mather envisions a material process. The entity he imagines as the recipient of the text is not the reader as such, but the reader's hands, a holding place associated more with physical than with cerebral labor. Other references to manuscript exchange follow suit. When addressing schoolmasters in *Bonifacius*, Mather urges an unusual form of teaching that privileges the equation of reading with doing. "Sirs," Mather writes, "let it be a great intention with you, to instill documents of piety into the children," signaling that the instillation itself would accomplish the goal of making them pious.[57] As was the case with "lodge," the verb "instill" suggests a physical mechanism for receiving texts that takes the form not of words or lines, but of whole documents.

Reading text for meaning as distinct from lodging or instilling text to induce communication also takes a back seat in Mather's description of key moments in a Pietist's life, where text operates again as a contractual prompt for the "right" interpretation. "An inveterate sinner I have read of," Mather observed in *Bonifacius*, "converted unto serious piety, by accidentally seeing that sentence of Austin [St. Augustine] written in a window: 'He that hath promised pardon to the penitent sinner, has not promised repentance to the presumptuous one.'"[58] Here the words at issue are not read so much as encountered in a place not typically associated with words, namely "a window." The act of encountering words "accidentally" reinforces our perception that the process of reading, while undoubtedly central to the "sinner," is secondary to the process of walking, glancing, or "seeing" the words. Whether these words were actually etched into the window pane with a diamond—a practice typically reserved in the seventeenth century for secular rather than sacred verse—or merely displayed on paper in a print shop, we may never know, but Mather's account of the incident leaves us with the impression that it was the interpretive encounter or exchange rather than the words themselves that brought this particular sinner into the fold.

If conceptualizing words as deeds helped Mather implement a communication system similar to the one Grotius and Pufendorf envisioned through a system of minimal language and easy access to the "right" interpretation, Mather nevertheless recognized that language, no matter what its form, would remain susceptible to the wrong interpretation if placed in the wrong hands. Such interpretations were very much on Mather's mind as he wrote *Bonifacius*. Intended to be brief, exemplary, and more easily understood than long narratives, essays on good deeds, like those in *Bonifacius*, were bound to be misunderstood on occasion. Thus in the preface Mather urged caution. "Misconstruction is one thing against which you will do well to furnish yourselves with the armor both of prudence and of patience," he observed. "You will unavoidably be put upon for the doing of many good things, which other people will see but at a distance . . . and this will expose you to their censures."[59]

The problem with misconstruction, as Mather saw it, was bound up with the cosmopolitan problem of communicating across large distances. Pietism was especially prone to these problems since at stake in the Pietists' project of communication was the creation of interpretive communities that would not only encompass local venues but would also wrap around the world. The intended audience for the Pietists' message—to do good things—was, to use words quoted by Mather in *Bonifacius,* "to love the public," "to study an universal good," and "to promote the interest of the whole world."[60] Mather took a cosmopolitan approach to the mandate, thinking in terms of total population. "The world," he wrote in contemplating the number of people to whom good things should happen, "had according to the contemplation of some, above seven hundred millions of people now living in it."[61] Reducing language to a minimum, as Grotius had urged with respect to treaties, would help overcome the cultural barriers that such a diverse, cosmopolitan audience would entail. The problem of how to communicate with people across vast distances where the possibility for misunderstanding was high remained.

With respect to this problem Mather had a notable, if not entirely novel, solution: create concentric circles of communication that would gradually and without loss of meaning include growing numbers of people around the world. We recall the spheres of communication Pufendorf introduced when he identified two different kinds of linguistic contracts: the "general compacts" that included everyone, and the "special compacts" that operated within much smaller spaces among a more like-minded group of people, united by a profession or some other trait. Mather combined the lessons of both compacts to create a system that moved through ever-widening circles of membership from the special to the general until the cosmopolis was within reach.

Mather's ever-widening circles created a cosmopolitan community by means of relationism, a concept key to the idea of the contract as well. We start the work of communicating with others, Mather wrote, with "frequent self examination." "First, let every man devise what good may be done... IN HIS OWN HEART AND LIFE."[62] After properly examining the self, however, one was to move in concentric circles outward. "The useful man may now with a very good grace" Mather wrote, "extend and enlarge the sphere of his consideration."[63] It mattered little where one looked next for enlargement, although Mather did have some suggestions. The important point, rather, was to recognize that the spheres in which one lived were always defined by one's relationships with others. "One great way to prove ourselves *really good,*" Mather wrote, "is to be *relatively good,*" where relatively pertains to one's relatives or relations.[64] Accordingly, his next piece of advice was to consider the world relationally. "My next Proposal now shall be: Let every man consider the Relation, wherein the Sovereign God has placed him, and let him devise what good he may do, that may render his relatives, the better for him."[65] The cosmopolitan reach of such relationism is clear. If no one person, no matter how small his or her sphere of operation, could think of him or herself as alone, then the move from one's local circumstances to that of the cosmopolis would be that much easier.

Increasing measures of distance determined Mather's linguistic map. The first place to look for relatives, Mather suggested, was in the home. "Let us begin," he urged, "with our domestic relations, and provide for those of our own house."[66] Naturally, the first person to consider would be one's spouse. "The Husband will do well to think," Mather wrote, "'What shall I do that in my carriage towards my wife, the kindness of the blessed Jesus towards His Church may be followed and resembled."[67] What is striking in Mather's suggestion is not that he thought of the conjugal relationship first, but that he urged both parties—husband and wife—to reflect on each other equally. "Sir," Mather wrote in addressing the husband, "Sometimes ask her [the wife] to help you in the answer; ask her to tell you, what she would have you to do."[68] This practice seemed especially rooted in the contractual nature of communication, a reinforcement in this particular case of the conjugal contract. Still staying within the sphere of the home, Mather moved beyond the conjugal to the parental relation and then to all of one's "natural" relations, connected by family. "Sir," Mather continued, "take a catalogue of all your more distant relatives. Consider them one after another; and make every one of them the subjects for your good devices."[69]

In order to grow the community in a cosmopolitan way, however, Mather understood that one had ultimately to move beyond one's blood relations. After tending to relatives in the home, people would call on neighbors to engage relationally. "Neighbors," Mather wrote, "you stand related unto one another; and you should be full of devices, that all the neighbors may have cause to be glad of your being in the neighborhood."[70] About these devices, Mather was specific. After pitying your neighbor, Mather suggested, "you may do well to visit them," which privileges the most direct form of communication. Even this, however, is not all. "[W]hen you visit . . . [your neighbors]" Mather urged, "carry them some good word, which raise a gladness, in an heart stop[ing] with heaviness."[71] We note the material act at the heart of this communication—exemplified by the verbal metaphor of carrying—as Mather returned to his emphasis on the word as deed. In keeping with the widening spheres of communication, Mather next urged that one talk directly not only to one's neighbors but also to one's friends about one's neighbors. Keep "a list of the poor in your neighborhood," Mather wrote, "always lying by you," for "such a list would often furnish you, with matter for a useful conversation, when you are talking with your friends, whom you may provoke to love and good works."[72]

After considering these more intimate relations, Mather turned the spheres of relationism defined by space—the home, the neighborhood—into spheres of increasing generality. In the subsequent chapters of *Bonifacius*, he addressed ministers, schoolmasters, church officials, magistrates, physicians, rich men, officials, lawyers, and members of reforming societies in that order. For Pufendorf, significantly, groups like these, defined largely by profession, fell under the rubric of the "special" groups that would naturally defer to the more general ones. For Mather, however, they were to be valued as the means to the larger end precisely because they defied territorial markers. The members of these groups, Mather concluded, were "in more public circumstances" and so had a special obligation to do good. The opportunities for finding parallels and carrying on a dialogue with people defined by these terms of relationality in other parts of the world seemed in Mather's mind far greater than otherwise, and so he privileged them for the purposes of cosmopolitan communication.

Mather's model of concentric circles bears a striking resemblance, as careful readers will note, to the model espoused by the ancient Stoics, who in thinking through the cosmopolis conjured a similar image. The first sphere of belonging in the Stoics' scheme, as Martha Nussbaum explains, "encircles the self, the next takes in the immediate family, then follows the extended family, then, in order, neighbors or local groups, fellow city-dwellers, and fellow countrymen."[73] For Nussbaum, who is thinking not only about the Stoics but also about the virtue of their model for contemporary cosmopolitan theory, the potential of such a communications scheme is huge. To these circles, she writes, "we can easily add ... groupings based on ethnic, linguistic, historical, professional, gender, or sexual identities."[74] For Nussbaum, as for Mather, the genius of the system is that it allows one to maintain local and remote associations without having to choose between them.

Whether Mather was influenced in his model of concentric circles by the Stoics, Pufendorf, or some combination of both, we will never know for sure. Yet the connections among all three are too prominent to ignore. In Mather's Pietism and in the language theories embedded in the law of nations, itself a product of the ancient Greek and Roman Stoic philosophy, we see an effort not only to bind the world to a certain doctrine (Pietism in one case, law in the other) but also to marry that doctrine to and in some sense equate it with a framework for communicating with the world. Reducing text to its essentials and communicating those essentials to others nearby—both simple technologies—ensure that people in one place will be able to talk to people in another and be understood. In this way, the means become the ends, and cosmopolitanism becomes both form and content.

By the middle of the eighteenth century, the complex relationship between the Puritans' religion and the law of nations had given way to the intense domestic political and legal battle being fought against Great Britain. In integrating the language theory of the law of nations into his notions about Pietism, Mather produced what was to be the Puritans' cosmopolitan swan song. One could even argue that Pietism, which was on some level nothing more than a reinvention of the Christian universalism that had failed miserably as a cosmopolitan ideal in the past, held within it the seeds of its own destruction. For all his interest in communicating with people around the world, Mather never really contemplated welcoming any but Christians into the fold. Yet Mather's Pietism at the turn of the eighteenth century remains a powerful example of a Puritan cosmopolitanism, parts of which are still in evidence today. Precisely because it moved from content to form, Mather's Pietism allowed for the kind of dialogue of which contemporary cosmopolitan communication theorists speak—a dialogue that transcends cultural and linguistic boundaries. And precisely because it began with a notion of dialogical relationality and of face-to-face communication, his Pietism served to ease the tension between polis and cosmopolis, between domestic politics, the law, and the politics of a larger order. The legacy of Mather's expressions of Pietism from *Bonifacius* to *Nuncia bona* to his correspondence and diary entries is the human voice that in his imagination had the power to bridge the gap from the individual to the community and from the community to the world as a cosmopolitan whole.

{ Epilogue }

THE LAW OF THE COSMOPOLIS AND ITS LITERARY PAST

When one judges and when one acts in political matters, one is supposed to take one's bearings from the idea, not the actuality, of being a world citizen.

—HANNAH ARENDT

The Puritan Cosmopolis opens with a quote from Hannah Arendt in which she identifies the salient feature of our "cosmopolitan existence." For Arendt, we recall, people belong to a cosmopolis and lead cosmopolitan lives "by the sheer fact of being human." In the spirit of coming full circle, I end *The Puritan Cosmopolis* by returning to Arendt and to the conclusion of the quote from which the epigraph to the introduction was taken. After identifying the grounds from which cosmopolitanism takes shape, Arendt observes that the intellectual and epistemological force behind our cosmopolitan existence is the *idea* of being a world citizen rather than its "actuality" (my emphasis). I invoke Arendt's observations in part because they remind us of where this book began, but also because they point us in a useful future direction, joining "a literature of the past [in this case that of the Puritans] with an unresolved legacy or project still before us." This union, David Simpson observes, can increase the relevance "of a historical and disciplinary field."[1] In this chapter I ask what the Puritans can teach us about some of the questions of world citizenship we still face today—questions having to do with refugees, climate change, or the distribution of global resources, among many others.

For Arendt, the most authentic way to be cosmopolitan was to act in accordance with the *idea* of world belonging as opposed to its manifestations in an imperfect world. As Robert Fine suggests, Arendt's preference for the ideational over the material in the context of cosmopolitanism "entails grappling with the ambivalences faced by subjects in making cosmopolitan judgments about the extremities of organized violence in thoroughly non-ideal conditions."[2] In seeming to dismiss the difficulties posed by "non-ideal conditions," Arendt's position seems partly utopian. It nevertheless guides my comments here for two reasons: (1) My analysis of the Puritans' cosmopolitanism suggests that they often "took their bearings from the idea of cosmopolitanism" rather than from its actuality; (2) The Puritans' writings on the cosmopolis provide us with a far more material basis for thinking through the idea of world belonging than either Arendt or Fine contemplate.

In drawing on the law of nations, an early modern compilation of writings about war, peace, and the world, the Puritans used literature in the form of multifaceted and generically eclectic discourse to bring the cosmopolis into material being. From its earliest articulations in the law of nations, the Puritans wrestled with ideas about belonging to a world that bound people together in ways that went beyond the ties mechanization, commerce, and globalization made possible. Giving voice to a cosmopolitanism that emerged within Puritan debates over concepts central to their worldview, such as the covenant, the millennium, evidence, and Pietism, the Puritans gave this sense of cosmopolitan belonging a materially discursive form, taking their bearings, as Arendt puts it, from its underlying legal vision, not from its limited legal presence in the early modern world.

These imaginative iterations of the Puritans' experiments with cosmopolitanism are what I refer to here as the law's literary past—a past confined not to literary artifacts per se—although the sermons, essays, and correspondence analyzed here provide ample evidence of those—but encompassing the imaginative enterprise that gives rise to literature in general. The Puritans' engagement with the law of nations and its vision of the cosmopolis was literary in three ways: in its world creation, it encouraged, as literature often does, a multiplicity of belongings and different solidarities; in its intertextuality, it produced imaginative revisions and collections of various texts; in its discursive diversity, it expressed itself in ways originally designed for other reasons. In these ways the Puritans emerged as the consummate literary assemblers, constituting their vision of a cosmopolis from legal, political, and religious texts and decision-making strategies. Finally, the Puritans' engagement with the cosmopolis was literary because the people who wrote the sermons, pamphlets, and letters that articulated a cosmopolitan vision were, like the people who listened to and read them, in some ways always responding to the law of nations, a text already written for the world.

Of course the Puritans were not alone in their literary uses of the law. Law in the early modern period, as many scholars have observed, was especially fluid and subject to patchwork constructions. As I explain in chapter 1, the early modern period saw a proliferation of sovereign and semi-sovereign entities from the colony to the republic to the empire and fledgling nation-state, which were all engaged in new legal constructions. The period also witnessed a multitude of constitutions drafted for a variety of constituencies and written by lawmakers from all walks of life, greatly increasing the cross-pollination between the law and nonlegal genres and discursive areas.[3] If many people were engaged in the enterprise of mixing law and literature in the period, however, the Puritan responses to the law of nations and its idea of the cosmopolis are among the best for revealing the complex and imaginative ways of engaging with the law largely lost to us today. As we rediscover these imaginative and literary resources, my hope is that we can rewrite this episode in American legal and literary history and recuperate a cosmopolitan way of thinking that will propel us past the terms that now dominate international law—the law of nations' later incarnation—and have closed off many cosmopolitan possibilities within the law.

The law began to lose its imaginative compass in the international context soon after the Puritans were forced to abandon their cosmopolitan vision. The main reason for this loss was the growing positivism and instrumentalism of the law. On its journey from the law of nations to international law, the law governing relations among states as well as nonstate entities around the world became overwhelmingly positivist, based on rules, regulations, and explicit agreements between and among sovereign members. The more enchanted, theological underpinnings of the law of nations as established by the Spanish Scholastics, Vitoria and Suarez, and further developed by the Protestant theorists, Gentili and Grotius, had positivist elements as well. As we saw in chapters 1 and 5, among Grotius's most useful innovations were the pared down expressions of how to start and end wars that obviated many of the unanswerable questions about justice plaguing warring parties in the Middle Ages. Despite these positivistic features, however, the law of nations was for Gentili and Grotius dominated by a nonpositivist spirit that was part natural law—the law of God and nature—and part literature, allowing a cosmopolis based on beliefs in human sociability and capacity to evolve.

The positivist and instrumentalizing turn in international law had two adverse consequences for the development of international law and the discursive fields informing it. The first was the more positivist the language of the law became, the less available it became to those outside the ranks of those already authorized to use it, namely lawyers, judges, and diplomats. The discursive fields surrounding and impinging on the law of nations, on the other hand—itself a composite of many sources as discussed in chapter 1—suggest that its many respondents and interlocutors required no such authorization or credentialing, leaving the Puritans among many others to read, revise, and redeploy the law in a variety of areas as they saw fit. For the Puritans, in particular, the law mingled freely with fiction. As a text, the law was not simply reflected in and adapted to the Puritans' literary expressions but also familiar to them from the literary sources that had been used in constructing the law of nations. As I explained in chapter 1, the law of nations flowed backward to the Hebrew Bible, which the Puritans read as a theological, historical, and literary text, and forward to the imagined texts of treaties to be written in an uncertain future. That the law of nations was imaginative in both past and future senses allowed it to take root in a variety of discursive areas where the concept of belonging was still under construction. And as *The Puritan Cosmopolis* shows, it was in part this looser construction of the juridical that enabled the cosmopolitan features of the law to emerge.

The second and far more significant check on international law as it developed in the eighteenth and nineteenth centuries was its tendency to translate most international law questions into jurisdictional claims. On one level, international law is patently jurisdictional. The recognition of an international legal order must by definition concern itself with the boundaries between and among states, as the Puritans knew all too well. International law has to establish borders between and among nations before it can posit a cosmopolis above or alongside it, such as Seneca once imagined. In a world where territorial boundaries changed frequently, it was often difficult to pin these boundaries down, but by the late eighteenth century, the focus on jurisdiction led to concrete proposals for a governing body that could adjudicate them fairly. Such proposals, which have played a large part in international law since that time, led to the major enforcement projects of the twentieth century, such as the League of Nations, the United Nations, and more recently the International Criminal Court (ICC). The substantial success of these institutions goes a long way toward explaining why among the relatively few scholars who continue to explore possibilities for a legal cosmopolitanism is a shared concern with governing bodies above all.[4] With the rise of nonstate actors in international law, including individuals, organizations, and associations with multiple and sometimes nonexistent territorial designations, the goal of creating governing institutions has become more difficult, but paradoxically the more complex and extraspatial our global networks are, the more jurisdictionally encumbered the law has become. As Neil Walker points out, "the exponential increase in the density of transboundary relations" has only increased the number of boundary disputes in the global sphere.[5]

Even when seen within the framework of legal pluralism, which serves as a kind of supplement to international law in its recognition of the multiple legalities within a single population, jurisdiction remains a dominant and restrictive concern. Understood as an overlapping or clash of legal regimes especially common to empires in which territory is contested, legally plural frameworks, according to Lauren Benton and Richard Ross, frequently present themselves as "a formation of historically occurring patterns of jurisdictional complexity and conflict."[6] Many of these plural legal systems are located in current or former colonies where many different kinds of legal systems exist, but they include places where other kinds of normative expression also operate. In encouraging the "interplay of a wide variety of normative commitments and law-giving entities," Paul Berman suggests, legal pluralism opens up many productive avenues for international law.[7] In its necessarily comparative approach, however, its subject matter often remains tied to the territorially defined jurisdictions from which legal systems typically spring.

The jurisdictional paradigm for fielding questions within international law has been so tenacious that it has even circumscribed the discourse of human rights, which was originally conceived within the legal framework as a kind of antidote to it. The rise of human rights discourse in international law, which some trace back to Immanuel Kant, others to the International Bill of Human Rights passed by the UN General Assembly in 1952, and still others to the more concrete human rights victories of the 1970s, has productively reoriented international law toward the conditions of human existence and away from the positivism that dominated eighteenth- and nineteenth-century international law.[8] Because "[t]he right to have rights," as Arendt puts it, was essentially "the right of every individual to belong to humanity," it has long been a driving force within the international arena.[9] Specific human rights, including those enumerated in the International Bill of Human Rights, such as the right "to work in just and favourable conditions, to social protection, [and] to an adequate standard of living," aim to provide minimum standards of fairness for people around the world.[10]

As a manifestation of the ability of the law to think past the institutional structures characteristic of international law, human rights discourse represents a major breakthrough. However, many questions about the law's relationship to human rights remain. How, for example, are these rights to be enforced, and how can we be sure that the rights enumerated in critical pieces of legislation are used to protect people in less than optimal situations rather than to promote certain ideologies and nationalist agendas? While the nation-states of the West developed as relatively effective guarantors of individual rights in the eighteenth and nineteenth centuries, the larger world order and its global governing structures continue to struggle in that role. One problem is that the human rights which states seem willing to enforce within the international law context tend to be those compatible with sovereign self-interest, which is often in conflict with the rights belonging to citizens of the cosmopolis.[11] Another problem is that structural constraints imposed by cross-national disparities interfere with the distribution and enforcement of human rights equally around the world. Both of these problems have led some scholars to favor the nation-state over the cosmopolis as a generator of human rights. "Living in political communities narrower than the species," Kwame Anthony Appiah writes, "is better for us than would be our engulfment in a single worldstate."[12] More damaging still to the optimism we associate with the human rights agenda of international law is Antony Anghie's observation that the discourse of human rights has been used in the colonial situation from Francisco Vitoria's time to today to further the economic goals of the West.[13]

The greatest drawback to the human rights discourse within the international law framework, however, is that in the end it too conforms to a jurisdictional paradigm. The moment an individual makes a rights claim under the law, it delimits an array of potential rights that may or may not belong to others, turning rights claims into boundary disputes and human rights law into boundary management. Any right—to own property, for example—is meaningless except insofar as it constrains the right of others to do the same. In the case of property, it means no one else can own the same piece of property. In the case of "social protection"—among the rights enumerated in the International Bill of Human Rights—one can easily see how a particular construction of such a right could impinge on another. The jurisdictional constraints of human rights discourse holds true in both the national and international context, but they present a greater impediment in the international context since the rights in question belong to states, organizations, associations, and individuals simultaneously.

In their literary interpretations and adaptations of the law of nations, the Puritans managed to avoid many of the jurisdictional difficulties that continue to afflict international law today. The Puritans cultivated a sense of cosmopolitanism that was defined in part by a spatially determined belonging; that's what it meant to be cosmopolitan as I use the term here. That sense, however, did not necessarily follow in a straight line from conceptualization to legal regulation and administration, the touchstones of jurisdictional thought. In part, the Puritans were liberated from a primary emphasis on jurisdiction by thinking through the cosmopolis in intertextual terms. The expression of Puritan cosmopolitanism found its way into the discourses of millennialism, covenant theology, evidence, and Pietism in ways whose meaning, as Benton and Ross suggest, "may not be captured by an emphasis on jurisdictional tensions." Incorporating readings of the Bible informed by the law of nations, precepts from treatises on the law of nations, and the language of treaties issued in the wake of the law of nations, the Puritans integrated and rewrote the law of nations to meet existing demands and answer existing questions about nonjurisdictional issues, such as how to think about correcting mistakes (covenant), prepare for the Second Coming of Christ (millennium), discredit the royal governors (evidence), and communicate more clearly with others (Pietism). In this way they moved from a reading of the legal possibilities that in the first half of the seventeenth century underwrote their community's self-sufficiency to a reading that in the second half of the century underwrote their connection with and dependencies on a world larger than the boundaries of the transatlantic or even hemispheric spheres encompass.

Each chapter of *The Puritan Cosmopolis* details the extent to which the Puritans shifted the grounds of the cosmopolis away from its restrictive emphasis on jurisdiction in international law. As a discursive site for cosmopolis building, the covenant, for example, replaced a focus on jurisdiction and boundary disputes with a temporal approach to the cosmopolis. In their musings on the covenant, as described in chapter 2, the Puritans offered a vision of the cosmopolis destroyed by human error but reestablished by acts of individual and collective renewal and commemoration. Taking shape in sermons on the cosmopolitan covenant delivered by ministers and absorbed by churchgoers, the law of nations brought the Puritans to a new recognition of the cosmopolis through the contingency of the narratives that helped renew and commemorate it over time. In addition, because the covenant—the principle of legal cohesion that gave rise to the polis and cosmopolis—appeared to be capable, like treaties, of being broken and renewed repeatedly, the Puritans gained an appreciation for the way in which their story had become intertwined with that of others at different points in history. No longer tied exclusively to the story of the Israelites, they were now also characters in the stories of people whose trajectories bore no resemblance to their own. In this way the cosmopolis became the product of time rather than place and of intertextuality rather than typology.

Similarly in chapter 3 on the millennium, the cosmopolis became a vision of a world at peace that merged with the Puritans' theological vision of a world to come. In this process the millennium was transformed from a physical site with a few biblically inspired coordinates into a project achieved by human agency. The focus for thinking through the cosmopolis in the context of the millennium was on the human intellect and imagination, and in this the Puritans took their cue from the many peace treaties negotiated in their day. In the Treaty of Westphalia, we recall, peace was achieved as a result of people forming thoughts about peace. "It has at last happened," the treaty reads, "that the one side, and the other . . . have formed Thoughts of an Universal peace; and for this purpose, [sign] . . . a mutual Agreement and Covenant of both Parties, in the Year of our Lord, 1641." In using the law of nations in which theorists had already formed thoughts of the cosmopolis as a catalyst for the formation of additional cosmopolitan thoughts, the Puritans engaged in a form of collaborative writing and narrative world making for a millennium that had previously been thought to require little to no manufacture at all.

In chapter 4, jurisdiction is subordinated to the search for truth. The central concern in that chapter about what the widening world could do to help the Puritans gather dispositive evidence from beyond their own borders helped transform the cosmopolis into a tool for legal veracity. Predicated on the vision of the cosmopolis at the heart of the law of nations, evidentiary cosmopolitanism insisted on hearing testimony from people all around the world, especially in matters pertaining to sovereignty and world politics. According to this logic, the bigger the world, the more critical it was to gather facts from all over to distinguish lies from truth. While jurisdiction undoubtedly played a part in the Puritans' insistence on hearing diverse voices, it took a back seat to an understanding of the cosmopolis's role in the kind of storytelling where truth prevailed over fiction.

Finally in the Pietism at the heart of the fifth chapter, boundary disputes among states and nonstate actors were replaced with a model of the personal encounter that superseded the question of authority central to jurisdiction. In Cotton Mather's vision of the cosmopolis, what was important was not the content of what was said but its form, allowing a consensus to take shape through the primal act of encounter. In this Mather foreshadows Emmanuel Levinas's theory of the face-to-face encounter, which is guided by an ethics stemming from the fact of the encounter rather than its substance. Mather's particular contribution to the face-to-face encounter was in transforming the encounter's phenomenology through a process of pietistic communication that said as little as possible and rendered the signifier far more important than the signified. Emptied of almost all its content, the act of communication formed a cosmopolis premised on the human capacity to recognize other humans, regardless of where they came from or what they had to say.

The interpenetration of legal and literary imaginations in the Puritans' uses of the law of nations allowed for an unusual degree of social dissemination and penetration. Although the texts that form the basis of my analyses in this book were written by members of the Puritan elites, their discursive variety allowed them an audience far larger than if they had been limited by legal contexts. The dissemination of legal ideas through conceptual frameworks outside the bounds of law proper—including commemorative rituals or millennialist expectations, to name two of the four frameworks covered here—enabled the assimilation of legal ideas by a more diverse population. Legal ideas in the Puritan world often circulated in fragmentary form and mingled freely with other imaginative discourses to affect a larger audience than otherwise. Not yet a literature written by or belonging to the middle or working classes, as such, the Puritan texts studied here nevertheless helped spread the legally informed concept of the cosmopolis throughout the popular imagination.

The diffusion of legal notions through a variety of discursive channels in Puritan society stands in stark contrast to the discursive reach of most international law today. Quite aside from its jurisdictional focus, perhaps the biggest problem with international law today is that even the most inclusive and well-intentioned efforts to realize the cosmopolis seem imposed on people from above. Consider what Luke Martell calls the "topdown" measures taken at the climate change talks at Kyoto and Cancún or of the "on-going rounds of world trade talks, the nuclear non-proliferation treaty that is reviewed every five years, and the United Nations."[14] To this list we might add the recent decision by voters in the UK to leave the European Union, once considered one of the greatest cosmopolitan accomplishments ever. If those charged with naming and identifying international law were to find legal expression in other forms of human discourse, however, the law might be more productively tied to concepts of the cosmopolis circulated and generated from below.

It is doubtful whether opening the law more widely to concepts that take root in other discourses could solve all the problems of international law, but the law might more easily find its way into the imaginations of more people. This I believe is what Philip Allot means when he refers to "the human potential of international law." "In finding the human potential of international society through the human potential of international law," Allott remarks, "humanity may discover the human position of society and of law. Humanity may discover a truly human law as the potential of all law in all society." In their writings about the millennium, the covenant, evidence, and Pietism, the Puritans attempted to build a cosmopolis with the human potential of law in mind. Their engagement with the law in terms of the concepts central to their society allowed them to skirt the imposition of meaning, the instrumentalism of belonging, and the jurisdictional constraints that international law later came to demand. The result as this study demonstrates was a nonunitary, highly differentiated series of texts revolving around the Puritans' place in the cosmopolis.

We could do worse than follow the Puritans' lead in associating the law with other forms of the human imagination or with its literary past and future. That we find currents of legally inspired cosmopolitan thought in these diverse areas of Puritan expression may also point the way to finding additional sites of cosmopolitanism in our time. The norm has been to search for cosmopolitanism in places where others are explicitly thinking about it. This norm, which took hold shortly after the Puritans' time, tended to accelerate international law's loss of its literary past. Examining the literary past of the law of nations in late seventeenth-century Puritan texts, however, sheds some light on the relevance of extralegal discourse in the creation of legal priorities, for it is these features of the Puritan cosmopolis that may hold the most potential for our uses of cosmopolitanism today. Today, the law tends to be relegated to the sidelines of cosmopolitan theory, having proved somehow unequal to the task. As I hope to show here, however, the law served a cosmopolitan vision in the American past that may help us open it back up again to the imagination. If the legal rationalism and positivism of the eighteenth through twentieth centuries has pushed a globalizing agenda that counts as a form of cosmopolitanism for some, it has done so too often at the expense of the kind of legal cosmopolis that emerged from the law of nations and which in Puritan hands became a basis for thinking widely in legal and literary terms about how to build a world to which and in which we all belong. To re-embrace the imaginative, the literary, and the intertextual within contemporaneous formulations of international law would mean to welcome, as the Puritans did, a cosmopolis that could be built from the bottom up to hold us all.

{ NOTES }

Prologue

1. For more about this particular broadside, see Charles E. Clark, *The Public Prints: The Newspaper in Anglo-American Culture, 1665–1740* (New York: Oxford University Press, 1994), 70; and for New England broadsides in general, David D. Hall, *Ways of Writing: The Practice and Politics of Text-Making in Seventeenth-Century New England* (Philadelphia: University of Pennsylvania Press, 2008).

2. The link I make here between cosmopolitanism and the law is not to be confused with the discourse about legal cosmopolitanism that has occupied a number of cosmopolitan theorists of late. These theorists are concerned with what it might mean and whether it would be possible to institute a governing body that would serve effectively as the world's sovereign. Previous attempts to do just this have been made, from the League of Nations to the world court at The Hague. For examples of scholarship in this area, see Adeno Addis, "Imagining the International Community: The Constitutive Dimension of Universal Jurisdiction," *Human Rights Quarterly* 31, no. 1 (2009): 129–62; Noah Feldman, "Cosmopolitan Law?" *Yale Law Journal* 116, no. 5 (2007): 1022–71; Richard Janda, "Toward Cosmopolitan Law," *McGill Law Journal* 50 (2005): 967–86; Garrett Wallace Brown, "Moving from Cosmopolitan Legal Theory to Legal Practice: Models of Cosmopolitan Law," *Legal Studies* 28, no. 3 (2008): 430–51.

3. Bruce Robbins, "Actually Existing Cosmopolitanism," in *Cosmopolitics: Thinking and Feeling Beyond the Nation*, ed. Pheng Cheah and Bruce Robbins (Minneapolis: University of Minnesota Press, 1998), 3.

4. Samuel Scheffler, *Boundaries and Allegiances: Problems of Justice and Responsibility in Liberal Thought* (Oxford: Oxford University Press, 2003), 115.

5. See especially Elizabeth Dillon, *The Gender of Freedom: Fictions of Liberalism and the Literary Public Sphere* (Stanford, CA: Stanford University Press, 2004); and Jonathan Beecher Field, "The Antinomian Controversy Did Not Take Place," *Early American Studies: An Interdisciplinary Journal* 6, no. 2 (2008): 448–63.

6. William C. Spengemann, *A New World of Words: Redefining Early American Literature* (New Haven, CT: Yale University Press, 1994); Wai Chee Dimock, *Through Other Continents: American Literature Across Deep Time* (Princeton, NJ: Princeton University Press, 2008); David Armitage, *The Declaration of Independence; A Global History* (Cambridge, MA: Harvard University Press, 2007); Thomas Bender, *A Nation Among Nations: America's Place in World History* (Boston: Hill and Wang, 2006).

7. See Immanuel Wallerstein, *World-Systems Analysis: An Introduction* (Durham, NC: Duke University Press, 2004).

8. Mark Valeri, *Heavenly Merchandize: How Religion Shaped Commerce in Puritan America* (Princeton, NJ: Princeton University Press, 2010), 2.

9. See Mark Peterson, "Theopolis Americana: The City-State of Boston, the Republic of Letters, and the Protestant International, 1689–1739," in *Soundings in Atlantic History:*

Latent Structures and Intellectual Currents, 1500–1825, ed. Bernard Bailyn (Cambridge, MA: Harvard University Press, 2009). For Peterson, late seventeenth-century Boston was cosmopolitan because in the wake of the Glorious Revolution and the ascension to the throne of William III, the Puritans found themselves partners in a much-expanded network of cultural, religious, political, and commercial alliances with the Protestant world. Protestant networking forms a part of my understanding of the cosmopolitan as well, but for me the real impetus toward cosmopolitan thought lies with the law of nations.

10. See, e.g., Hilary E. Wyss, *Writing Indians: Literacy, Christianity, and Native Community in Early America* (Amherst: University of Massachusetts Press, 2003); Birgit Brander Rasmussen, *Queequeg's Coffin, Indigenous Literacies and Early American Literature* (Durham, NC: Duke University Press, 2012); Jenny Hale Pulsipher, *Subjects Unto the Same King: Indians, English, and the Contest for Authority in Colonial New England* (Philadelphia: University of Pennsylvania Press, 2006); Matt Cohen, *The Networked Wilderness: Communicating in Early New England* (Minneapolis: University of Minnesota, 2009); Kristina Bross, *Dry Bones and Indian Sermons: Praying Indians in Colonial America* (Ithaca, NY: Cornell University Press, 2004); Laura Stevens, *The Poor Indians: British Missionaries, Native Americans, and Colonial Sensibility* (Philadelphia: University of Pennsylvania Press, 2006); Sarah Rivett, *The Science of the Soul in Colonial New England* (Chapel Hill: University of North Carolina Press, 2011).

11. Samuel Moyn and Andrew Sartori, eds. *Global Intellectual History* (New York: Columbia University Press, 2013), 5.

12. Ibid.

13. Panu Minkkinen, *Thinking without Desire: A First Philosophy of Law* (Portland, OR: Hart, 1999).

14. Seneca, *De otio* 4, quoted in Malcolm Schofield, *The Stoic Idea of the City* (Chicago: University of Chicago Press, 1991), 93.

15. See Bradin Cormack, *A Power to Do Justice: Jurisdiction, English Literature, and the Rise of Common Law* (Chicago: University of Chicago Press, 2007), 8, for an analysis of how jurisdiction—the law's central operation—works in this way.

16. Abram Van Engen, *Sympathetic Puritans: Calvinist Fellow Feeling in Early New England* (New York: Oxford University Press, 2015), 3.

17. For the excellent scholarship on the common law see, e.g., George Lee Haskins, *Law and Authority in Early Massachusetts: A Study in Tradition and Design* (New York: Macmillan, 1960).

18. See, for example, Richard Ross, "The Legal Past of Early New England: Notes for the Study of Law, Legal Culture, and Intellectual History," *William and Mary Quarterly* 50 (1993): 28–41; and Peter Hoffer, *Law and People in Colonial America* (Baltimore, MD: Johns Hopkins University Press, 1992). See also Christopher L. Tomlins and Bruce H. Mann, eds., *The Many Legalities of America* (Chapel Hill: University of North Carolina Press, 2001), for an invaluable approach to law in the early period that reminds us, among other things, of its many threads, including Indian law, Hebrew law, and charity law, to name just a few. See also William Nelson, *The Common Law in Colonial America*, vol. 1: *The Chesapeake and New England 1607–1660* (New York: Oxford University Press, 2008) for a reminder that the various colonies from Maryland to Virginia to those in New England made very different law and followed very different legal agendas, thus providing a welcome corrective to earlier, more uniform accounts.

19. As William Nelson points out, the vast majority of scholarship on the early American legal history is devoted to the common law's reception, *Common Law in Colonial America*, 3–4.

20. On civil law in early modern England, see Brian P. Levack, *The Civil Lawyers in England, 1603–41: A Political Study* (Oxford: Clarendon Press, 1973). The most comprehensive work on the civil law in seventeenth-century England is the four-part series by Daniel Coquillette in the *Buffalo Law Review*. Daniel R. Coquillette, "Legal Ideology and Incorporation I: The English Civilian Writers, 1523–1607," *Boston University Law Review* 61, no. 1 (1981): 1–89, 39–49; "Legal Ideology and Incorporation II: Sir Thomas Ridley, Charles Molloy, and the Literary Battle for the Law Merchant, 1607–1676," *Boston. University Law Review* 61 (1981): 315–71; "Ideology and Incorporation III: Reason Regulated—The Post-Restoration English Civilians, 1653–1735," *Boston University Law Review* 67 (1987): 289–361; "Legal Ideology and Incorporation IV: The Nature of Civilian Influence on Modern Anglo-American Commercial Law," *Boston University Law Review* 67 (1987): 877–970.

21. See Edwin D. Dickinson, "The Law of Nations as Part of the National Law of the United States," *University of Pennsylvania Law Review* 101 (1952): 26–56; and Stewart Jay, "The Status of the Law of Nations in Early American Law," *Vanderbilt Law Review* 42, no. 3 (1989): 819–50. Both of these articles call for recognition of the law of nations in American law only as early as the late eighteenth century.

22. See Jeffrey Glover, *Paper Sovereigns: Anglo-Native Treaties and the Law of Nations, 1604–1664* (Philadelphia: University of Pennsylvania Press, 2014).

23. Max Farrand, "Introduction," *The Laws and Liberties of Massachusetts* (1648; repr., Cambridge, MA: Harvard University Press), 1029, vii.

24. See, for example, the discussion about Indian rights as understood by the Puritans in Stuart Banner, *How the Indians Lost Their Land: Law and Power on the Frontier* (Cambridge, MA: Harvard University Press, 2005), 16.

25. Roger Williams, *The Complete Writings Roger Williams* (New York: Russell and Russell, 1963), 1:105.

26. See David Kennedy, "Primitive Legal Scholarship," *Harvard International Law Journal* 27, no. 1 (1986), 1–98, 6.

27. Samuel Rutherford, "Lex, Rex, or the Law and the Prince: A dispute for the just prerogative of king and people.... With a scripturall confutation of the ruinous grounds of W. Barclay, H. Grotius, H. Arnisaeus, Ant. de Domi. P. Bishop of Spalato, and of other late anti-magistratical royalists; as, the author of Ossorianum, D. Fern, E. Symmons, the doctors of Aberdeen, &c. In XLIV. questions" (London: Printed for Iohn Field, 1644).

28. Peterson, "Theopolis Americana," 353.

29. See Timothy Hampton, *Fictions of Embassy: Literature and Diplomacy in Early Modern Europe* (Ithaca, NY: Cornell University Press, 2009) for an account of this literature.

30. See also Polly J. Price, "Natural Law and Birthright Citizenship in Calvin's Case (1608)," *Yale Journal of Law and the Humanities* 9, no. 1 (1997): 73–146.

31. Foster, *The Long Argument*, 234, 244.

32. See Owen Stanwood, *The Empire Reformed: English America in the Age of the Glorious Revolution* (Philadelphia: University of Pennsylvania Press, 2011).

33. Mather does refer to them this way, but that is not the pervasive take away.

34. Cotton Mather, *India Christiana* (Boston, 1721), 56.

35. Daniel Levy and Natan Sznaider, "Memory Unbound: The Holocaust and the Formation of Cosmopolitan Memory," *European Journal of Social Theory* 5, no. 1 (2002): 87–106, 92.

36. We are, as Saskia Sassen has put it, "living through an epochal transformation" in which "global-level institutions and processes" are having a "transformative effect." The nation, Sassen notes, is becoming "denationalized," while the corporation, often thought to be one of the pillars of the nation, becomes more global with each passing day. More pertinent still to the cosmopolitan is the mandate brought about by this state of affairs to think through new ways of assembling and governing social orders in terms of the world as a whole. Saskia Sassen, *Territory, Authority, Rights* (Princeton, NJ: Princeton University Press, 2006), 1.

Chapter 1

1. Hedley Bull, *The Anarchical Society: A Study of Order in World Politics* (New York: Columbia University Press, 1977), 1.

2. Antonio Cassese, "States: Rise and Decline of the Primary Subjects of the International Community," in *The Oxford Handbook of International Law*, ed. Bardo Fassbender and Anne Peters (Oxford: Oxford University Press, 2012), 51.

3. Olaf Asbach and Peter Schröder, eds. *War, the State, and International Law in Seventeenth-Century Europe* (Burlington, VT: Ashgate, 2010), 5.

4. Kalevi J. Holsti, *Peace and War: Armed Conflicts and International Order* (Cambridge: Cambridge University Press, 1991), 39.

5. Immanuel Wallerstein, *World-Systems Analysis: An Introduction* (Durham, NC: Duke University Press, 2004), 54–55.

6. David Held, *Cosmopolitanism: Ideals and Realities* (Cambridge: Polity, 2010), 96.

7. There has been considerable controversy about the extent to which the early law of nations theorists could be said to have considered the individual "as a source of concern," as I put it here. In arguing for the importance of human rights in international law after World War II, for example, Hersch Lauterpacht attributed this early concern to the Grotian tradition, but he was harshly criticized by his contemporaries who believed there was no such consideration in Grotius's thought.

8. See Francis J. Bremer, *Lay Empowerment and the Development of Puritanism* (New York: Palgrave Macmillan, 2015).

9. Alberico Gentili, *De jure belli libri tres*, Book III, trans. John C. Rolfe (Oxford: Clarendon Press, 1933), 373.

10. Hugo Grotius, *The Rights of War and Peace*, Book I, ed. Richard Tuck (Indianapolis: Liberty Fund, 2005), 240.

11. For more on this, see Wilhelm G. Grewe, *The Epochs of International Law*, trans. Michael Byers (Berlin: Walter de Gruyter, 200), 320–21ff.

12. Mark Peterson, "Theopolis Americana: The City-State of Boston, the Republic of Letters, and the Protestant International, 1689–1739," in *Soundings in Atlantic History: Latent Structures and Intellectual Currents, 1500–1825*, ed. Bernard Bailyn (Cambridge, MA: Harvard University Press, 2009), 331.

13. Cicero, *De Republica* III, xxii, quoted in Alexander Passerin d'Entreves, *Natural Law: An Introduction to Legal Philosophy* (New Brunswick, NJ: Transaction, 1994), 25.

14. Ibid.

15. James Brown Scott, ed. *Selections from Three Works of Francisco Suarez*, vol. 2 of *The Classics of International Law* (Oxford: Clarendon Press; London: Humphrey Milford, 1944), 348–49.

16. Bruce Robbins, *Feeling Global: Internationalism in Distress* (New York: New York University Press, 1999), 75.

17. Hugo Grotius, *Commentary on the Law of Prize and Booty* (Indianapolis, IN: Liberty Fund, 2006), 434.

18. Grotius, *The Rights of War and Peace*, 1:97.

19. For more on the Ottomans conquests in this area, see Gábor Ágoston, "Ottoman Conquest and the Ottoman Military Frontier in Hungary," in *A Millennium of Hungarian Military History*, ed. Béla Király and László Veszprémy (Boulder, CO: Atlantic Research and Publications, 2002), 85–110.

20. On diplomats as being more like spies than negotiators, see Jeremy Black, *A History of Diplomacy* (London: Reaktion Books, 2010), 59.

21. See Timothy Hampton, *Fictions of Embassy: Literature and Diplomacy in Early Modern Europe* (Ithaca, NY: Cornell University Press, 2009) for an account of this literature.

22. Richard Knolles, *The Turkish History, from the Original of that Nation, to the Growth of the Ottoman Empire* (London: Printed for Jonathan Robinson, 1687); "The Sum of The Nine Articles Lately Ratified And Mutually Counterchanged, Between The Ottoman Emperor And Count Emerich Techli, Leader Of The Hungarian Malcontents" (Printed 1683; found in the Mather Library holdings at the American Antiquarian Society).

23. Nicholas Onuf, "'Tainted by Contingency': Retelling the Story of International Law," in *Reframing the International: Law, Culture, Politics*, ed. Richard Falk, R. B. J. Walker, and Lester Ruiz (New York: Routledge, 2013), 41.

24. See Kennedy, "Primitive Legal Scholarship," *Harvard International Law Journal* 27, no. 1 (1986): 1–98, 12.

25. Arthur Nussbaum, *A Concise History of the Law of Nations* (New York: Macmillan, 1947), 90–91.

26. See Richard Rorty, "The Unpatriotic Academy," *New York Times*, February 13, 1994. See also Rorty, "Justice as a Larger Loyalty," in *Cosmopolitics*, ed. Cheah and Robbins, 45–58 for a view of patriotism that comports with cosmopolitanism; and Robbins, *Feeling Global*, 127–45.

27. Nussbaum, "Patriotism and Cosmopolitanism," 14.

28. Kwame Anthony Appiah, "Cosmopolitan Patriots," in *For Love of Country?* 26.

29. Grotius, *The Rights of War and Peace*, 1:93.

30. See, for example, Daniel J. Elazar, *The Covenant Tradition in Politics*, vols. 1–3 (New Brunswick, NJ: Transaction, 1996).

31. David Held's *Global Covenant: The Social Democratic Alternative to the Washington Consensus* (Malden, MA: Polity Press, 2004) is the only book I know to use the word covenant with reference to a cosmopolitan order. Held describes several new models for world governance, but he does not elaborate on the religious connotations of the covenant in his title.

32. Grotius continues: "I say *of many* because there is scarce any Right can be found, except that of Nature...common to all Nations." Grotius, *The Rights of War and Peace*, 1:162–63.

33. See Randall Lesaffer, "The Grotian Tradition Revisited: Change and Continuity in the History of International Law," *British Yearbook of International Law* 73, no. 1 (2003): 103–39, for more on the depersonalization.

34. "Treaty of the Pyrenees, Isle of the Pheasants, November 7, 1659," in *Major Peace Treaties of Modern History, 1648–1967*, vol. 1, ed. Fred L. Israel (Philadelphia: Chelsea House, 2002), 53.

35. Alberico Gentili, *De jure belli libri tres*, Book I, trans. John C. Rolfe (Oxford: Clarendon Press, 1933), 67.

36. Robbins, "Introduction, Part I: Actually Existing Cosmopolitanism," in *Cosmopolitics*, 7.

37. Grotius, *The Rights of War and Peace*, 1:79–81.

38. See Eric Nelson, *The Hebrew Republic: Jewish Sources and the Transformation of European Political Thought* (Cambridge, MA: Harvard University Press, 2011).

39. Grotius, *Commentary on the Law of Prize and Booty*, 434.

40. Jason Rosenblatt, *Renaissance England's Chief Rabbi: John Selden* (Oxford: Oxford University Press, 2006), 161–62.

41. John Selden, *De jure naturali*, 3.6, 302, quoted in ibid., 151 (my translation).

42. Grotius, *The Rights of War and Peace*, 1:113.

43. Grotius, *The Rights of War and Peace*, Book II, ed. Richard Tuck (Indianapolis, IN: Liberty Fund, 2005), 849.

44. See the discussion of such pietistic practices in Michael P. Winship, *Seers of God: Puritan Providentialism in the Restoration and Early Enlightenment* (Baltimore, MD: John Hopkins University Press, 1996), 88.

45. On the never-ending paradox of fighting a just war unjustly or an unjust war justly see Michael Walzer, *Just and Unjust Wars: A Moral Argument with Historical Illustrations* (New York: Basic Books, 2006).

46. Gentili, *De jure belli libri tres*, 1:9.

47. This is from *The Rights of War and Peace*, trans. Francis Kelsey (Oxford: Oxford University Press, 1925), 57.

48. Grotius, *The Rights of War and Peace*, Book III, ed. Richard Tuck (Indianapolis: Liberty Fund, 2005), 1745.

49. Ibid., 1:250.

50. Ibid., 3:1268.

51. Ibid., 3:1267.

52. Seyla Benhabib, *Another Cosmopolitanism* (Oxford: Oxford University Press, 2006), 23.

53. Noah Feldman, "Cosmopolitan Law?" *Yale Law Journal* 116, no. 5 (2007): 1022–71, 1024 (2007).

54. Pheng Cheah, "Introduction Part II: The Cosmopolitical—Today," in *Cosmopolitics*, 21.

55. Sheldon Pollock, Homi K. Bhabha, Carol A. Breckenridge, and Dipesh Chakrabarty, eds., *Cosmopolitanism* (Durham, NC: Duke University Press, 2002), 3.

56. Gentili, *De jure belli libri tres*, 1:68–69.

57. Grotius, *The Rights of War and Peace*, 1:385.

58. Ibid., 1:386.

59. Ibid., 2:671.

60. Ibid., 2:672.

Chapter 2

1. It would be difficult to identify a starting or ending point for the Puritans' covenantal sermons. Even after the turn of the eighteenth century, they continued to write obsessively about the covenant. What I hope to show here is that for a period of about thirty years—years that coincided with a great deal of political and legal turmoil—they turned to a different, more cosmopolitan understanding of a covenant that both before and after this period revolved largely around internal affairs.

2. See generally, Elazar, *Covenant and Commonwealth: From Christian Separation through the Protestant Reformation, The Covenant Tradition in Politics*, vol. 2 (New Brunswick, NJ: Transaction, 1996).

3. See Robert N. Bellah, *The Broken Covenant: American Civil Religion in Time of Trial* (Chicago: University of Chicago Press, 1992).

4. For a general introduction to the Antinomian crisis, see Michael P. Winship. *The Times and Trials of Anne Hutchinson: Puritans Divided* (Lawrence: University Press of Kansas, 2005); and David D. Hall, ed., *The Antinomian Controversy, 1636–1638: A Documentary History* (Durham, NC: Duke University Press, 1990); for an early account of the Halfway Covenant crisis, see Robert Pope, *The Half-Way Covenant: Church Membership in Puritan New England* (Princeton, NJ: Princeton University Press, 1969).

5. The so-called corporate covenant was of concern to earlier generations of Puritans as well, but not necessarily in the social, political, and cultural sense in which I invoke it here. E. Brooks Holifield, for example, argues for a general turn toward corporatism in the Puritans' use of "covenantal themes as a defense against Baptist attacks on infant baptism" as early as the 1640s. Holifield's sense of the corporate, however, is linked to the Puritans' increasing reliance on sacramentalism and its consequences for the shift from an inner, purely experiential faith to more publicly visible signs of grace. E. Brooks Holifield, *The Covenant Sealed: The Development of Puritan Sacramental Theology in Old and New England, 1570–1720* (New Haven, CT: Yale University Press, 1974), ix, 226–27.

6. Increase Mather, "Renewal of Covenant the Great Duty Incumbent on Decaying or Distressed Churches," 8, 9.

7. See Stephen Foster, *The Long Argument: English Puritanism and the Shaping of New England Culture, 1570–1700* (Chapel Hill: University of North Carolina Press, 1991), 228; and David D. Hall, *The Faithful Shepherd: A History of the New England Ministry in the Seventeenth Century* (Chapel Hill: University of North Carolina Press 1972), 245, which talks about the covenant's potential for forging a coalition politics, but still focuses on the internal consolidation of identity and power it provides.

8. Harry Stout, *The New England Soul: Preaching and Religious Culture in Colonial New England* (New York: Oxford University Press, 1986), 80.

9. Samuel Willard devoted himself almost exclusively between 1680 and 1693 to the subject of the covenant, dispelling mistakes about it and providing a detailed taxonomy for its many varieties. His many covenant sermons make up most of the material discussed in this chapter.

10. See Shabtai Rosenne, "The Influence of Judaism on the Development of International Law: A Preliminary Assessment," *Nederlands Tijdschrift Voor Internationaal Recht*, vol. 5 (1958): 125. See also Eric Nelson, *The Hebrew Republic: Jewish Sources and the Transformation of European Political Thought* (Cambridge, MA: Harvard University Press, 2011), 16.

11. See, for example, Achsah Guibbory, *Christian Identity, Jews, and Israel in Seventeenth-Century England* (Oxford: Oxford University Press, 2010); Gordon Schochet, Fania Oz Salberger, and Meirav Jones, eds., *Political Hebraism: Judaic Sources in Early Modern Political Thought* (Jerusalem: Shalem Press, 2008); Allison P. Coudert and Jeffrey S. Shoulson, eds., *Hebraica Veritas?: Christian Hebraists and the Study of Judaism in Early Modern England* (Philadelphia: University of Pennsylvania Press, 2004); and Nelson, *The Hebrew Republic.*

12. Nelson, *The Hebrew Republic*, 126.

13. Although it's not clear whether Grotius could read biblical Hebrew with any facility, he almost certainly made use of the popular Latin translations of biblical and Talmudic

commentary by Constantijn L'Empereur van Oppijck in the early seventeenth century. See Phyllis S. Lachs, "Grotius's Use of Jewish Sources," *Renaissance Quarterly* 40, no. 2 (1977): 181–200.

14. See Richard Tuck, *Philosophy and Government, 1572–1651* (Cambridge: Cambridge University Press, 1993), 154–221 for more on the relationship between Grotius and Selden.

15. Hugo Grotius, *The Rights of War and Peace*, Book I, XVI (Indianapolis, IN: Liberty Fund, 2005), 166–69.

16. Theoretically, the discovery of shared moral rules in the natural or precivil state of humankind provided a basis for relationships among human beings anywhere in the world as well. See Jason P. Rosenblatt, *Renaissance England's Chief Rabbi: John Selden* (Oxford: Oxford University Press, 2006), 137.

17. Abraham Berkowitz, "John Selden and the Biblical Origins of the Modern International Political System," *Jewish Political Studies Review* 6, no. 1 (1994): 27–47.

18. For the connection between the Noahide laws and *The Body of Liberties*, see those sections of the *Body of Liberties*, especially Articles 89–91, which pertain to the "liberties of forreiners and strangers."

19. Increase Mather, "To the Church in Dorchester," Preface to "Renewal of Covenant the Great Duty Incumbent on Decaying or Distressed Churches" (Boston: Printed by J.F. for Henry Phillips, 1677), A3. As if to emphasize their importance, Increase Mather repeated these same lines three years later in "Returning unto God the Great Concernment of a Covenant People" (Boston: Printed by John Foster, 1680), 17.

20. Guibbory, *Christian Identity, Jews, and Israel in Seventeenth-Century England*, 13.

21. David Novak, *The Jewish Social Contract: An Essay in Political Theology* (Princeton, NJ: Princeton University Press, 2009), 34.

22. Bernard M. Levinson, "The Sinai Covenant: The Argument of Revelation," in *The Jewish Political Tradition:* Vol. 1 of *Authority*, ed. Michael Walzer, Menachem Lorberbaum, and Noam J. Zohar (New Haven, CT: Yale University Press, 2000), 27.

23. Bruce Robbins, "Introduction, Part I: Actually Existing Cosmopolitanisms," in *Cosmopolitics: Thinking and Feeling Beyond the Nation*, ed., Pheng Cheah and Bruce Robbins (Minneapolis: University of Minnesota Press, 1998), 3.

24. David Armitage, *Foundations of Modern International Thought* (Cambridge: Cambridge University Press, 2013), 10.

25. See Ibid., 86–87.

26. See Meredith G. Kline, *Treaty of the Great King: The Covenant Structure of Deuteronomy, Studies and Commentary* (Eugene, OR: Wipf and Stock, 1963) for a detailed examination of this resemblance.

27. Ibid.

28. Cotton Mather, "The Serviceable Man" (Boston: Printed by Samuel Green for Joseph Browning, 1690), A3.

29. Jonathan Mitchel, "Nehemiah on the Wall in Troublesom [*sic*] Times" (Cambridge: Printed by S.G. and M.J., 1671), 4.

30. Joseph Rowlandson, "The Possibility of God's Forsaking a People" (Boston: Printed for John Ratcliffe and John Griffin, 1682), 5.

31. Todd Gitlin and Liel Liebovitz, *The Chosen Peoples: America, Israel, and the Ordeals of Divine Election* (New York: Simon and Schuster, 2010), 49.

32. David Scobey uses the term in a different sense, to describe the general conflict in the Halfway Covenant crisis. See David M. Scobey, "Revising the Errand: New

England's Ways and the Puritan Sense of the Past," *William and Mary Quarterly* 41, no. 1 (1984): 3–31.

33. Rowlandson, "The Possibility of God's Forsaking a People," 11.

34. Immanuel Kant, "Perpetual Peace: A Philosophical Sketch," in *Political Writings,* ed. H. S. Reiss (Cambridge: Cambridge University Press, 2011), 107–108.

35. Mather, "The Serviceable Man," 48.

36. The treaty-like nature of the covenant has been noted before, although largely only in formal terms. Scholars of the ancient Near East have long pointed to the formal resemblance between the Sinaitic covenant and the many covenants made by Hittite and Ugaritic princes with vassal nations. Delbert Hillers, for example, makes a convincing case that the Ten Commandments and the idea of the covenant as described in Exodus 20 and later in Joshua 24 closely resemble the structure of many of these treaty documents from their preamble to the listing of laws or conditions to the blessing and curse that appear at the end. See Delbert Hillers, *Covenant: The History of a Biblical Idea* (Baltimore, MD: Johns Hopkins University Press, 1969), 53. Still others have offered more extended analogies. Daniel Elazar, for example, has claimed that the first four books of the Torah can be seen as a covenant, treaty, or constitutional document with a long historic introduction (Genesis), a preamble, covenant, fundamental set of laws (Exodus and Leviticus), and a historical epilogue (Numbers). See Elazar, *Covenant and Polity in Biblical Israel.* George Mendenhall also makes the connection between the Hebrew covenant and the Near Eastern covenants before it. See George Mendenhall, "Covenant Forms in Israelite Tradition," *Biblical Archaeologist* 17, no. 3 (1955): 55–58. The claim I make for their resemblance here, however, goes far beyond the formal features to include the purposes to which both were put and the way they served for the ancient Jews as well as for the Puritans as documents of foreign policy.

37. The list is long, but a few examples, including the Treaty of the Pyrénées between France and Spain (1659), the Treaty of Aix-la-Chapelle between France and Spain (1668), the Treaty of Nijmegen between France and Holland (1678), the Treaty of Ryswick between Great Britain and France (1697), and the Treaty of Utrecht between Great Britain, France, and Ireland (1713), provide a preliminary sense of how pervasive treaty making was in this period.

38. For more on the importance of the Scottish covenanters, see Charles J. Guthrie, "The Solemn League and Covenant of the Three Kingdoms of England, Scotland, and Ireland," *Scottish Historical Review* 15, no. 60 (1918): 292–309; John D. Ford, "The Lawful Bonds of Scottish Society: The Five Articles of Perth, The Negative Confession and the National Covenant," *Historical Journal* 37, no. 1 (1994): 45–64; Edward Vallance, "'An Holy and Sacramentall Paction': Federal Theology and the Solemn League and Covenant in England," *English Historical Review* 116, no. 465 (2001): 50–75; and Ian B. Cowan, *The Scottish Covenanters, 1660–88* (Durrington, UK: Littlehampton Book Services, 1976).

39. Mather, "The Serviceable Man," 48–49.

40. As Jeffrey Glover and others have pointed out, the Puritans had used models drawn from international treaties to make peace with the Indians when the hostilities concerned the Indians in their role as independent foreign nations. In this instance, however, because the Puritans believed the Indians to be working in France's service, the treaty model is the covenant itself. See Glover, *Paper Sovereigns: Anglo-Native Treaties and the Law of Nations, 1604–1664* (Philadelphia: University of Pennsylvania Press, 2014).

41. The temporality I point to here is not to be confused with the religious use of the term to signify the worldly as opposed to spiritual relevance of the covenant itself.

42. Aihwa Ong, *Flexible Citizenship: The Cultural Logics of Transnationality* (Durham, NC: Duke University Press, 1999).

43. Samuel Willard, "The Duty of a People Who have Renewed their Covenant" (Boston: Printed by John Foster, 1680), 4.

44. Ibid., 6–7.

45. Mather, "The Serviceable Man," 1–2.

46. Increase Mather refers to the *brit* in the context of the covenant in his sermon, "Renewal of Covenant the Great Duty Incumbent on Decaying or Distressed Churches," 2.

47. Elazar, *Covenant and Polity in Biblical Israel*, 10. See also Regina W. Schwartz, *The Curse of Cain: The Violent Legacy of Monotheism* (Chicago: University of Chicago Press, 1998), for more about the *brit*.

48. Elazar, *Covenant and Polity in Biblical Israel*, 81.

49. See Increase Mather, "Renewal of Covenant the Great Duty Incumbent on Decaying or Distressed Churches," 3, 5; and Increase Mather, "Returning unto God the Great Concernment of a Covenant People," A3.

50. Willard, "The Duty of a People That Have Renewed their Covenant" (Boston: Printed by John Foster, 1680), 3.

51. Ibid., 1–2.

52. See Fred L. Israel, ed., *Major Peace Treaties of Modern History*, vol. 1 (Philadelphia: Chelsea House, 2002), 123. Similar provisions were to be found in the treaties of Ryswick and Utrecht as well. Ibid., 149; 177–239.

53. Randall Lesaffer, "Peace Treaties and the Formation of International Law," in Bardo Fassbender and Anne Peters, ed. *The Oxford Handbook of The History of International Law* (Oxford: Oxford University Press, 2012), 71–94, 77.

54. Samuel Willard, "Israel's True Safety" (Boston: Printed by B. Green for Samuel Phillips, 1704), 9.

55. Samuel Willard, "Covenant-Keeping," 51–52.

56. Ibid., 54.

57. Jeremy Black, *A History of Diplomacy* (London: Reaktion Books, 2010), 65.

Chapter 3

1. See Reiner Smolinski, "Israel Redivivus: The Eschatological Limits of Puritan Typology in New England," *New England Quarterly* 63, no. 3 (1990): 357–95.

2. Ibid., 377. Smolinski argues, contrary to scholars such as Sacvan Bercovitch and Mason Lowance, while the Puritans may have seen themselves as the spiritual heirs to the Jews, they never saw themselves as the literal reincarnation of the Jews who remained central to the millennialist story.

3. Zygmunt Bauman describes a similar shift in the context of Jewish messianism. See Zygmunt Bauman, "Exit Visas and Entry Tickets: Paradoxes of Jewish Assimilation," *Telos* 77 (1988).

4. Alberico Gentili, *De jure belli libri tres*, trans. John C. Rolfe (Oxford: Clarendon Press, 1933), 360–40.

5. See Meredith Marie Neuman, *Jeremiah's Scribes: Creating Sermon Literature in Puritan New England* (Philadelphia: University of Pennsylvania Press, 2013) for a description of how the ideas in the sermons delivered in the metropolis by the Puritan elite often made

their way through the notes taken by parishioners into the sermons of less educated and less imaginative ministers in smaller towns and villages throughout New England.

6. Cotton Mather, *Things to Be Look'd For: Discourses on the glorious characters, with conjectures on the speedy approaches of that state, which is reserved for the church of God in the latter dayes: Together with an inculcation of several duties, which the undoubted characters and approaches of that state, invite us unto: delivered unto the artillery company of the Massachusets colony: New England; at their election of officers, for the year* (Cambridge, MA: Samuel Green, 1691), 5.

7. Ibid., 7–8.

8. Ibid., 14.

9. Reiner Smolinski, ed., *The Threefold Paradise of Cotton Mather: An Edition of "Triparadisus"* (Athens: University of Georgia Press, 1995), 153.

10. See Smolinski, "Israel Redivivus," 357–95, for an argument that takes as its object earlier scholarly claims that New England had become the New Jerusalem for the Puritans.

11. This was a popular belief among the Fifth Monarchy Men, in particular. See J. F. Maclear, "New England and the Fifth Monarchy: The Quest for the Millennium in Early American Puritanism," *William and Mary Quarterly* 32, no. 2 (1975): 223–60, 237 for more explanation.

12. Quoted in Reiner Smolinski, ed., *The Kingdom, the Power & the Glory: The Millennial Impulse in Early American Literature* (Dubuque, IA: Kendall/Hunt, 1998), x.

13. On the fortunes of the millennium in this period, see Christopher Hill, *Antichrist in Seventeenth-Century England* (London: Oxford University Press, 1971). See also James Holstun, *A Rational Millennium: Puritan Utopias of Seventeenth-Century England and America* (New York: Oxford University Press, 1987).

14. See Kenneth Silverman, *The Life and Times of Cotton Mather* (New York: Harper-Collins, 1984), 323–33. See also Robert Middlekauf, *The Mathers: Three Generations of Puritan Intellectuals, 1596–1728* (New York: Oxford University Press, 1971), 328–29, and N. H. Keeble, *The Literary Culture of Non-Conformity in Later Seventeenth-Century England* (Athens: University of Georgia Press, 1987), 11.

15. Jeffrey Scott Mares, ed., *Cotton Mather's "Problema Theologicum": An Authoritative Edition* (Worcester, MA: American Antiquarian Society, 1994), 412.

16. Cotton Mather, *Theopolis Americana: An Essay on the Golden Street of the Holy City* (1710), ed. Reiner Smolinski, Electronic Texts in American Studies 29 (Lincoln: University of Nebraska, DigitalCommons@University of Nebraska), 48.

17. Ibid., 33

18. Smolinski, *The Threefold Paradise of Cotton Mather*, 33.

19. Ibid., 271

20. Ibid., 245.

21. Gentili, *De jure belli libri tres*, 17.

22. Ibid.

23. Timothy Marr, *The Cultural Roots of American Islamicism* (Cambridge: Cambridge University Press, 2006), 89.

24. Ibid., 8.

25. Ibid., 93.

26. Smolinski, *The Threefold Paradise of Cotton Mather*, 21–37.

27. Mather, *Things to Be Look'd For*, 31.

28. Scholars have mined the Barbary Coast captivity narratives for their mixed portraits of the Turks, who generally emerge as barbarians with a largely unexplained tolerance for cultural and religious difference. These include Adrian Tinniswood, *Pirates of Barbary: Corsairs, Conquests and Captivity in the Seventeenth-Century Mediterranean* (New York: Riverhead, 2010); Daniel Vitkus, ed., *Piracy, Slavery, and Redemption* (New York: Columbia University Press, 2001; and Paul Baepler, "The Barbary Captivity Narrative in Early America," *Early American Literature* 30, no.2 (1995): 95–120.

29. Mares, ed., *Cotton Mather's "Problema Theologicum,"* 371–72.

30. Ibid., 403

31. See Smolinski, *The Threefold Paradise of Cotton Mather*, 69–74.

32. James Franklin, *New-England Courant*, no. 8, September 18–25, 1721, col. 1–2, 1.

33. Mather, *Things to Be Look'd For*, 46.

34. See Jeffrey K. Jue, *Heaven upon Earth: Joseph Mede (1586–1638) and the Legacy of Millenarianism* (Dordrecht: Spring, 2006), 152.

35. See Ernestine Van Der Wall, "Between Grotius and Cocceius: The 'Theologia Prophetica' of Campegius Vitringa (1659–1722)," in *Hugo Grotius, Theologian: Essays in Honor of G.H.M. Posthumus Meyjes*, ed. Henk J. M. Nellen and Edwin Rabbie (Leiden: E. J. Brill, 1994), 199.

36. Increase Mather, *The Mystery of Israel's Salvation* (London: Printed for John Allen, 1669), 54–55.

37. Mares, ed., *Cotton Mather's "Problema Theologicum,"* 371.

38. Ibid., 358.

39. Fred L. Israel, ed., *Major Peace Treaties of Modern History, 1648–1967*, vol. 1 (Philadelphia: Chelsea House, 2002), 139, 149.

40. See A. C. Wood, "The English Embassy at Constantinople, 1660–1762," *English Historical Review* 40, no. 160 (1925): 533–61, 545.

41. Mather, *Things to Be Look'd For*, 32

42. Cotton Mather, *Selected Letters of Cotton Mather*, ed. Kenneth Silverman (Baton Rouge: Louisiana State University Press, 1971).

43. Hugo Grotius, *The Rights of War and Peace*, Book 3 (Indianapolis, IN: Liberty Fund, 2005), 1568.

44. There were admittedly several utopian theories during the second half of the seventeenth and into the early eighteenth century that contemplated the kind of peace that presupposed a cosmopolis or virtual world community, including those by William Penn in 1693 and Charles Francois Irénée Castel de Saint-Pierre in 1712, but it wasn't until the Peace of Utrecht in 1712 that an interest emerged in thinking through a peace that might prevent the recurrence of war. See, generally, F. H. Hinsley, *Power and the Pursuit of Peace: Theory and Practice in the History of Relations between States* (Cambridge: Cambridge University Press, 1963).

45. Smolinski, ed., *The Threefold Paradise of Cotton Mather*, 339.

46. Mather, *Things to Be Look'd For*, 15.

47. Ibid., 31.

48. Ibid., 22.

49. Hugo Grotius, *The Rights of War and Peace*, Book 2 (Indianapolis, IN: Liberty Fund, 2005), 912.

50. Abraham de Wicquefort, *The Embassador and His Function*, trans. Mr. D I (London: Printed for Bernard Lintott, 1716), 246.

51. Daniel Goffman and Virginia Aksan, eds., *The Early Modern Ottomans: Remapping the Empire* (Cambridge: Cambridge University Press, 2007), 65.

52. In this argument, Goffman takes issue with Garrett Mattingly's earlier assertion that diplomacy began with the Italians. See Garret Mattingly, *Renaissance Diplomacy* (Baltimore: Penguin Books, 1964).

53. Viorel Panaite, *The Ottoman Law of War and Peace* (New York: Columbia University Press, 200), 31.

54. Jeremy Black, *A History of Diplomacy* (London: Reaktion Books, 2010), 72–79.

55. Mather, *Things to Be Look'd For*, 75.

56. Ibid., 80.

57. Ibid., 72.

58. Ibid., 49.

59. Ibid., 77.

60. Israel, *Major Peace Treaties of Modern History, 1648–1967*, 8.

Chapter 4

1. Edward Randolph arrested Increase Mather twice to prevent him from traveling to England to appeal to James II, who though Catholic had issued a bill for toleration. See Kenneth Silverman, *The Life and Times of Cotton Mather* (New York: Harper and Row, 1984), 64–65, 72.

2. T. H. Breen, *Character of a Good Ruler: A Study of Puritan Political Ideas in New England, 1630–1730* (New York: ACLS Humanities E-Book, 2008), 164.

3. Silverman, *The Life and Times of Cotton Mather*, 70.

4. David Levin, "Cotton Mather's Declaration of Gentlemen and Thomas Jefferson's Declaration of Independence," *New England Quarterly* 50, no. 3 (1977): 509–14, 512.

5. Jack M. Sosin, *English America and Imperial Inconstancy: The Rise of Provincial Autonomy, 1696–1715* (Lincoln: University of Nebraska Press, 1985), 7.

6. See Richard Firth Green, *A Crisis of Truth: Literature and Law in Ricardian England* (Philadelphia: University of Pennsylvania Press, 2002), for more on this topic.

7. See Barbara J. Shapiro, "Law and Science in Seventeenth-Century England," *Stanford Law Review* 21, no. 4 (1969): 727–66, 728 for more on this topic. See also Steven Shapin, *A Social History of Truth: Civility and Science in Seventeenth-Century England* (Chicago: University of Chicago Press, 1995) for a counter-argument about the residual influence of credibility among witnesses.

8. See Barbara J. Shapiro, *A Culture of Fact: England, 1550–1720* (Ithaca, NY: Cornell University Press, 203), 137.

9. Andros filed several reports, including his "Charges against the Government" (1689) in William Henry Whitmore, ed., *The Andros Tracts* (Boston: The Prince Society, 1874), 31–33. After he was released from jail in Boston, he returned to England and filed his official report entitled "Sir Edmond Andros's Report of his Administration," in ibid., 17–27. For the "loud lie" see Increase Mather, "A Vindication of New-England," in Whitmore, ed., *The Andros Tracts* (Boston: The Prince Society, 1869, rpt, BiblioLife, 2011), 33.

10. Whitmore, *The Andros Tracts* [1869], 32, and Increase Mather, "A Vindication of New-England," 114.

11. Increase Mather, "An Answer of the Massachusetts Agents to Randolph's Account of the Irregular Trade Since the Revolution in New-England," in Whitmore, *The Andros Tracts* [1869], 128–29.

12. Increase Mather et al., "The Present State of New-English Affairs," in Whitmore, *The Andros Tracts* [1869], 15.

13. Sarah Rivett, *The Science of the Soul in Colonial New England* (Chapel Hill: University of North Carolina Press, 2011).

14. Andrea Frisch, *Invention of the Eyewitness: Witnessing and Testimony in Early Modern France* (Chapel Hill: University of North Carolina Press, 2004).

15. Harold J. Berman, "The Origins of Historical Jurisprudence: Coke, Selden, Hale," *Yale Law Journal* 103, no. 7 (1994): 1651–1738, 1728.

16. Shapiro, *A Culture of Fact*, 137.

17. John Locke, *Essay Concerning Human Understanding* (New York: Penguin Classics, 1998), 586.

18. Increase Mather, "A Vindication of New-England," 21.

19. Seth Ward, "A Philosophical Essay," 4th ed. (Oxford, 1667), 101.

20. Shapiro, *A Culture of Fact*, 49.

21. John Endecott, "To the Kings most Excellent Majesty," *Records of the Governor and Company of the Massachusetts Bay of New England, Vol. IV-Part II, 1661–1674*, ed. Nathaniel B. Shurtleff (Boston: From the Press of William White, 1854), 129.

22. "Petition and Address of John Gibson and George Willow," appended to Increase Mather, "A Narrative of the Miseries of New-England," in Whitmore, *The Andros Tracts* [1869], 8–11.

23. A.B., "An Account of the Late Revolutions in New-England; In a Letter" in Whitmore, *The Andros Tracts* [1869], 196.

24. Ibid., 198.

25. Ibid., 192. Original emphasis.

26. John Palmer, "The State of New-England, Impartially Considered, c." (Boston: Samuel Green, 1689; rpt., Ann Arbor, MI: Text Creation Partnership [2007]), 12.

27. Locke, *Essay on Human Understanding*, 109.

28. Justin Stagl acknowledges something similar when he explains, "yet although public and private research, travels and surveys coordinated by academics or ecclesiastic institutions were thus imperfectly interconnected, empirical knowledge of European and extra-European countries and people advanced slowly but continuously during the early modern period. This advancement was at first hardly visible on the intellectual surface but in the Age of Enlightenment, public and private, academic and ecclesiastic research into cultural, social and political reality began to emerge." See Justin Stagl, *A History of Curiosity: The Theory of Travel, 1550–1800* (London: Routledge, 1995), 153.

29. See Arthur Nussbaum, *A Concise History of the Law of Nations* (New York: Macmillan, 1961), 88–92.

30. See Pheng Cheah and Bruce Robbins, eds., *Cosmopolitics: Thinking and Feeling beyond the Nation* (Minneapolis: University of Minnesota Press, 1998), 23.

31. Barbara Shapiro notes that travel accounts were added to historical writings to provide information thought necessary for public life. See Shapiro, *A Culture of Fact*, 65. See also Frisch, *Invention of the Eyewitness*, 81.

32. "The Humble Address of the Publicans of New-England" (London, 1691), in Whitmore, *The Andros Tracts* [1869], 251.

33. For a skeptical account of the authorship and importance of this pamphlet, see Richard R. Johnson, "The Humble Address of the Publicans: A Reassessment," *New England Quarterly* 51, no. 2: 241–49.

34. "The Humble Address," in Whitmore, *The Andros Tracts* [1869], 251.

35. Alain Badiou, *Saint Paul: The Foundations of Universalism* (Stanford, CA: Stanford University Press, 2003), 17.

36. Lennard Davis and Kate Loveman discuss the rise of the historical hoax, the political sham, and the literary forgery, all of which served as the basis for an outpouring of literary works in this period. See Kate Loveman, *Reading Fictions, 1660–1710: Deception in English Political and Literary Culture* (Aldershot, UK: Ashgate, 2008) and Lennard J. Davis, *Factual Fictions: The Origins of the English Novel* (Philadelphia: University of Pennsylvania Press, 1997) for more on this topic.

37. See Justin A. I. Champion, "Legislators, Impostors and the Political Origins of Religion: English Theories of Imposture from Stubbe to Toland," in *Heterdoxy, Spinozism, and Free Thought in Early Eighteenth-Century Europe*, ed. Françoise Charles-Daubert and R. H. Popkin (Vienna: Springer: 1996), 351.

38. "A Full Answer to the Depositions; And to all other the Pretences and Arguments whatsoever, Concerning the Birth of the Prince of Wales" (London: Printed for Simon Burgis, 1689), 6.

39. "The Pretender an Impostor" (London: Printed and Sold by the Booksellers, 1711), 5.

40. Ibid., 6–7

41. Ibid.

42. Michel de Montaigne, *Essays*, trans. John M. Cohen (New York: Penguin, 1993), 30.

43. Joseph Glanvill, "A Blow at Modern Sadducism" (London: Printed for E.C., 1668), 70.

44. "The Pretender an Impostor," 20.

45. Ibid.

46. Ibid., 15.

47. "Declaration of the Freeholders of Suffolk County, 3 May 1689," in "Nicolson and the Council of New York to the Board of Trade, 15 May 1689," in *Documents Relative to the Colonial History of the State of New York*, ed. E. B. O'Callaghan and John Romeyn Broadhead, 15 vols. (Albany, NY, 1853–87), 3:577.

48. A.B., "An Account of the Late Revolutions in New-England," 5.

49. Ibid.

50. Increase Mather, "A Vindication of New-England," in Whitmore, *The Andros Tracts* {1869], 52.

51. A.B., "An Account of the Late Revolutions in New-England," 194.

52. Increase Mather, "A Narrative of the Miseries of New-England," in Whitmore, *The Andros Tracts* [1869], 11.

53. See, e.g., "A Brief Relation of the State of New England," in Whitmore, *The Andros Tracts* [1869], 161 and 194.

54. Increase Mather, "A Vindication of New-England," 34, my emphasis.

55. Thomas Hobbes, *Leviathan* (New York: Penguin, 1982), 297.

56. Sr. J. B. de Rocoles, *The History of Infamous Impostors* (London: Printed for William Cademan, 1683), second unnumbered page.

57. "The Devil of Delphos, or, The Prophets of Baal" (London: Printed for the Author, 1708), 14.

58. Ibid, 48.

59. "The Humble Address," in Whitmore, *The Andros Tracts* [1869], 233.

60. Ibid., 258.

61. Ibid., 253.

62. Ibid., 255
63. Ibid., 239.
64. "The Pretender an Impostor," 15.
65. A.B., "An Account of the Late Revolutions in New-England," 191.
66. Increase Mather, "A Brief Relation of the State of New-England," in Whitmore, *The Andros Tracts* [1869], 160–61.
67. Ibid., 161.
68. Rivett, *The Science of the Soul in Colonial New England*, 224.
69. David D. Hall, *Witch-Hunting in Seventeenth-Century New England: A Documentary History, 1638–1693* (Boston: Northeastern University Press, 1999), 282.
70. Stanwood, *The Empire Reformed: English America in the Age of the Glorious Revolution* (Philadelphia: University of Pennsylvania Press, 2011), 171.

Chapter 5

1. David D. Hall, *The Faithful Shepherd: A History of the New England Ministry in the Seventeenth Century* (Chapel Hill: University of North Carolina Press, 1972), 223.
2. Jan Stievermann, "Cotton Mather and *'Biblia Americana'*—America's First Bible Commentary: General Introduction," in *Cotton Mather and Biblia Americana: Essays in Reappraisal*, ed. Reiner Smolinski and Jan Stievermann (Tubigen: Mohr Siebeck, 2010), 5.
3. Hannah Dawson, *Locke, Language and Early-Modern Philosophy* (Cambridge: Cambridge University Press, 2007), 5.
4. See, for example, Kathleen Genister Roberts and Ronald C. Arnett, eds., *Communication Ethics: Between Cosmopolitanism and Provinciality* (New York: Peter Lang, 2008); Pippa Norris and Ronald Inglehart, *Cosmopolitan Communications: Cultural Diversity in a Globalized World* (Cambridge: Cambridge University Press, 2009).
5. "Cosmopolitans," Appiah writes, "suppose that all cultures have enough overlap in their vocabulary of values to begin a conversation. But they don't suppose, like some universalists, that we could all come to agreement if only we have the same vocabulary." *Cosmopolitanism: Ethics in a World of Strangers*, 57.
6. See especially Ernst Benz, "Ecumenical Relations between Boston Puritanism and German Pietism: Cotton Mather and August Hermann Franke," *Harvard Theological Review* 54, no. 3 (1961): 159–93; Richard F. Lovelace, *The American Pietism of Cotton Mather: Origins of American Evangelicalism* (Eugene, OR: Wipf and Stock, 1979).
7. See Patrick M. Erben, *A Harmony of the Spirits: Translation and the Language of Community in Early Pennsylvania* (Chapel Hill: University of North Carolina, 2012) for an in-depth discussion of how language and Pietism worked in these communities.
8. See, for example, Kristina Bross and Hilary E. Wyss, eds., *Early Native Literacies in New England: A Documentary and Critical Anthology* (Amherst: University of Massachusetts Press, 2008), Matt Cohen, *The Networked Wilderness: Communicating in Early New England* (Minneapolis: University of Minnesota Press; Andrew Newman, *On Records: Delaware Indians, Colonists, and the Media of History and Memory* (Lincoln: University of Nebraska Press, 2012); Birgit Brander Rasmussen, *Queequeg's Coffin: Indigenous Literacies and Early American Literature* (Durham, NC: Duke University Press, 2012), Sarah Rivett, "Learning to Write Algonquian Letters: The Indigenous Place of Language Philosophy in the Seventeenth-Century Atlantic World," *William and Mary Quarterly*, 3d ser., 71, no. 4 (2014): 549–88.

9. For more on Eliot's efforts in this regard, see Rivett, "Learning to Write Algonquian Letters," 551.

10. Richard Baxter, "How to Do Good to Many: Or, the Public Good is the Christian's Life" (London: Printed for *Rob. Gibs* at the Ball in *Chancery Lane*, 1682), 11.

11. Translated from the German and quoted in Jonathan Strom, Hartmut Lehmann, and James Van Horn Melton, *Pietism in Germany and North America, 1680–1820* (Surrey, UK: Ashgate, 2009), 35.

12. Mark A. Peterson, "Theopolis Americana: The City-State of Boston, the Republic of Letters, and the Protestant International, 1689–1739," in *Soundings in Atlantic History: Latent Structures and Intellectual Currents, 1500–1830*, ed. Bernard Bailyn and Patricia Denault (Cambridge, MA: Harvard University Press, 2009), 363.

13. There is some controversy over whether Mather actually wrote *Nuncia bona* since much of it consists of passages written to him by August Francke. I treat it here as a product of Mather's own pen because he put his name to it and inserted passages that made it his own. For the claim that it is definitely not Mather's, see Ernst Benz, "Pietist and Puritan Sources of Early Protestant World Mission (Cotton Mather and A. H. Francke)," *Church History* 20, no. 2: 28–55, 39.

14. Cotton Mather, *India Christiana* (Boston: Printed by B. Green, 1721), 57.

15. See Alberico Gentili, *De jure belli libri tres*, Book II, trans. John C. Rolfe (Oxford: Clarendon Press, 1933), 51. See also Timothy Hampton, *Fictions of Embassy: Literature and Diplomacy in Early Modern Europe* (Ithaca, NY: Cornell University Press, 2009), 8ff for more on Gentili's contribution in this regard.

16. Hugo Grotius, "Preliminary Discourse," in *The Rights of War and Peace*, vol. 1 (Indianapolis, IN: Liberty Fund, 2005), 94.

17. Grotius, *The Rights of War and Peace*, vol. 2 (Indianapolis, IN: Liberty Fund, 2005), 848.

18. The adjective, "stripped-down," is Richard Tuck's. He writes, "the principles that were to govern dealings of this kind had to be appropriately stripped down: there was no point in asserting to a king in Sumatra that Aristotelian moral philosophy was universally true." Introduction to Grotius, *The Rights of War and Peace*, 1: xviii.

19. For more on the work of these sorts of language philosophers, see Murray Cohen, *Sensible Words: Linguistic Practice in England, 1640–1785* (Baltimore, MD: Johns Hopkins University Press, 1977), 4.

20. Gentili, *De jure belli libri tres*, Book I.3.32.

21. Grotius, *The Rights of War and Peace*, 2:849.

22. Meredith Marie Neuman, *Jeremiah's Scribes: Creating Sermon Literature in Puritan New England* (Philadelphia: University of Pennsylvania Press, 2013), 19. Neuman's explanation of plain style is preceded by many others, which have helped us understand what plainness meant to the Puritans. See for example, Teresa Toulouse, *The Art of Prophesying: New England Sermons and the Shaping of Belief* (Athens: University of Georgia Press, 1987); Lisa M. Gordis, *Opening Scripture: Bible Reading and Interpretive Authority* (Chicago: University of Chicago Press, 2003); Sandra Gustafson, *Eloquence Is Power: Oratory and Performance in Early America* (Chapel Hill: University of North Carolina Press, 2000); Jasper Rosenmeier, "'Clearing the Medium': A Reevaluation of the Puritan Plain-Style in Light of John Cotton's A Practicall Commentary Upon the First Epistle Generall of John," *William and Mary Quarterly* 37, no. 4 (1980): 577–91. Janice Knight,

Orthodoxies in Massachusetts: Rereading American Puritanism (Cambridge, MA: Harvard University Press, 1994).

23. Grotius, *The Rights of War and Peace*, 2: 853.
24. Ibid., 858–59.
25. Ibid., 856–57.
26. Samuel Pufendorf, *Of the Laws of Nature and Nations*, vol. 4, 276.
27. Ibid., 4:278.
28. Ibid.
29. Ibid., 4:280.
30. Ibid.
31. Ibid., 4:280–81.
32. Ibid., 4:276.
33. See Rosalind J. Beiler, "Dissenting Religious Communication Networks and European Migration, 1660–1710," in *Soundings in Atlantic History*, ed. Bernard Bailyn and Patricia L. Denault (Cambridge, MA: Harvard University Press, 2009), 210.
34. Cotton Mather, *Nuncia bona* (Boston: Printed by B. Green, 1715), 7.
35. Ibid., 7–8.
36. Ibid., 8.
37. Ibid.
38. This bilingual text formed a part of *Notitia Indiarum: A Collection of Some Things Worthy to be known, relating to the Work of Christianity among the Indians*, which was at some point either printed with or bound together with Cotton Mather's *India Christiana* (Boston: Printed by B. Green, 1721), 52–55.
39. Philip H. Round, *Removable Type: Histories of the Book in Indian Country, 1663–1880* (Chapel Hill: University of North Carolina Press, 2010), 25.
40. Mather uses this language in, among other places, the general introduction to the *Magnalia Christi Americana* (1702).
41. Mather, *Notitia Indiarum*, 60–61.
42. Mather, *Nuncia bona*, 1.
43. Cotton Mather, *Diary of Cotton Mather* (Boston: Massachusetts Historical Society, 1911), entry for April 19, 1716.
44. Mather, *Terra beata:* **A** brief essay, on the blessing of Abraham; even the grand blessing of a glorious Redeemer, which, all the nations of the earth, are to ask for, and hope for. And the promises of it explained, with some uncommon illustrations (Boston: Printed for J. Phillips, 1726), 35.
45. For more on the Native American Guaman Poma de Ayala's incorporation of the Andean quipu into his Spanish language text, see Birgit Rasmussen, "The Manuscript, the Quipu, and the Early American Book," in *Colonial Mediascapes: Sensory Worlds of the Early Americas*, ed. Matt Cohen and Jeffrey Glover (Lincoln: University of Nebraska Press, 2014).
46. Mather, *Terra beata*, 20.
47. In his first letter to August Francke, quoted in Ernst Benz, "Ecumenical Relations between Boston Puritanism and German Pietism: Cotton Mather and August Francke," *Harvard Theological Review* 54, no. 3 (1961): 174.
48. Ibid.
49. Cotton Mather, *Notitia Indiarum*, 68.
50. Ibid., 66–68.
51. Ibid.

52. August Francke, *Pietas halliensis*, vol. 1 (London: Printed for R. Burrough, 1706), B2.

53. Cotton Mather, *Bonifacius: An Essay upon the Good* (Cambridge, MA: Harvard University Press, 1966), 36.

54. David Levin, introduction to Cotton Mather, *Bonifacius*, xxii.

55. Mather, *Bonifacius*, 27.

56. Mather, *Diary*, 1711.

57. Mather, *Bonifacius*, 83.

58. Ibid., 86.

59. Ibid., 8.

60. Ibid., 19.

61. Ibid., 17.

62. Ibid., 35.

63. Ibid., 41

64. Ibid.

65. Ibid.

66. Ibid.

67. Ibid., 42.

68. Ibid.

69. Ibid., 56.

70. Ibid., 57.

71. Ibid., 58

72. Ibid., 59.

73. Martha Nussbaum, *For Love of Country?* (Boston: Beacon Press, 2002), 9.

74. Ibid.

Epilogue

1. David Simpson, "The Limits of Cosmopolitanism and the Case for Translation," *European Romantic Review* 16, no. 2 (2005): 141.

2. Robert Fine, "Cosmopolitanism and Violence: Difficulties of Judgment," *British Journal of Sociology* 57, no. 1 (2006): 58.

3. See Vicki Hsueh, *Hybrid Constitutions: Challenging Legacies of Law, Privilege, and Culture in Colonial America* (Durham, NC: Duke University Press, 2010), 3.

4. For examples of scholarship in this area, see Adeno Addis, "Imagining the International Community: The Constitutive Dimension of Universal Jurisdiction," *Human Rights Quarterly* 31, no.1 (2009): 129–62; Noah Feldman, "Cosmopolitan Law?" *Yale Law Journal* 116, no. 5 (2007): 1022–70; Richard Janda, "Toward Cosmopolitan Law," *McGill Law Journal* 50, no. 4 (2005): 967–84; Garrett Wallace Brown, "Moving from Cosmopolitan Legal Theory to Legal Practice: Models of Cosmopolitan Law," *Legal Studies* 28, no. 3 (2008): 430–51.

5. Neil Walker, "Beyond Boundary Disputes and Basic Grids: Mapping the Global Disorder of Normative Orders," *International Journal of Constitutional Law* 6, no. 373 (2008): 375.

6. Lauren Benton and Richard J. Ross, eds., *Legal Pluralism and Empires, 1500–1850* (New York: New York University Press), 4.

7. Paul Schiff Berman, "From International Law to Law and Globalization," *Columbia Journal of Transnational Law* 43, no. 2 (2005): 485–556, 511.

8. See the discussion of human rights discourse in Samuel Moyn, *The Last Utopia: Human Rights in History* (Cambridge, MA: Harvard University Press, 2010), 176–211.

9. Hannah Arendt, *The Origins of Totalitarianism* (New York: Harcourt, Brace, Jovanovich, 1973), 298.

10. "Fact Sheet No. 2 (Rev.1), The International Bill of Human Rights," http://www.ohchr.org/Documents/Publications/FactSheet2Rev.1en.pdf.

11. See Eric A. Posner and Jack L. Goldsmith, *The Limits of International Law* (Oxford: Oxford University Press, 2006), 110–11.

12. Kwame Anthony Appiah, "Cosmopolitan Patriots," in *Cosmopolitics: Thinking and Feeling beyond the Nation* (Minneapolis: University of Minnesota Press, 1998) 97.

13. Antony Anghie, *Imperialism, Sovereignty and the Making of International Law* (Cambridge: Cambridge University Press, 2004), 269ff.

14. Luke Martell, "Cosmopolitanism and Global Politics," *Political Quarterly* 82, no. 4 (2011): 618–27, 618.

{ INDEX }